DON'T TELL THE NEWFOUNDLANDERS

Also by Greg Malone
You Better Watch Out

DON'T TELL THE NEWFOUNDLANDERS

THE TRUE STORY OF
NEWFOUNDLAND'S CONFEDERATION
WITH CANADA

GREG MALONE

Alfred A. Knopf Canada

PUBLISHED BY ALFRED A. KNOPF CANADA

Copyright © 2012 Greg Malone

All rights reserved under International and Pan-American Copyright Conventions. No part of this book may be reproduced in any form or by any electronic or mechanical means, including information storage and retrieval systems, without permission in writing from the publisher, except by a reviewer, who may quote brief passages in a review. Published in 2012 by Alfred A. Knopf Canada, a division of Random House of Canada Limited, Toronto. Distributed in Canada by Random House of Canada Limited.

www.randomhouse.ca

Knopf Canada and colophon are registered trademarks.

Library and Archives Canada Cataloguing in Publication
Malone, Greg
Don't tell the Newfoundlanders : the true story of Newfoundland's
confederation with Canada / Greg Malone.
Includes bibliographical references and index.
Issued also in an electronic format.
ISBN 978-0-307-40133-5
1. Newfoundland and Labrador—History—1934–1949. 2. Newfoundland and
Labrador—Politics and government—1934–1949. I. Title.

FC2174.8.M36 2012   971.8'03   C2012-902097-4

Text design by Jennifer Lum
Cover design by Terri Nimmo
Cover images: (bottom) The Franklin D. Roosevelt Library;
(flag) © Andreykuzmin/Dreamstime.com;
(ripped paper) © Carlosphotos/Dreamstime.com

Printed and bound in the United States of America

2 4 6 8 9 7 5 3 1

This book is dedicated to James T. Halley,
a great Newfoundlander who believed that
his countrymen and all Canadians deserve the truth.

CONTENTS

PROLOGUE

"In December 1945 when the big announcement came from London, I was a law student at Dalhousie University in Halifax," James Halley told me. "I and several other students were milling about in the hallway talking about this great news in the paper from St. John's: 'Newfoundlanders to Vote on Future Government.'[1]

"We were all very excited because we had been waiting for this for many years. I and my friends had grown up under British rule since 1934, and now it seemed we were going to have elections and control of our government again. So this was a great moment for us.

"We were very optimistic about the future in Newfoundland in 1945. The war had been good to Newfoundland. We were prosperous with so much American and Canadian and British activity during the war. Newfoundland was central to wartime and civil aviation, with two of the largest airports in the world at Gander and Goose Bay. American, British and Canadian Airlines had landing rights in Newfoundland. The fishery was good, and it seemed that Labrador might well hold vast mineral and hydro wealth. So we were looking forward to a new and exciting future for our country.

"There were several of us there talking about what it all meant—me and Lloyd Soper, Abe Shipman and George Hawkins, all law students.

We talked about staying linked to Britain in some way, but mostly we talked about getting control of our own government back and becoming an independent country once again, as we had been for almost a hundred years. Then George Hawkins interrupted us.

"'Oh no,' he said, 'Newfoundland is going into Confederation with Canada. The deal is already done.'

"We were stunned. I couldn't believe what he was saying to us.

"'Yes,' he went on. 'England sent people over from the Exchequer and the Dominions Office to Ottawa in October, and the deal is done.'

"'What deal? What are you talking about?' we asked.

"'Well, England is broke after the war, so Canada agreed to write off Britain's war debt to Canada and give them a big loan at low interest, and, in return, Britain agreed to work with Canada to put Newfoundland into Confederation.'

"I could not believe he was saying this, I just could not accept it. But I knew he wasn't lying. He knew what he was talking about because his father, Charles Hawkins, later a senator from Nova Scotia, was then a prominent member of the Liberal Party.

"'Yes,' said George, 'my father was with the team that negotiated the deal. It's all done.'

"I was shocked. Surely, I thought, the British government would not do such a thing. They would not set up a National Convention in Newfoundland just for show. Surely there was still some chance for the people to have a say and change that outcome.

"I returned home for Christmas on the *Florizel*, two days by steamer—we used to travel by steamer then, it was great. All the talk in St. John's was about the coming National Convention, but I could get no further information on what George Hawkins had said.

"That's a long time ago now, but what he told us that day has been on my mind ever since. I think of it all the time, and now I want the people of Newfoundland to see how it was done. And I want the people of Canada to know it because I don't think they would approve of it any more than we do."

This account was one of the highlights in a series of conversations I had with Jim Halley about his recollections of the events that led to Newfoundland joining Canada in 1949.

"The truth, as so often happens," he continued, "is not commonly known."[2]

James Halley, QC, was a prominent member of the Newfoundland and Labrador legal community. A man of great presence, wit and conviction, he was my friend and mentor for many years. I first met Halley during the public campaign in 1994 to stop the privatization of Newfoundland and Labrador Hydro and prevent its falling into the hands of its nemesis, Hydro-Québec. The success of that campaign empowered the people of Newfoundland and Labrador to hold on to a very valuable asset. Halley was an ardent nationalist, and he supported anyone who might do some good for his beloved Newfoundland. "The great injustice," as he put it, which had been done to Newfoundland in 1949 preoccupied him throughout his entire adult life. He believed that the true story of Newfoundland's union with Canada had never been adequately told to the people of Newfoundland and Labrador (or to Canadians elsewhere), and that this ignorance of their own history has put Newfoundlanders at a perpetual disadvantage in that great Confederation.

Over the years, Halley amassed a large collection of research materials relating to Newfoundland's federation with Canada. He became an expert on that tumultuous period of our history in which he himself had been an active player fighting for the return of responsible government. Halley wanted to tell the story of Newfoundland's entry into Confederation by using the words of the Canadians and British themselves, in their own official documents, and creating a brief chronological record of the most relevant and revealing passages in a way that would make this history accessible to the average reader. At the same time it would create a paper trail of Canadian and British activities in Newfoundland from 1941 to 1949.

Before he died in 2009, Halley extracted a promise from me to write such a book. He presented me with his collection of research materials and, over the course of 2008, I recorded many lengthy interviews with him on the subject. In the years since, I have added context and additional commentary to this basic framework. I hope the result proves worthy of his vision—and that it will be useful to all those people who sense there was something not quite right about Newfoundland's entry into Confederation but are not sure what went wrong.

After 1949, the idea that Great Britain had conspired with Canada to place Newfoundland into Confederation with Canada was met with disbelief and derision in historical and political circles. Until the early 1990s, the official "Joey Smallwood" version of Confederation history as written by the victors was accepted almost without question. It held that Newfoundland had freely chosen federation with Canada—without any interference from either Britain or Canada.

Then in the 1980s and '90s, official documents covering the period from 1941 to 1949 were released in Ottawa and in London—and they contradict that interpretation. Particularly useful are the documents on confederation with Newfoundland released by the Department of External Affairs in Ottawa, compiled and edited by Paul Bridle, a senior civil servant who had worked on the Newfoundland project throughout the 1940s.

The Bridle documents, along with other sources, reveal a very different version of history—one more in line with popular belief in Newfoundland than with official accounts. The numerous dispatches, letters and top-secret memoranda between the highest levels of government in London and Ottawa make it clear that there was considerable sustained collusion between Canada and Great Britain to put Newfoundland into

Confederation on Canada's terms, with a significant quid pro quo for Britain in return, as the "honest broker" of the deal.

The long and sorry record of the deliberate effort throughout this period to keep Newfoundlanders ignorant of these top-secret deals and arrangements puts the entire effort into the category of conspiracy at the highest levels. The lofty ideals of democracy and self-determination for which two world wars had recently been fought and won were ignored. Newfoundland was not to share in that principled victory for which it had sacrificed so much. Self-determination seemed to be there, but on close inspection it proved to be only a chimera, an elaborate show. Newfoundlanders did not determine their own future in 1948; rather, it was determined for them by the governments of Canada, Great Britain and, to a degree, the United States.

The gains of this conspiracy were all for Canada and Britain; the loss was all for Newfoundland. Along with her sovereignty, Newfoundland lost her right to negotiate terms with Canada on an equal basis. That right was abrogated by Great Britain, which negotiated in its own interests. Newfoundland did not make the deal or even accept it. The Terms of Union with Canada were accepted by the British-appointed Commission of Government of Newfoundland.

The constitutional arrangements whereby confederation between Canada and Newfoundland was effected were extraordinary, dubious, and as controversial in London and Ottawa as they were in St. John's. The 1949 confederation was not effected through the British North America Act, which had been set up precisely for that purpose more than eight decades earlier, simply because Canada did not want to negotiate with an independent Newfoundland government. Instead, Canada preferred to negotiate with Britain while Newfoundland was temporarily under British control. So other means were employed, outside the British North America Act, secretly and at considerable effort.

———

To understand why Britain was able to hand Newfoundland over to Canada in 1948, we require some knowledge of how Great Britain came to repossess Newfoundland in 1933. That year, after a century of self-government, the legislature of the Dominion of Newfoundland, the oldest in the British Empire outside Westminster, was suspended. Great Britain once again assumed direct control of the Island, and Newfoundland was reduced to the status of a crown colony. This reversal was not only unique in the annals of imperial colonial history but was completely opposed to the direction of thinking in the twentieth century. It caused a stir in the Dominions Office at Whitehall, and Paul Emrys-Evans, the parliamentary under-secretary of state for dominions affairs, was moved to write: "The idea of a Dominion reverting to the status of a Crown Colony was almost unthinkable. There was no provision in the Imperial structure for such a contingency."[3] Yet provision was made, once again at Britain's insistence. As St. John Chadwick, the financial adviser to the Commission of Government put it: "In its time the Island has rung more Constitutional bells than any other Colony."[4]

THE FIRST STONE:
FROM DOMINION TO COLONY

It is commonly believed that Newfoundland was Britain's oldest colony, and certainly it is referred to as such by those official bodies that should know best—the Dominions Office, the British government, and the Crown. Yet that is not exactly true. Newfoundland was Britain's oldest possession and nearest overseas territory, but the Island was always too valuable an asset for England to allow it to be colonized. Europe initially came to Newfoundland for fish, and even before John Cabot officially discovered it in 1497 for Henry VII, the first of the Tudors, Portuguese, Dutch, Basque and Norman boats were fishing on the Grand Banks and their crews had already worn a path alongside the harbour in St. John's where Water Street lies today. By 1530 as many as 150 English vessels had stopped fishing in Icelandic waters and moved on to the Grand Banks, and, in 1583, Elizabeth I, the last of the Tudors, was moved to dispatch Humphrey Gilbert to take possession of this "Newfoundelande" for the English Crown.[1] By the late 1700s, twenty thousand English seamen were employed in the annual fishery, with a total value of £600,000. The French, Spanish and Portuguese were also extensively involved. Newfoundland fish was big money.

Unlike other North American colonies that required plantations and communities of people to grow sugar, cotton or tobacco, Newfoundland's primary resource was based not on land but offshore, and the entire operation could be hauled back to England after the fishing season was over each year. "In the spring either in ballast or laden with goods and provisions for the seamen, the sack [supply] ships left Britain for Portugal or some other foreign country to secure adequate supplies of staves and the all-essential supply of salt," one expert explained. "On arrival at Newfoundland they obtained in exchange cargoes of dried fish for the West Indian or Mediterranean ports. Late in the autumn these ships returned to England with wine, oil and other commodities from abroad or with the more precious bullion received in payment for the salted cod."[2]

The workmen, fit and trained on the fishing boats, went back to serve in England's growing navy. Neither the English merchants nor the English Crown wanted any competition for this trade or these men from colonists settled in Newfoundland, so colonization was suppressed by the Western Charter of 1634 and again in 1698 by the Act to Encourage Trade to Newfoundland. Amazingly, this prohibition stayed in effect until the early 1800s.

Settlement could not be stopped, however. Planters could be flogged or burned out by the ruthless "fishing admirals" who ruled arbitrarily over the Island, or they could be dispossessed without recourse to any justice save that of their tormentors. In response, and especially to be near the valuable fishing grounds, settlers fanned out into the innumerable coves and bays around the Island's 6,000 miles of coastline, where they could live and fish as far from English justice as possible. Although there were thousands of these outports around the coasts, their population, except for a handful of larger communities, was often no more than a few hundred people, too small for the development of municipal governments. Consequently, the tradition of settlement in Newfoundland was very different from that of the North American mainland. The Newfoundland experience until well into the nineteenth century was not that of lawful colonists building up the civic institutions of a state, but one of rugged individualists, shy of all civic authority. Even in the 1930s, the Englishmen on the Amulree Royal Commission who were sent out from London to determine the political and financial circumstances of the Island were shocked to find hardly any municipal government outside the city of St. John's.

The legislature in St. John's did not have the support of local and municipal democratic institutions, simply because there were none. Democracy had never been fostered. Newfoundland had had to fight to get representative government in 1832. Full responsible government was gained in 1855, when Britain finally agreed that it "ought not to withhold from Newfoundland those institutions and that civil administration which, under the popular name of Responsible Government, had been adopted by all Her Majesty's neighbouring possessions in North America."[3]

From the mid-1860s onwards, British policy favoured a Canadian Confederation as the way to resolve the military and financial security of its remaining North American colonies, including Newfoundland. Sir John A. Macdonald, Canada's first prime minister as of 1867, shared that goal of a nation stretching from coast to coast. But it was not the wish of the young country of Newfoundland, which resisted all efforts to draft it into the Canadian fold.

Newfoundland did attend the Quebec Conference of 1864, and in 1895 the government of Prime Minister Sir William Whiteway sent a delegation to Ottawa to negotiate possible terms for Confederation. But for reasons both good and bad, Newfoundlanders ultimately decided not to join Canada. The Newfoundland bank crash of 1894 brought Canadian banks and currency to the Island as the price of Canadian credit and greater financial stability, but the relationship between the two neighbouring countries remained prickly. In 1905, after Prime Minister Sir Robert Bond successfully negotiated a free-trade agreement for the sale of its fish with the United States, the Island's biggest trading partner, Nova Scotia immediately pressured Ottawa to persuade London to demand that Washington cancel the treaty. That often seemed to be the pattern when Newfoundland fortunes competed with Canadian interests. It was almost impossible for Newfoundland to forge an independent economic or political course without leave from the formidable trio of Britain, Canada and the United States.

In 1908, during the electoral contest between the nationalist Sir Robert Bond and the pro-Confederate Sir Edward Morris, Canadian Governor General Lord Grey promised: "The Canadians who have interest in Newfoundland can be relied on to do whatever is possible to stiffen Morris and to assist him in the battle against Bond. All the money he wants to enable him to conduct an educational campaign [for Confederation] will be forthcoming."[4] But the vote produced a tie and left Morris in no position to carry off Confederation. Once again, Newfoundland remained independent.

By the turn of the nineteenth century, Newfoundland was an autonomous country with a population of almost a quarter of a million. In 1907 at the Imperial Conference in London it was elevated to dominion status along with Canada, Australia and New Zealand. Despite the huge sacrifices Newfoundland made during the First World War, the country enjoyed both good government and prosperity throughout the opening decades of the twentieth century. It was the bank crash of 1929 and the worldwide Depression that followed which proved to be the country's undoing.

The years directly leading up to 1929 were plagued with political and financial turmoil. World markets for Newfoundland fish collapsed, and successive administrations struggled to pay the growing national debt. In a one-year period, no fewer than five governments were elected. The ever-resourceful Sir Richard Squires, prime minister during much of the decade, even tried to sell Labrador to Canada for $100 million. But the price was too rich for the Canadians, who, like the British, preferred to acquire empire on the cheap. By the early 1930s civil service salaries were cut in half, and there was mass unemployment and widespread hunger. Charges of embezzlement against Squires brought a mob to the doors of the legislature. The ensuing riot brought down the government.

Such scenes were not unusual across North America during the "Dirty Thirties." Certainly people in the Maritimes of Canada and the Dust Bowl of the United States suffered as much as Newfoundlanders did during this grim period. However, Newfoundland relied almost exclusively on world markets to sell its fish, and it could not survive such a protracted calamity without help. It was a large country to be sure, almost three times the size of the Maritime provinces, but it was undeveloped and had only a small population. It simply did not have the credit base of large federations such as Canada or the United Kingdom to withstand a deep and sustained financial crisis. In 1885 Canada had come through with the necessary financial backing to avert the crisis, but in 1933 it declined to assist its sister dominion. That left Newfoundland entirely dependent on Great Britain for financial support.

The Newfoundland debt was by then more than $100 million, at 5 percent interest. During the 1931 session in the House of Assembly, Major Peter Cashin, the finance minister in the Squires government, had proposed rescheduling a portion of that debt from 5 percent interest to 3 percent. The United Kingdom had already struck such an agreement with the United States for its own enormous war debt. Frederick Alderdice, the leader of the opposition, initially opposed such a default, but by 1933, when he was prime minister, he had come around to Cashin's way of thinking.[5] Faced with the spectre of bankruptcy, Alderdice, even though a staunch fiscal conservative, proposed that Newfoundland be allowed to reschedule a portion of its debt and thereby carry on. The British government declined, on the basis that a default by one of the dominions would have a damaging effect on the credit of the whole empire. This philosophy was puzzling even to Canadian observers. O.D. Skelton, the Canadian under-secretary of state for external affairs, observed to W.D. Herridge, the Canadian ambassador to Washington: "I have never been able to understand why Newfoundland should not be allowed to repudiate a portion of its debts when the United Kingdom government is declining to pay its government debts and the US is meeting gold obligations with paper money."[6] Instead, Britain advanced the necessary credit for Newfoundland to make the next interest payment on its debt and avert disaster on one condition: Britain would appoint a royal commission to assess Newfoundland's financial and political situation, and Newfoundland would be obliged to accept its findings. Alderdice had suggested such a commission in his election campaign the year before, so he readily consented to the terms. He had also promised that the final recommendations would "be submitted to the electorate for their approval" and that "no action [would] be taken that [did] not first have the consent of the people."[7] This promise was never kept.

The Newfoundland Royal Commission, led by the Scottish peer William Warrender Mackenzie, 1st Baron Amulree, and popularly called the Amulree Commission, arrived in St. John's in the spring of 1933. The other members were bankers Charles A. Magrath from Ontario, as Canada's nominee, and William Stavert from Prince Edward Island, as Newfoundland's representative. From the Canadian viewpoint, the British seemed already to have made up their minds. In Paul Bridle's opinion: "The decision to set up the Amulree Commission was as tough-minded as the Commission's findings and virtually foreshadowed them."[8] The commissioners immediately set out to observe conditions across the Island and gather information for their conclusions. Their final report on Newfoundland that fall was written not by Lord Amulree but by commission secretary Peter Alexander Clutterbuck, the Newfoundland expert in the Dominions Office.

Born in India in 1897 in the era of the Raj, the period of British rule, Clutterbuck was educated at Cambridge University and served with distinction in the Coldstream Guards during the First World War. Diligent, discreet, and devoted to the Dominions Office and the empire, he embodied the ideals of the British civil service and brought considerable diplomatic and literary talent to his assignments in Newfoundland.

He would remain on the Newfoundland file until 1949, rising to the highest ranks in his department. Clutterbuck's pervasive presence in the great events in which he participated is little known outside official dispatches and top-secret memos. He moved behind the scenes, where he promoted his department's policy with remarkable detachment.[9]

Clutterbuck's report, written in colourful language by official standards, gave the British government the pretext it required to resume direct control over the Island. Newfoundland's financial crisis, he concluded, was not the fault of a worldwide Depression and the collapse of the fish markets but the result of corrupt and venal politicians. He began with this sweeping generalization: "Politics in Newfoundland have never been such as to inspire wholehearted confidence in the ability of the people to govern themselves wisely, but there is general agreement that a process of deterioration, which has now reached almost unbelievable extremes, may be said to have set in a quarter of a century ago."[10]

"Never" is no doubt excessive and fails to take account of the work of able politicians such as Sir Robert Bond or even Sir Edward Morris. Clutterbuck continued:

> For a number of years there has been a continuing process of greed, graft and corruption which has left few classes of the community untouched by insidious influences.
>
> The twelve years 1920–32, during none of which was the Budget balanced, were characterized by an out-flow of public funds on a scale as ruinous as it was unprecedented, fostered by a continuous stream of willing lenders. A new era of industrial expansion, easy money and profitable contact with the rich American continent was looked for, and was deemed in part to have arrived. . . .
>
> The public debt of the Island was in 12 years (1920–32) more than doubled; its assets dissipated by improvident administration; the people misled into acceptance of false standards, and the country sunk in waste and extravagance. The onset of the world depression

found the Island with no reserves, its primary industry neglected and its credit exhausted.[11]

As for the Island's financial difficulties, the report allowed that they "have been intensified by the world depression, but they are also due primarily to the persistent extravagance and neglect of proper financial principles on the part of successive Governments during the years 1920–31."[12] Lord Amulree attributed all this bad government to his view that:

> There is no leisured class, and the great majority of the people are quite unfitted to play a part in public life.
>
> The so-called "modernization" of politics and the introduction into political life of men who sought to make a living out of their political activities, have been responsible for this deplorable state of affairs.[13]

In short, Newfoundlanders did not have the leisure for democracy. The report recommended that Great Britain should guarantee the Newfoundland debt, but that the Newfoundland legislature should be revoked and the Island put into a form of receivership:

a) The existing form of government would be suspended until such time as the Island may become self-supporting again.

b) A special Commission of Government would be created. . . .

c) . . . subject to supervisory control by Your Majesty's Government in the U.K. and the Governor-in-Commission . . . responsible to the Secretary of State for Dominions Office in the U.K.

> " . . . it would be understood that . . . as soon as the Island's difficulties are overcome and Newfoundland is again self-supporting, responsible government on request from the people of Newfoundland would be restored.[14]

This arrangement, the report breezily concluded, would provide Newfoundlanders with a "rest from politics." The Amulree Commission had already decried the lack of municipal government outside St. John's, but its recommendation to abolish the legislature in the capital city was hardly consistent with those democratic concerns.

It is curious to note that most of the Newfoundland debt with which Sir Richard Squires grappled in the 1920s was incurred by Sir Edward Morris during the First World War and in the construction of the Newfoundland railway. Morris resigned as prime minister of Newfoundland in 1917 during a trip to London. The next year he was honoured with a rare hereditary peerage and became a minister in the UK government. Here at least was one improvident politician of whom London seemed to approve.[15]

The drastic course recommended by Amulree was not his own invention. When he returned to London, he found that everything had been carefully worked out between Neville Chamberlain at Treasury and Sir Edward Harding at the Dominions Office, and these two men informed Amulree and Clutterbuck what the key points in the report should be.[16] When Canada's representative, Charles Magrath, read the draft, he objected strongly to the harsh and demeaning portrait that Clutterbuck had painted of Newfoundland politics and politicians and to the conclusion that Newfoundland was unfit to govern itself. He registered his objection bluntly in a personal letter to Lord Amulree: "Who can throw the first stone at Newfoundland?" he asked. "There is not a province in Canada or a state in the U.S. that has lived within its income. . . . I seem to recall that the May Commission in the U.K. found, rightly or wrongly, the government of that country guilty of extravagance which threatened the ruin of that country." As for Britain's refusal to allow Newfoundland to default on its war debt, he noted that "practically every country in the world is today in financial difficulties. Some have defaulted on their public obligations. In none has it been found necessary to send in the sheriff. . . . The criticism is apparently exaggerated for the purpose of building up a case for drastic and extravagant remedies in substantial reversion of Newfoundland to a Crown Colony."[17]

Some of the stronger language in the commission's draft report disparaging Newfoundland culture and politics was softened for Canadian sensibilities, and both Magrath and William Stavert bowed to British pressure and signed Clutterbuck's final text. It recommended revoking the Newfoundland legislature and handing the country over to Britain in receivership. Canada's prime minister, Richard Bennett, had already announced that Canada would not participate in any financial assistance to Newfoundland, so Magrath and Stavert were left with little leverage. Besides, they knew that Canadian banks would do very well under the proposed British plan, enabling them to recover immediately the loans they had earlier made to the dominion.

With the gun to his head, Prime Minister Alderdice accepted the verdict. He realized that certain members of his government would find it difficult to vote for the establishment of a Commission of Government from Great Britain which would be the instrument of their own extinction and leave them without jobs. Alderdice himself and several other favoured men received appointments within the new British administration. As for the others, Governor Sir David Anderson, the chair of the new commission, cynically assured Alderdice that "the few thousand dollars annually to be spent to ensure acceptance would be well invested."[18] Compensation for the losing party was not uncommon in deals between imperial and colonial elites: it provided for the smooth running of the empire. In this case, however, Noel Trentham, the British financial supervisor already in Newfoundland, objected to the bribes, and they were never given out.[19]

Confederation was never considered. Britain now had other plans for its new possession. The elected legislature in St. John's would be replaced by a governor and six commissioners—three Englishmen and three Newfoundlanders—and the country would be run directly from the

Dominions Office in London. Lord Macaulay's famous description of the rule by the East India Company—"the strangest of all governments designed for the strangest of all empires"—proved an apt description a century later for Britain's oldest, now newest, colony.[20] Newfoundland's Commission of Government was a novel arrangement in every sense and a very odd constitutional duck, but the British were determined to make it quack.

Both Magrath and Stavert felt strongly that federation with Canada was the best long-term solution for Newfoundland. And, when the new British governor, Sir Humphrey Walwyn, arrived in St. John's in February 1936, he agreed with them. Although many Canadian officials felt the same way, they were in no hurry to make the deal. Ambassador W.D. Herridge in Washington wrote to his boss, O.D. Skelton, in Ottawa in November 1933: "Some day we shall have to take it [Newfoundland] over, but at present I would regard the price as too high."[21] It was the familiar Canadian complaint, and Skelton was of similar mind. But the mood was entirely different in Newfoundland. Despite the hard times brought on by the Great Depression, public opinion almost unanimously opposed any association with the "cold and comfortless Canadian fold" that had recently rejected the country in its hour of need.

In reflecting on this complete reversal in British policy towards Newfoundland, Paul Bridle notes: "There was a period especially during the Second World War, and after it, when the British Government veered towards keeping Newfoundland in the British fold and nurturing it." He then offers this generous explanation: "More than anything else this probably reflected the affection which had developed for Newfoundland because of its unflinching and self-effacing support of Britain in two wars."[22]

Similar sentiments should have carried more weight with British thinking in 1933. Newfoundland had raised its own regiment, at its own expense, and sent its young men into battle for Britain in the First World War. The Newfoundland Regiment was virtually destroyed in one day in its first engagement at the Battle of Beaumont Hamel as part of the huge disaster that began the Battle of the Somme. Nevertheless, the regiment was reconstituted with new recruits from home and, at war's end, it was rewarded as the only one in all the British Empire to have "Royal" incorporated into its name. "The men of the Newfoundland Regiment rapidly showed their adaptability and ultimately developed a battle discipline equal to that of the old British regiments and probably surpassing that of all the overseas troops," stated the *Cambridge History of the British Empire*. "The seamen of Newfoundland . . . readily undertook almost impossible boarding operations in wild seas which others would not face. Nothing but praise was accorded to the Fleet."[23]

Newfoundland had suffered some of the heaviest losses per capita of any country in the British Empire. Of the 5,482 Newfoundlanders who went to war in 1914, 1,500 died, 2,314 were wounded, and 234 were decorated. By 1933 the portion of the Newfoundland debt dating from the First World War was approximately $40 million. Certainly Newfoundland had a strong case for honourable default, and if Britain had allowed the country to reschedule just that portion of the debt, it would have enabled the Island to carry on until better times. But Britain was not guided by such sentiments in 1933—or, later, in 1948.[24]

The period of the Great Depression was an inauspicious time for institutions of democracy generally. It was often democracy, not capitalism, that was seen as the root of the economic catastrophe: the people were too ignorant to elect good governments, and democracy was too inefficient to guarantee the smooth running of industry. Many in the financial and political elites of Europe and America wanted a strongman, a dictator who would guarantee a cheap supply of resources and labour. It was in this negative political climate that Hitler came to power in Germany, and Mussolini in Italy, giving both these countries a "rest from politics" and setting the stage for the ultimate confrontation between raw, unregulated capitalism, or facism, and the forces of democracy. As Churchill is famously said to have remarked: "Democracy is the worst form of government, except for all the rest."

In the Dominion of Newfoundland in 1933, however, the population was judged by Lord Amulree and Alexander Clutterbuck as simply not fit for democratic rights. Clutterbuck concluded smoothly that, in Newfoundland, "considerations of constitutional status were regarded more as a matter for academic discussion than as a practical issue."[25] The Amulree Report, written very much in the spirit of the times, reduced the institutions of democracy to little more than a bureaucratic option for Newfoundland. The freedom of self-determination, deemed so essential for the great democracies, was here brushed aside. Democracy would enjoy a better reputation after the war, but little better treatment.

Many royal commission reports sit on shelves gathering dust once they are completed, but the drastic recommendations in the Amulree Report were acted on in London with all possible haste. The Newfoundland Bill was put before the British Parliament on December 13, 1933. Clement Attlee, the leader of the Labour Party, disputed the need for the bill and, indeed, the need for dismantling democracy in Newfoundland. Echoing Magrath's objection, he observed: "all the best countries default nowadays. . . . It is about time the Government faced the fact that the world cannot stand the interest demanded by the money lenders."[26] The main objection from the opposition ranks in the British Parliament was the lack of any cutoff date for the Commission of Government. Morgan Jones, the MP for Caerphilly, wondered how the Newfoundland legislature would be restored in the future, what the phrase "on request from the people of Newfoundland" might mean, and how such a request would be made: "As I see the position," he remarked, "there will be no machine of government. There will be no vocal expressions of the opinions or desires of the people of Newfoundland, no elected assembly or organization."[27] Nevertheless, this clause, deliberately vague, was left to allow Britain the option of delaying, even reneging on, its promise to restore responsible government to Newfoundland. The word "revoke" was objected to and replaced by the word "suspend," in relation to the Letters Patent that established the Newfoundland legislature. No definite cutoff date was ever included, but J.H. Thomas, the dominions secretary, assured the House that "temporary is written all over the Bill."[28]

On December 15, 1933, after an all-night session, the Newfoundland Act was finally passed and the clock turned back one hundred years on the British Empire in North America. Newfoundland again became a British colony. Once in control, the British rescheduled the Newfoundland debt for themselves along the lines that Alderdice had earlier requested and been denied. "In short," historian Peter Neary writes, "a rescheduling of debt that would have been anathema while Newfoundland was a self-governing Dominion would be perfectly acceptable should she forego that constitutional status."[29]

The debate on the Amulree Report continues. In the April 28, 2003, edition of *The Globalist*, an online magazine devoted to the global economy, politics and culture, David Hale, writing about the International Monetary Fund, gave this perspective of the Newfoundland crisis of 1933:

> The most extraordinary debt restructuring of the pre-1945 era was not in Latin America. It was in a dominion of the British Empire, the country of Newfoundland. During the early 1930s Newfoundland experienced a form of political punishment and national humiliation for its debt problems which is unsurpassed by any other country since the emergence of government debt markets in the 17th century.
>
> . . . The [Royal] commission's proposed solution to the crisis . . . has no parallels in any other sovereign debt restructuring . . . The notion that a self-governing community of 280,000 English-speaking people should give up both democracy and independence in order to avoid debt and default was unprecedented.

... If the IMF had existed in 1933 it would have granted emergency debt relief to Newfoundland and the country would have never given up democracy or independence. Indeed, democracy is now a pre-condition for IMF aid.

... [The story] is a reminder of why, in the aftermath of World War II, the nations of the world created the International Monetary Fund. They did not want nations to ever again confront a choice between debt and democracy.[30]

In 1933 Great Britain chose to humiliate Newfoundland and drag the country's reputation, and that of its people, through the mud. It did so not because Newfoundland deserved such singular condemnation, but as a pretext to gain full control over the country while it was temporarily broke. Clutterbuck, the author of the report, was rewarded by a grateful government at Whitehall with a silver salver and a promotion to head officer in charge of Newfoundland affairs at the Dominions Office. He was offered a silver inkwell, but he requested the salver instead because he already had received an inkwell from another commission.[31] Presumably his reward betokened the success of his mission to annex Newfoundland, not to saddle the empire with a liability.

In St. John's, the Newfoundland Legislative Chamber was dismantled and taken over as offices by British civil servants. The furnishings and artifacts of one hundred years of parliamentary democracy were cleared out, put in storage or destroyed. This act of official vandalism, combined with the lack of any time limit on the new Commission of Government, added to the growing suspicion that the country had been annexed and that the British were there to stay. In 1935, one year after this takeover, Frederick Alderdice, the former Newfoundland prime minister, wrote these bitter words to Lord Amulree: "To you alone I would say, if I had had any idea the present plan of government was to turn out as it has, I am afraid I would not have been so ready to accept it."[32]

FOR ALL MANKIND:
THE COMMISSION OF GOVERNMENT

L ord Amulree and Alexander Clutterbuck were not the only important visitors touring Newfoundland in the summer of 1933. Charles
Lindbergh was travelling around the Island as well, scouting out the
best locations for aerodromes for Pan American World Airways. He
would settle on Botwood, which became a refuelling stop on the Great
Circle route six years later. Lindbergh also attended an international
conference in St. John's involving Pan American, Imperial Airways and
government officials from the United States, Great Britain, Canada
and Newfoundland, where agreement was reached on establishing a
transatlantic air route in Newfoundland. As Jim Halley put it:

> It is impossible to overestimate the importance of aviation in the
> '20s and '30s. It was equal to the space race and the Internet today.
> The world was being connected faster and faster, and everyone
> was excited about it and Newfoundland was at the centre of
> all the activity. After World War I, airfields sprang up around
> St. John's and in Harbour Grace, and we had a steady stream of
> famous aviators coming to the Island with their entourages.
> When I was just a boy my father took me by the hand and pointed

up to the sky to see Lindbergh fly over. When the *Graf Zeppelin* came across from Europe it flew down low over St. John's and we all waved up at the passengers. All the boys had balsa planes with the propeller powered by a rubber band. Since 1919 everyone who was trying to cross the Atlantic non-stop came to Newfoundland to take off. The reason was obvious of course. Newfoundland is a thousand miles farther out in the Atlantic, and therefore a thousand miles closer to Europe than New York is, so my generation had great expectations for aviation in Newfoundland and so did Great Britain."[1]

By the end of the First World War Britain realized that the supremacy of its great cruise ships was over. Air travel would replace steamer travel, and if Great Britain wished to retain its superiority it must somehow take the lead in aviation. In 1919 the English team of John Alcock and Arthur Brown, flying out of Lester's Field in St. John's, was the first to make the transatlantic hop successfully. Their prize of £10,000, or $50,000, was put up by Lord Northcliffe, the owner of Britain's *Daily Mail*, though it was presented by Winston Churchill, then secretary of state for air in Lloyd George's government. Britain had its eye on Newfoundland, and once the Commission of Government was in place in St. John's in 1934, it immediately began to construct the largest aerodrome in the world at Gander.

According to Halley, everyone knew what Britain was up to and why it wanted Newfoundland. Amulree had foreseen a great British rebuilding of Newfoundland, and the Commission of Government announced many lofty development plans. By and large these plans came to nothing. In fact, unemployment and poverty increased under British rule. The Newfoundland Airport at Gander, however, was completed and operational by 1938, at a cost of £900,000, or almost $5 million, despite the Great Depression, and it gave Britain instant superiority in transatlantic civil aviation. The imperial gambit had worked.

As important as Newfoundland was to Great Britain and civil aviation before the Second World War, after 1939 it became absolutely vital to the war effort. When France fell to the Nazis in 1940, Britain, cut off from the rest of Europe, faced blockade and isolation. Overnight the North Atlantic Convoy Route became Britain's only lifeline. Everything it needed, from flour to bombers, now came from North America, and the western end of that lifeline was the island of Newfoundland—which, by a stroke of amazing good fortune, was under British government control.

By then, both Canada and the United States were abundantly aware of the Island's strategic importance to them as well. Any eventual attack on North America from across the Atlantic would first encounter Newfoundland. Once again the oldest colony, now the newest, proved an invaluable bargaining chip for the United Kingdom as Newfoundland became the Gibraltar of North America. In 1940 Britain signed the Leased Bases Agreement with the United States for the defence of the Island, by means of which Britain obtained fifty American destroyers that it badly needed for continuing the war in return for leases for US bases in Newfoundland and the Caribbean. The agreement for the bases in Newfoundland, the largest outside the United States, provided that:

> His Majesty's Government will secure the grant to the Government of the United States freely and without consideration of the Lease for immediate establishment and use of Naval and Air Bases and facilities for entrance thereto and the operation and protection thereof on the Avalon Peninsula and on the Southern Coast of Newfoundland and on the East Coast. . . . All the Bases will be leased to the United Sates for a period of 99 years, free from all rent.[2]

The British government's assertion of the right to lease large tracts of Newfoundland territory to foreign powers for close to a century without any reference to the local people raised strong objection across the Island and became a cause for further embarrassment to the Commission of

Government. Lord Cranborne at the Dominions Office "recognized that very real hardship to the inhabitants of the territories and Newfoundland might well be involved."[3]

Prime Minister Winston Churchill was worried that Newfoundlanders would consider the "extremely harsh" American terms, which included total jurisdiction for the United States on its bases, as a "surrender." He met personally in London with two of the visiting Newfoundland commissioners, L.E. Emerson and J.H. Penson, and pleaded with them to accept the deal. To help them win public support for the agreement back home, he wrote Emerson a letter in March 1941 intended for publication in Newfoundland.

> I would only ask the people of Newfoundland, on whose loyalty we have, in this testing time as throughout her long and eventful history, had ample proof, to bear in mind the wide issues which hang upon this agreement. . . . It is with these considerations in our minds that, recognizing to the full the considerable sacrifices made by Newfoundland to the cause which we all have at heart and her splendid contribution to the war effort, we ask her to accept the Agreement. It will be yet one more example of what she is ready to do for the sake of the Empire, of liberty, and of the welfare of all mankind.[4]

The commissioners had no choice but to bow to Churchill's eloquent appeal and accept the agreement. They could do no more. But as Peter Neary records in his monumental work on the Commission of Government years, Emerson and Penson "were to leave the British capital fearful and bitterly disappointed men."[5]

The agreement in fact set a bad precedent for Newfoundland in terms of the British government's right to make a long-term disposition of Newfoundland territory while holding only temporary authority on the Island as a government without appropriate local representation.

Churchill's patriotic and moving letter, which was actually written by Sir Charles Dixon, the assistant under-secretary of state, imploring Newfoundland to accept the US bases, was printed in the local newspapers and the deal went through.[6] The historic meeting between Franklin D. Roosevelt and Churchill five months later at Placentia Bay off the south coast of Newfoundland underscored the Island's strategic significance to both allies. There the leaders signed the Atlantic Charter, proclaiming the rights of all peoples to self-determination. The irony of those two great champions of democracy plotting to save the free world as they met in the recently re-colonized Newfoundland was lost for the moment under weightier concerns. It was fortuitous also that Newfoundland, which had been stripped of its democracy for failure to pay its First World War debt to Britain and Canada, was now able to facilitate the arming of Great Britain and the defence of Canada and the United States at such little cost to each empire, and with only such residual benefits to the people of Newfoundland as could not be conveniently avoided.

In 1939, despite the rectitude of the Commission of Government, Newfoundland was even worse off than it had been in 1933. After five years of the benevolent dictatorship, 50,000 men were still on relief, and poverty had only increased. These and other criticisms appeared in a series of articles written in London's *Daily Express* by Morley Richards, who charged that the UK government had exploited the Island and done nothing to improve conditions. Alexander Clutterbuck was assigned the task of rebutting Richards. In an April letter in defence of the Commission of Government, he completely reversed himself on the drastic conclusions he had earlier drawn about Newfoundland in the Amulree Report and, in particular, about the justification for suspending Newfoundland's legislature in 1933. Now, he argued, the disappointing conditions that prevailed in Newfoundland despite the performance of the Commission of Government were due to "a depressed world market which no Newfoundland government could control,"[7] not even the government of the much reviled Sir Richard Squires.

The justification and pretext for the dismantling of the Newfoundland legislature might be knocked down, but no thought was given to restoring it; nor was there any apology. The Commission of Government would remain at the helm in Newfoundland. What Clutterbuck wrote was for English eyes only. That same year Thomas Lodge, one of the first British commissioners, published a book, *Dictatorship in Newfoundland*, about his experience in the Commission of Government. Lodge wrote: "No one inside the British Administration had a positive sincere desire to make a real success of this bizarre experiment in dictatorship."[8] Disillusioned by the failure of the Commission, he concluded: "to have abandoned the principles of democracy without accomplishing economic rehabilitation is surely an unforgiveable sin."[9] The Dominions Office, although stung by the criticism, did little beyond public relations to improve the situation on the Island.

The arrival of the American troop ship the USS *Edmund B. Alexander* in St. John's harbour in January 1941 signalled the end of the long depression in Newfoundland and the beginning of prosperity. By 1944, after just three years of American activity on the Island, not only was there full employment but the Commission of Government was running surpluses—an astonishing turnaround. The Canadian banks in Newfoundland were also making millions from the large volume of American dollars now coming through their accounts, adding significantly to Canada's foreign currency reserves. Public criticism of the Leased Bases Agreement receded with the enormous financial benefits resulting from the aircraft-base building boom. Geoffrey Shakespeare, on a whirlwind fact-finding mission for the Dominions Office in 1941, reported on the need to capitalize on the quickly changing state of affairs: "I . . . suggest we really make a bold and comprehensive effort to repair the deficiencies of years of unimaginative government. I may add that Americans and Canadians, who are pouring millions of pounds into the Island for war purposes, are shocked at the general state of its development. . . . The housing conditions in St. John's are a disgrace."[10]

The level of development on the Island was not commensurate with its strategic importance, Shakespeare argued, and in view of the American and Canadian investment, Britain's could be no less. As Lord Amulree had before him, and others would later on, Shakespeare outlined a bold plan for reconstruction to justify the continuance of the Commission of Government. He presumed, albeit wrongly, that Canada and the United States would lose interest in Newfoundland after the war and proposed that it once again be granted dominion status—making it a British bulwark in the North Atlantic. He saw federation with Canada as a possibility in the future. The policy he proposed would remain essentially unchanged in Britain until 1945.

In the meantime, the Americans got the bases they wanted in Newfoundland for the defence of North America. The British got their ships and planes from the Americans. And the Newfoundlanders got the Americans and immediate relief from British thrift. Britain did, however, succeed in having the Americans reduce the salaries they were paying the Newfoundlanders to something more in line with British pay. The Americans were big spenders, but the American "invasion" was more than a great economic success in Newfoundland—it was a huge social success too. By the time Pepperrell Air Force Base closed in 1960, approximately 20,000 American service personnel stationed there had married Newfoundland women, producing 60,000 American-Newfoundland children and few recorded divorces. Ironically, the arrival in Newfoundland of thousands of American and Canadian personnel to fight the war in Europe would finally turn Newfoundland's focus away from Europe and towards North America. However, if the American–Newfoundland connection was a marriage of the heart, the same could not be said of the Canadian–Newfoundland relationship. As Governor Walwyn wrote to Sir Eric Machtig, under-secretary of state, at the Dominions Office in 1944: "The behaviour of the Americans, except in isolated incidents in the early days, has been infinitely better than the Canadians, and is so today."[11]

For the defence of Canada, the Canadians were necessarily involved in the defence of Newfoundland. They were there before the Americans and had a base at the harbour in St. John's, as well as air bases in Torbay and at Gander with the Royal Air Force (RAF). The sweeping concessions granted to the Americans by the British in Newfoundland by the Lend Lease Agreement of March 1941 generated both alarm and envy in Ottawa. It is fair to say that the Canadians finally discovered Newfoundland after the Americans' arrival.[12] Early in the war the Commission of Government had wanted to hand over the management of Newfoundland airports for military purposes entirely to the Canadians, but the plan was rejected out of hand by J.W. Herbertson at the Air Ministry in Whitehall. In his first telegram to Sir Charles Dixon at the Dominions Office on September 23, 1939 (released in 1998), Herbertson wrote:

> Secret. I have always assumed that our policy was to do nothing which would tend to give Canada a greater footing in Newfoundland. To hand over the airport to the Canadian Military's Airforce would mean the disappearance of our interests there for perhaps a considerable period at the end of which we might find it difficult to re-establish ourselves. The advantage of the present arrangement under which we control the airport is that it gives us a stranglehold over the North Atlantic Route and enables us to restrain our partners Erie and Canada. It would be a grave tactical error to do anything to weaken our position in this matter.[13]

Several weeks later Herbertson followed up with an equally emphatic statement on Newfoundland. It is clear that considerable discussions had taken place in the interval, resulting in a statement of Britain's overarching ambitions in Newfoundland since at least 1933. Herbertson began his second memo of October 13, 1939, with the more formal "We," which seemed to speak for the department:

Secret: We have always understood that it was the decided policy of H.M.G. in the U.K. that Newfoundland, the oldest British colony, should remain a separate entity and should not be absorbed by Canada. That policy has certainly governed our actions in regard to the provisions of aerodrome and marine air base facilities in Nfld. since I first went there for preliminary talks in 1933. At that time (which was shortly before the establishment of the Commission of Government) the local government was about to conclude agreements with Pan American Airways under which the latter would obtain certain exclusive rights for aviation services in the Island. I was just in time to stop this.

. . . We have spent large sums of money on the provision for an airport at Hattie's Camp [Gander] and also on the marine air base at Botwood and on ancillary services. I think that it would be a great mistake to hand over the airports to the Royal Canadian Air Force for the duration of the war. It is one thing to let them in but it would be quite another thing to get them out.

Newfoundland is destined to play an important part in the operation of the Trans-Atlantic services and it is an important bargaining counter which it would be folly to allow to pass out of our control.[14]

Air supremacy was the fundamental consideration underlying all British policy in Newfoundland from at least the 1920s to the late 1940s. It was the key reason for taking full control in 1933—one fully reinforced by the experience of the Second World War. The value Britain placed on Newfoundland's strategic importance is revealed in Herbertson's casual reference to another British policy—that of using Newfoundland as a "bargaining counter" in the North Atlantic geo-political game. The imperious rejection of the commission's and Canada's request proved entirely impractical, however, and wartime circumstances soon forced the British not only to accept Canadian authority on the bases already on the Island but eventually to grant Canadians the prize they most wanted—a ninety-nine-year lease for a Canadian air base at Goose Bay in Labrador—a deal that was bitterly opposed in Newfoundland.

Overall, the Canadian presence was felt far less in terms of money, men and popularity than the American, but it was still a significant investment that Prime Minister Mackenzie King was anxious to profit from and protect. On August 28, 1940, he instructed O.D. Skelton at the Department of External Affairs to prepare a report "as to what the British had done in Newfoundland and what we [Canada] had done and then consider the advisability of acquiring ownership of areas in Newfoundland in which we were spending money. An effort would be made after the war to have us take over Newfoundland."[15] King's assertiveness may have come from more than his $5 million investment in the Island. His confidence may have been buoyed by his secret understanding with President Roosevelt on Newfoundland's position after the war. After a meeting with the US president in December 1942, King wrote in his diary that he reminded him of a previous conversation: "You said to me, some time ago, that Canada ought to possess Newfoundland." He remembered that Roosevelt thought the island would be suitable for raising sheep.[16]

In response to King's request, Hugh Keenleyside prepared a lengthy memo for Norman Robertson, the acting under-secretary of state for external affairs, on the new Canadian position in Newfoundland:

Since the outbreak of war in September 1939, Newfoundland has been playing an increasingly large part in considerations relating to Canadian defence. . . . It is quite clear that rather than decreasing in importance as hoped, our relations with Newfoundland during the remainder of this year and until the end of the war, will be more important than they have been in the past. With Canada taking a very large measure of responsibility for the defence of Newfoundland with Canadian military, naval and air force bases established in, and possibly operating from, Newfoundland bases, with the expenditure of some $5,000,000 by Canadian representatives in the Island immediately in prospect, with United States forces established in Newfoundland bases, and with the United Sates Government maintaining a consular representative (Consul General) in St. John's . . . it is most desirable that consideration be given to . . . appointing an official representative of the Canadian Government to be stationed permanently, or at least until the end of the war. . . .

Although Newfoundland is not a Dominion it would perhaps please the people of the Island if the Canadian representative in Newfoundland were to be designated a High Commissioner.[17]

Unable to continue to ignore Newfoundland as irrelevant to national concerns, and with an eye to eventual annexation, Robertson presented the department's recommendations to King in July 1941:

It is clear from an inspection of the files of the DEA for the past six months that Canada has more varied, more important and more urgent business with Newfoundland than with all the self-governing Dominions in which we maintain High Commissioners put together. It may be difficult to get a good man to go to St. John's as High Commissioner but it is clearly a post which requires an able man who is capable of gaining the confidence and trust of Newfoundlanders. One man who I think could fit in well is C.J. Burchell, now High Commissioner in Australia. He is a Maritimer, familiar not only with the question of Dominion–Provincial relationships but with Commonwealth constitutional theory and practice—both important qualifications in view of the special problems which Newfoundland relations with Canada present. He is, however, doing a good job in Australia and he's not been there very long. He might feel that translation to Newfoundland was not a promotion."[18]

King agreed with the need for this posting, but Robertson proved to be correct about Charles Burchell. After arriving in St. John's on a chilly November day in 1941, the new high commissioner immediately wrote to his boss and offered to return to Australia. King replied, "As much as I appreciate your offer to return to Canberra . . . I am convinced that you can perform a larger, national service by continuing in your present post."[19]

The "larger service" was understood by all concerned as the incorporation of Newfoundland into the Canadian Confederation. And so Burchell stayed on. He moved into a spacious residence—Canada House—on the corner of Circular Road and Johnny's Hill, and before long there was a steady stream of correspondence and requests for information between the Canadian high commissioner in Newfoundland and the British governor. The Canadians had officially arrived.

Burchell's appointment was another constitutional anomaly for Newfoundland. Canada maintained a high commissioner as its senior diplomatic agent in other Commonwealth dominions but had never had such representation in neighbouring Newfoundland. Why Canada should suddenly recognize Newfoundland as worthy of such attention, let alone transfer one of its top diplomats to the post, and at a time when Newfoundland was in a compromised constitutional position with suspende dominion status, was no mystery to the people of Newfoundland. Burchell's appointment was greeted with the same skepticism with which most Canadian moves towards the Island were met. The *Daily News* fumed:

How the appointment of a Canadian High Commissioner eliminates Dominions Office controls over the decisions of the Newfoundland Government is something inconceivable unless it be that Mr. Burchell is to stand here in the place of Lord Cranborne (the Dominions Secretary) and his officials in Downing Street. And if that be the case then the Canadian High Commissioner would become in theory the final arbiter in all questions involving Canada and Newfoundland."[20]

The *Fishermen-Workers Tribune* went so far as to declare that "Newfoundland is to be run by a Canadian Commissioner or Board."[21]

Burchell found this reception disconcerting, and on December 14 he expressed his concerns to Robertson:

> I find that the attitude of the great majority of people here is that they think Canada is standing by ready to gobble Newfoundland up at the proper time. They look with great suspicion on the spending by Canada of money for the defence of Newfoundland, as apparently they fear the Greeks bringing gifts. . . .
>
> I can recall some instances in which the attitude of Canada has been anything but helpful to Newfoundland and in respect of which Newfoundlanders have so many grievances."[22]

Robertson responded: "It is quite clear that we can never divorce ourselves from an active interest in conditions in Newfoundland and that, in fact, we may have to take a very much closer and more immediate part in the fate of our nearest neighbour to the east."[23] Robertson's melancholy reflection that Canada could "never divorce" itself from Newfoundland seemed an ill omen for any happy union, the inevitability of which he seemed darkly certain. If the American relationship with Newfoundland was a marriage of the heart, as was often said, it seemed certain that any marriage between Canada and Newfoundland would require a shotgun.

As the war carried on, both the Canadians and the British in Newfoundland were increasingly embarrassed by the Americans, who were far more popular than the Canadians and were clearly spending more and doing more for the Island than its British rulers had ever done.

In June 1942 Paul Emrys-Evans, parliamentary under-secretary for dominions affairs in Great Britain, wrote a memo echoing Geoffrey Shakespeare's alarm about the imperial reputation and urging the Dominions Office to speedy action:

> The Americans and the Canadians are competing with one another in order to impress the Newfoundlanders. Our recent record shows no dramatic or impressive achievement and this is being noted both in Canada and in the US.
>
> . . . the remarkable speed and efficiency with which the Bases and especially the Base hospitals have been built, has greatly impressed the people, while the development of the Atlantic Air Service is bound to make itself felt . . . a new and vigorous policy with regard to Newfoundland has become imperative.
>
> . . . it is essential . . . that a Governor should be appointed for Newfoundland who will also be the active chairman of the Commission. He would in fact combine the duties of the King and the Prime Minister . . . Such men cannot be found unless they are taken from important posts, but unless they are spared for work in the Empire its future is dark indeed.[24]

At the time, Sir Humphrey Walwyn was still governor of Newfoundland and, before he departed in 1946, he would fill out a ten-year term, in spite of Emrys-Evans' warnings. As soon as Clement Attlee became prime minister after the war, he appointed Sir Gordon Macdonald to the position. Sir Gordon was exactly the kind of governor that Emrys-Evans had envisaged, but by then the hour was late and the future of the British Empire would get no brighter.

On June 13, 1942, Sir Eric Machtig, responding to Emrys-Evans' urgent concerns, outlined the situation in Newfoundland for Attlee, who was then the secretary of state for dominions affairs, and he began with this embarrassed nod to democracy:

I do agree that the Commission of Government from its nature has never been a very happy instrument for the government of a country like Newfoundland.

. . . we must actively consider the future after the War . . . the immense efforts made by the Newfoundlanders during the War in the Allied cause and the completely changed financial position, even if only temporary (they are now lending us money instead of our financing them) means that when the War ends there will be an overwhelming move in favour of the restoration of self-government. This will be difficult to resist and we ought to be prepared with our line of action. . . . We ought to know our own minds as regards the main issue and not rely on a Royal Commission to make them up for us. Our policy should be to bring Newfoundland into this Canadian Confederation if by any means this can be accomplished.

It is clear that public opinion in Newfoundland has always been intensely against union with Canada, but this is largely due to the fact that the Canadians have regarded them as poor relations, have done in the main little to help them and have always taken the line that circumstances would force Newfoundland into Canada in due course on Canada's terms.

The position as I see it, is that the change which has taken place in the circumstances of Newfoundland will make it politically impossible to retain control from the UK through a Commission of Government. There will be great political pressure for the restoration of free Parliamentary institutions in Newfoundland.[25]

Machtig was obviously reluctant to release Newfoundland from British control and averse to restoring democracy to the Islanders, at least outside the confines of the Canadian Confederation. He was, however, correct in his assessment of local discontent. Opposition to the British Commission of Government had been muted at first. In the darkest hours of 1933, many Newfoundlanders felt that, for years, they had not been represented by their own government and that, perhaps, someone else's government might do better. But by the late 1930s, this tacit acceptance had passed because of the commissioners' general inaction and lack of communication. The criticism that had been simmering in the local papers had grown to an audible grumble by the opening days of the Second World War. There were frequent calls from the St. John's Board of Trade and other organizations for a return to some form of representative government, if not full responsible government.

Perhaps the most intelligent and informed record of Newfoundlanders' concerns throughout this period can be found in the writing of Albert Perlin, whose "Wayfarer" column in the *Daily News* recorded the entire drama. The fact that Canadian High Commissioner Charles Burchell quotes him extensively and frequently in his dispatches to the Department of External Affairs in Ottawa is testimony enough of the soundness and influence of his views. Perlin was the subject of this dispatch, for instance, in June 1942:

> I have the honour to bring to your attention extracts from recent articles by *"Wayfarer"* in *The Daily News* on the subject of the restoration of Responsible Government. . . .
>
> . . . the Commission Government has proved itself an utter and complete failure. It sees itself as a permanent oligarchy. It has done nothing at all to prepare the people for an assumption of the responsibilities of self-government. It seems more concerned with getting a pat on the back from the Dominions Office than catering to the natural democratic rights of the people. . . . When you are denied self-government and you have not got good, in the form of efficient government to replace it, the urge to political independence becomes that much stronger.
>
> It will be noted that *Wayfarer* suggests some form of representative government should be adopted as a major step towards the

restoration of Dominion status after the war, rather than an immediate return to Responsible Government. He states that no one wants to do anything that would interfere with the war and that meant acceptance of the war effort.[26]

Newfoundland, always intensely patriotic, had thrown itself wholeheartedly into the war effort. Its support included acceptance of the status quo, the Leased Bases Agreement, and even the Goose Bay deal with Canada for the duration of the conflict. But as the war dragged on, it became incumbent on the government in Whitehall to do or say something about the increasingly absurd political situation in Newfoundland.

ATTLEE IN NEWFOUNDLAND:
HOLDING ON FOR BRITAIN

In the summer of 1942 Clement Attlee, the dominions secretary, came to Newfoundland for a tour of the country and a rest. He was preceded by his secretary, Alexander Clutterbuck, the author of the infamous Amulree Report. On his arrival, High Commissioner Charles Burchell wrote a confidential memo to Norman Robertson at the Department of External Affairs in Ottawa:

> Mr. P.A. Clutterbuck of the Dominions Office is arriving in St. John's on Monday. He was Secretary to the Royal Commission, 1933, commonly known as the Amulree Commission.
>
> There are few people in Newfoundland who have a good word to say for the Amulree Commission today. It is in fact exceedingly unpopular. . . .
>
> The mystery to me is why Attlee should come here at the present time or even send someone from the Dominions Office, such as Clutterbuck. . . .
>
> Officially I do not know anything about Clutterbuck's visit, nor do I know what his present standing in the Dominions Office is. I am wondering if he is an important enough person for me to

ask to the luncheon for the Governor General. I now have 36 invitations and 36 acceptances, as per the enclosed list. These, with my wife, my daughter and myself, make a total of 39. I have seating accommodation for exactly 40 people but that is the limit. I therefore have one seat vacant and would appreciate hearing from you by cable on Monday as to Clutterbuck's standing and whether or not he is of sufficient importance as representing the Dominions Office to be asked to the luncheon. I do not want to make enquiries about him around here. . . .[1]

Robertson replied: "United Kingdom authorities here did not know of Clutterbuck's arrival. They were under the impression that he was to be a member of the party accompanying the other person mentioned in your letter. Under the circumstances it would probably be a suitable and gracious act for you to invite Clutterbuck to your dinner."[2]

By way of underlining the need for confidentiality, Burchell added in a following correspondence:

You will note that . . . *The Fishermen-Workers Tribune* is suggesting that Clutterbuck's visit is for the purpose of conspiring to rush Newfoundland into Confederation. . . . It is amazing to discover from time to time to what a large section of the people the thought of Confederation is sort of a nightmare hanging over them all the time. . . .[3]

For example, I am enclosing herewith a very interesting editorial which appeared in *The Evening Telegram* . . . in which the writer, probably Mr. Jeffrey, the editor of the paper, says: "It is something more than a coincidence that this talk of—or more correctly in some quarters, fears of—Confederation with Canada should crop up so regularly when discussions are held between the Commission and the British or Canadian leaders.[4]

Burchell got on well with the governor, Sir Humphrey Walwyn, but he had little understanding of the workings of the Dominions Office in Newfoundland. Clutterbuck was in fact head of Newfoundland Affairs at the office at the time and secretary to Attlee during his visit. Officials in the governments of both Great Britain and Canada in the early 1940s, and even in different departments in the same government, were often ignorant of each other's affairs. But that situation was about to change. Clutterbuck came to lunch, and Burchell was impressed with him—as, a month later, he was with Attlee too, after their tour of the Island. In September, on the eve of their departure, Burchell wrote again to Robertson:

> I thought Attlee was very adroit in turning aside the issue of confederation. . . . "Asked [in a press interview] whether he would discuss confederation with Ottawa officials his answer was that he would not take the initiative of raising that or any other question." You will note that [the *Evening Telegram*] says that that reply . . . seems to have turned discussions of his visit away from confederation to the possible return of responsible government. . . . I find also that, in some quarters at least, Clutterbuck is highly regarded in spite of the fact that he was Secretary of the Amulree Commission. . . . I take it that Mr. Attlee and Mr. Clutterbuck are both giving a good deal of study and thought to the present form of government and perhaps may evolve some improvement. . . .
>
> On the other hand, the fact must be kept in mind, in fairness to the Commissioners, that the people of this country are difficult people to deal with. This country has been so badly governed during the whole period of its history of over four hundred years that I think it is inevitable, and no matter how good a government may be, it is inbred in the people here to be always in revolt against governmental authority.[5]

The Newfoundlanders' well-developed skepticism and spirit of independence were not qualities appreciated by Ottawa, at least not for purposes
of assimilation.

Following this visit, Attlee and Clutterbuck continued to play key
roles in British Newfoundland right up to the handover to Canada six
years later. In November, Attlee wrote to Governor Walwyn:

> Secret and Personal. Since my return from Newfoundland I
> have been thinking over my impressions. Although there
> appears at present to be little or no demand in the Island for any
> constitutional change while war conditions continue, it is clear
> that we ought to be turning over in our minds the various pos-
> sibilities that may arise as soon as the war ends, and I am anx-
> ious to make as much progress as possible in working out with
> the Commission [of Government] an agreed line of policy in
> order that we not be caught unprepared by events. . . . The pres-
> ent constitution is the result of a contract with the Newfoundland
> people which was confirmed by the Newfoundland Act [of
> 1933], and no matter how strong the case might be on merits, it
> would not be open to us to vary the terms of this contract of
> our own volition without the express consent of the other
> party to the bargain. In other words, if Newfoundland could be
> regarded as self-supporting and there were a general demand in
> Newfoundland for the restoration of self-government, it would
> not be practicable to refuse it.[6]

This assessment was an entirely accurate description of Great
Britain's contractual and constitutional obligation to Newfoundland. It
is unfortunate that, when he later became prime minister, Attlee would
do exactly the opposite and unilaterally "vary the terms" of the original
"contract with the people of Newfoundland" and consider the case for
Confederation "on its merits." His reference to "the various possibilities"

after the war is a fair warning that the constitutional course in Newfoundland was about to take some curious turns.

In his reply to Attlee on January 7, Walwyn suggested, after a flight of imperial fancy, what one such meritorious case might be. He also indicated an apparent willingness to stray from the terms of the Newfoundland Act:

6. It may be that the final solution lies in the political incorporation of this country in a larger unit.

7. In this connection the possibility of some association with Great Britain on the Northern Ireland pattern should not be ruled out. We do not think that distance any longer precludes such a possibility.

8. The only other political incorporation which deserves consideration is Confederation with Canada. It may be, as you assert, that confederation is unlikely to be acceptable to public opinion in either country. We feel that on a plebiscite in this country at this time the assertion would be proved true. . . .

9. Canada's present and growing interest in this country, her fear of an increase of United States influence, her desire to acquire the Labrador, are all powerful factors. At no time has our bargaining position been so favourable and it is doubtful if it ever will be so again.[7]

That the Dominions Office entertained thoughts of joining Newfoundland to Great Britain along the lines of Northern Ireland, with Newfoundland MPs sitting in the Parliament at Westminster, shows the reach of imperial thinking even in 1943. Walwyn's casual reference to the British "bargaining position" in relation to Newfoundland suggests the true British perspective. Fully one hundred years after self-government had been granted, Britain still regarded Newfoundland as its own, to possess or dispose of at will.

Governor Walwyn was wrong in his prognostication on Confederation. The British would have an even better opportunity to "sell" Newfoundland to Canada in 1948, and for a much better price. If conditions were propitious for Confederation in 1943, however, the timing was not. Newfoundland opinion was almost unanimously against any union with Canada. It would be an uphill fight for Canadians to win the hearts and minds of Newfoundlanders and capture the prize of Labrador. There is clear frustration and even resentment in Burchell's gloomy dispatches to Hugh Keenleyside at External Affairs about his own country's miserable history on the Island:

> It appears that February 16th is the 9th Anniversary of the Commission of Government. I am enclosing an editorial on the Anniversary which appeared in the *Daily News* of today's date. I am also enclosing an article by the Wayfarer in the same paper.
>
> I do not usually agree with much of what the Wayfarer has to say but I think he pretty nearly hits the nail on the head this time. I do not think the British Government can be at all proud of the fact that they set up this form of Government here. Neither do I think that as Canadians we can take any pride in the fact that there were two Canadians, C.A. Magrath and Stavert, sitting on the Amulree Commission which recommended the doing away with responsible Government and the setting up of the Commission of Government. Nor do I think Canadians can take much pride in the fact that they stood aside when the people of Newfoundland were in the depths of despair in 1933. That was the time, if ever, that we might have been of real help to Newfoundland, and we did nothing except allow two Canadians without any experience or background in constitutional matters to sit in judgment on them.[8]

Jack Pickersgill, Prime Minister Mackenzie King's private secretary, was listening to Burchell's lament. He, along with the influential justice minister, Louis St. Laurent, and External Affairs officers R.A. MacKay and Hugh Keenleyside, was much in favour of Canada taking Newfoundland into Confederation, and they consistently pushed the Department of External Affairs in this direction. Pickersgill's memorandum of May 1943 puts the best face on the situation in Newfoundland and reads like a pep talk to Burchell:

> [Secret] The Canadian attitude to Newfoundland is very like the American attitude to Canada, an amicable indifference coupled with a complete ignorance of local susceptibilities. . . .
>
> Assuming that it is of first importance to Canada to maintain and extend our position in Newfoundland after the war and, if possible, to incorporate Newfoundland into Canada, and assuming further that we can only accomplish these ends with the consent of the Newfoundlanders, it is clear that every effort should be made now to win their goodwill, and, equally, that no opportunity should be lost in presenting them in as favourable light as possible to Canadians.
>
> It is suggested that a programme looking to these ends should be mapped out jointly by Executive Affairs and WIB [Wartime Information Board] and that WIB with discreet assistance from the High Commissioner undertake to implement it. . . .
>
> Needless to say, it should all be done unobtrusively and in a simple spirit of neighbourliness, but there should be no doubt that it was being done by Canadians. [Marginal note: Simple like a serpent].[9]

In June 1943 a question in the House of Commons in Ottawa from J.W. Noseworthy, MP for South York, about the state of Newfoundland after the war drew this premature and now fateful reply from the ever-cautious Mackenzie King: "If the people of Newfoundland should ever decide they wish to enter the Canadian federation and should make that decision clear and beyond all possibility of misunderstanding, Canada would give most sympathetic consideration to the proposal."[10] In London at the Dominions Office, Clutterbuck observed with interest that "Mr. MacKenzie King's statement . . . follows very much the line one would expect. . . . Reading between the lines this certainly suggests that Canada is now prepared to adopt a more forthcoming attitude than in the past, but I fear that there is little likelihood of the statement influencing Newfoundland opinion."[11]

The Dominions Office was also moving slowly towards formulating its postwar policy on *not* returning responsible government to Newfoundland. To help it along, the year after his own tour Attlee sent over a "Goodwill Mission" to report back to the UK government and Parliament and to suggest the next constitutional step for the Island. Many in Newfoundland were surprised at the arrival of another fact-finding mission so soon after Attlee and Clutterbuck's extensive visit. It seemed to them that Newfoundland was getting a lot of attention but very little information or action.

The Goodwill Mission, composed of Sir Derrick Gunston, Charles Ammon, and A.P. Herbert, arrived in St. John's in June 1943. Herbert, the Independent member for Oxford University, was a published author, something of a wit, and a highly regarded member of the House. He was also Newfoundland's champion in the British Parliament for the return of self-government, as promised by the terms of the Newfoundland Act of 1933. As Jim Halley recalled:

> I met Herbert in Corner Brook that summer. I was walking back from a tennis game with Tommy Williams when I saw him across the street. I knew who he was and what he was doing here of course, and introduced myself. We were both staying at the Glynmill Inn so we had lunch together and he asked me: "What do

you and your friends see for Newfoundland after the War?" "Oh,"
I said, "we're going with the United States." "Why do you think
that?" he asked. "Well just look around you," I said, "there's
Americans and American activity and American money all over
the Island. We'd be crazy *not* to go with them."[12]

In St. John's, Herbert and his colleagues had extensive discussions
with Governor Walwyn about the possibility of some form of future
elections on the Island. The idea for an elected council, or National
Convention, was being discussed in the local papers. Initially suggested
by R.B. Job, a prominent Water Street merchant, it appealed to Herbert
as a possible mechanism for Newfoundland to request the restoration of
responsible government.[13] He also had several conversations with Charles
Burchell, not all of them satisfactory. On their last encounter, Burchell
reported to Norman Robertson: "Herbert and Captain Rowland followed me . . . and as we were leaving, he put out his hand to say good-bye
and told me he was leaving tomorrow. As he was shaking hands with me
he said to me, 'Keep your hands off Newfoundland.' Somehow or other
I managed to keep my Irish temper under control but I could not help
making the statement that some of us who lived in the Dominions are
trying to build up the British Empire but some people who live in
England are trying to break it up. As I was walking away from him
I heard him muttering to himself, 'Canadian banking in Newfoundland
and Canadian life insurance companies!'"[14]

The return of the Goodwill Mission to Britain once again focused
the attention of the Parliament of Parliaments on Newfoundland. Many
MPs besides Herbert were troubled that the United Kingdom continued
to maintain a benevolent dictatorship on the Island. Frustrated with the
reasons offered for the continued delay in returning responsible government, Beverley Baxter, the MP for Wood Green and a popular novelist,
declared, "We do not give self-government as a prize, as a lollipop. We
give it as a command. When Newfoundland owed us money we put in

the Commissioners. We have heard it is now paying us money. I should say that we have had on deposit (in war loans) about $10,000,000. Suppose we cannot pay it when the war is over. Will Newfoundland be entitled to send three Commissioners to Britain and close this House? It sounds absurd certainly, but the principle is the same."[15] Bartle Bull, the MP for Enfield, asked Attlee the obvious question that troubled the members: "How in the world without a Parliament in Newfoundland can we find out whether the people of Newfoundland have made a request to Great Britain for Dominion status, or return to self-government or however you wish to put it?"[16]

In his final report to Churchill's War Cabinet on the return of the Goodwill Mission in November 1943, Attlee concluded:

> [Secret] . . . In view of Newfoundland's important rôle as a Naval and Air Base we should clearly wish to avoid any disturbance of public opinion which would distract from the war effort. . . . There should be no change in the present form of Government while the war lasts; as soon as practicable after the end of the war, that is the war in Europe, we must provide machinery . . . for enabling the Newfoundland people to examine the situation and to express their considered views as to the form of government they desire. . . . One proposal for the solution of this problem which appeals to me is that made by Mr A.P. Herbert MP, viz., that a national Convention should be set up after the war, composed of members representative of all classes and interests in Newfoundland, and empowered to discuss and determine amongst themselves, with the guidance of a constitutional lawyer from home, the form of government to be recommended both to the Newfoundland people and to the United Kingdom Government.[17]

This memo marks the first official mention of the National Convention that Herbert had discussed with Governor Walwyn and others in St. John's that summer. However, when the terms of reference for the convention were ultimately released by the Dominions Office in December 1945, they included two key changes that, in effect, subverted any intention of returning responsible government to Newfoundland. By then, the British had determined that they must control the constitutional situation in Newfoundland completely.

The threat of increased American and even Canadian activity displacing Britain in the North Atlantic, as well as some sense of responsibility for their own obligations, eventually drove the Dominions Office to prepare a comprehensive, even generous, policy of reconstruction in Newfoundland. With the international spotlight increasingly focused on the Island, a horrified cry arose from the bowels of the Dominions Office: "There must be no Imperial slum on the back doorstep of the United States."[18] Faced with the failure of direct British rule in the form of the Commission of Government and the de facto rebuilding of Newfoundland around the American bases, Britain felt compelled to announce its own plans to rebuild the country.

The commissioners in St. John's were so used to receiving so little from the British Treasury that they were visibly "surprised at the generosity and magnitude of the assistance contemplated" when Lord Cranborne, the dominions secretary, told them at a special meeting in London of his plan to spend £20 million ($100 million) on the Island's reconstruction. "The Commissioners appeared, however, to be of the opinion that if the scope and purpose of the scheme were to be made public prior to the holding of a referendum on the constitutional issue . . . the Newfoundland people's mind would be made up for them in advance and that there was little doubt that there would be an overwhelming vote in favour of a return to responsible Government."[19] The commissioners felt that with such generous financial support, Newfoundlanders would feel comfortable with Responsible Government again and reject Confederation with Canada. The political argument for denying Newfoundland any funds for reconstruction as a necessary condition to induce Newfoundlanders to vote for union with Canada was apparently not recognized by the Dominions Office either in this instance from the Newfoundland commissioners, or later by the Canadians themselves.

Perhaps the British plans for a generous reconstruction would have surprised the Newfoundland commissioners less if they had been privy to the plans Lord Beaverbrook had prepared for Churchill's War Cabinet to restore dominion status to Newfoundland. Beaverbrook, the Canadian champion of empire, was born William Maxwell Aitken, the son of a Presbyterian minister in Newcastle, New Brunswick. He became a self-made millionaire and, later, a press baron in England. For fifty years he was part of the British political establishment: in the First World War he was a minister in Lloyd George's War Cabinet and, during the Second World War, he was Lord Privy Seal and the minister of aviation supply in Churchill's War Cabinet. A close friend of Churchill and a celebrity in his own right, he possessed a larger than life personality and an original mind with very definite opinions. His report stands in complete opposition to Attlee's views. This controversial and highly sensitive document was released by the UK government only in the winter of 2010, and it demonstrates a dramatic split in the War Cabinet over policy in Newfoundland. Beaverbrook presents a far more explicit and striking appraisal of the actual situation in Newfoundland, along with the imperial determination to maintain the Island within the strictly British sphere. Most startling, the report contains a blunt warning to Churchill and the War Cabinet that the UK government's position in Newfoundland was not only unconstitutional but illegal.

At this time—the autumn of 1943—the War Cabinet was meeting in underground bunkers, bombs were falling overhead and the outcome of the war was still uncertain. Nevertheless, Beaverbrook was uncompromising in his condemnation of the Commission of Government in Newfoundland. His report is also fascinating for what it implies about the reasons for the British takeover of Newfoundland in 1933. It is a powerful indictment of British policy in the Island and is reproduced here in full:

[Secret] Memorandum from Lord Privy Seal to War Cabinet of
Great Britain, London, Nov 18, 1943

1. Newfoundland should be offered the right to resume Dominion
   status at any time during the war or after it.

2. The claim is put forward that the present Commission of Government is unconstitutional, and its acts will inevitably be challenged. This contention is based on Clause 1 of the Newfoundland Act, 1933, which makes it clear that the suspension of the
   Constitution was limited by the terms of the Address to His
   Majesty by the Legislative Council and House of Assembly of
   Newfoundland to a period until such time as the island may become
   self-supporting again. But Newfoundland is now self-supporting,
   so it is argued. It has a surplus of 11 million dollars. Therefore the
   legal basis of Commission Government has been destroyed.
   Now, if we neglect to give self-government to Newfoundland, we
   must be prepared to meet and destroy this argument. It is my view
   that we will fail in convincing the people of Newfoundland.

3. Newfoundland has lent us 8 million dollars, most of it interest-
   free. It has given 500,000 dollars to the Spitfire Fund for the
   purchase of aircraft and, by voluntary subscription among the
   public, has provided another 150,000 dollars to that Fund.

4. The agitation in Newfoundland for the restoration of self-
   government is widespread. Practically all the newspapers partici-
   pate in the campaign. Among them may be mentioned the *Daily
   News* of St. John's, the *Grand Falls Advertiser*, the *Fishermen-
   Workers' Tribune*, the *Observer's Weekly*, the *Evening Telegram*, the
   Newfoundland Trade Review, and the *Western Star*.

5. The Newfoundland public is entirely dissatisfied with the
   Commission and the unpopularity of that body grows steadily.

6. Six Trade Union leaders met at St. John's on the 13th April and
   passed a resolution for the restoration of self-government.

7. The Newfoundland Board of Trade, meeting on the 29th March, passed a resolution asking that representative government be set up, as a matter of urgent need.

8. There is resistance in newspapers, amounting to claims of repudiation of the transactions relating to the bases.

9. The claim that the Newfoundland Government fell through corruption is not now accepted. It is believed that the measure was taken to benefit bond-holders and supply Canadian banks with repayment of their overdraft. In fact, it is believed that Canadian banks helped to precipitate the financial crisis. . . .

10. The advantages of a restored Dominion status are manifold. It would be a protection against Canada's unjust claim over Goose Bay and the pretensions which the United States will advance to civil air bases in Newfoundland.

11. With Dominion status, Newfoundland will safeguard our Imperial interests in the Western Atlantic against any "ganging up" by Canada and the United States, always a possibility under a different government.[20]

It is hard not to notice the urgency in the tone of this memorandum in expressing the fear of losing Newfoundland to either the Americans or the Canadians. When the Imperial Conference of 1931, via the Statute of Westminster, confirmed dominion status for Newfoundland, Canada, New Zealand, Australia and three other countries, there was some criticism that, in the case of Newfoundland, the Dominions Office was putting the trappings of an elephant on the back of a mouse. Beaverbrook's reasons for restoring that status in 1943 suggest what had motivated the British to bestow this status on Newfoundland in the first place. In 1931 the British already had significant investments in Newfoundland. They were keenly aware of the Island's strategic importance to them and had plans for larger investments in aviation at Gander. Conferring dominion status on Newfoundland allowed Whitehall to keep the Americans and the Canadians out while securing their own investment in the Island and their position in the North Atlantic. The financial crisis of 1933 had only occasioned a change in strategy to one of direct control. Dominion status was therefore as much about protecting British interests in the North Atlantic as was the establishment of the Commission of Government.

The 1939 memo from J.W. Herbertson at the Air Ministry to Sir Charles Dixon at the Dominions Office had already revealed that Newfoundland was the key to British air supremacy. Indeed, it had always been British policy to keep the Americans and the Canadians out and to preserve the Island as a British bastion. By 1943, however, Beaverbrook's confrontational stance was out of step with the interdependent agreements forged by the Allies during and after the war, and in particular with Churchill's and Roosevelt's understanding about Newfoundland. Perhaps even more to the point, Beaverbrook's uncompromising view of the contract between Great Britain and Newfoundland in the Newfoundland Act of 1933 could only make the UK government uncomfortable as it prepared to manoeuvre around it with the establishment of a controlled National Convention at war's end. Ultimately, the only "ganging up" in the North Atlantic would be by Britain and Canada against Newfoundland.

In St. John's, Governor Walwyn was dubious about the value of any sort of National Convention or, more particularly, about his ability to control it. In a long telegram to Attlee on February 12, 1944, he reported that public reaction to the rumours of such a convention was not positive.

> We observe that you also feel that some sort of referendum to the people as a whole may be unavoidable. . . .
>
> . . . A dozen or so letters . . . have appeared in the Press, and without exception they have condemned the proposal to set up conventions or other machinery on the ground that the simple issue which has to be decided is the retention of Commission Government or the return to full Responsible Government.

> . . . the new proposals represent a serious departure from the simple terms of the Amulree recommendations [and] there is no power in anyone in Newfoundland to agree to a variation of these terms except . . . a responsible government.[21]

With his plan of establishing a National Convention in Newfoundland, Attlee was indeed straying from the terms of reference of the original contract of 1933 in an effort to control the constitutional outcome. But this variation is exactly what he had claimed only fifteen months earlier to Walwyn as "not open to us."

In this debate the government of Newfoundland stood with Beaverbrook. Walwyn clearly disapproved of the "departure from the simple terms," just as he disapproved of the novel constitutional process now envisaged by the Dominions Office. He reminded Attlee:

> It is by no means certain that the Newfoundland Legislature in 1933 would have consented to the suspension of the Letters Patent if the door were left wide open to permit any other form of government to succeed Government by Commission than the one relinquished. . . . There was no thought in 1933 of any change in the permanent form of government.
>
> The clear and inescapable implication in the new proposals is that Newfoundland's financial troubles were in large measure bound up with her form of government and may possibly be avoided in the future if another form is substituted. This implication has been seen by several writers in the press during the past year or two and strongly resented by them.[22]

Walwyn was clearly correct in his view of the last Newfoundland government's understanding of the Newfoundland Act. That was certainly Prime Minister Alderdice's understanding when he wrote, "a full measure of Responsible Government will be restored to the Island when we have again been placed upon a self-supporting basis."[23] Moreover, it was also Churchill's understanding of the Newfoundland Act when he reassured Cordell Hull, the American ambassador to London, that the Leased Bases Agreement between Britain and America would remain unaltered "upon the resumption by Newfoundland of the Constitutional status held by it prior to the 16th of February 1934."[24]

In case Attlee, the dominions secretary, was in any doubt about Walwyn's own views, the governor of Newfoundland declared:

> We ourselves are firmly convinced that for all practical purposes there will only be two possible alternatives open to the country, either to return to Responsible Government or to continue with the same or substantially the same system of Government as that now in force. . . . In the long run it will be much better for Newfoundland to have Responsible Government restored immediately.[25]

This was forceful language from the Newfoundland governor. Walwyn went as far as he could in stating his disapproval of the UK government's constitutional schemes. He was, however, an appointed leader, not an elected one. Well aware of the way his views would be received by his superiors in Whitehall, he added dutifully: "We submit this statement of our views to you with sincere regret that we should seem to doubt the wisdom of a course of action to which you are already committed by a statement to the British Parliament and with an assurance that we shall do our utmost to implement successfully whatever decision you may reach."[26]

Clearly, Walwyn would have to go. Despite official assurance, he was not the man for the job Attlee had in mind in Newfoundland. Rather, Attlee would require a willing and aggressive partner in the final push to put Newfoundland into Confederation—a governor who owed his position to Attlee and who would not be averse to using that position to promote the prime minister's personal agenda on the Island.

Shortly after the return of the Goodwill Mission, a bitter controversy erupted in the Newfoundland press over Canada's new base in Goose Bay. The St. John's Board of Trade protested that the Goose Bay deal was an unacceptable giveaway by Great Britain of assets vital to Newfoundland's future and that the extension of the ninety-nine-year lease to Canada was totally unnecessary. The Canadians, they charged, were seeking to establish postwar civil aviation rights on Newfoundland soil. The British resisted signing the lease until the summer of 1944. However on June 27 of that year, Norman Robertson, under-secretary of state for external affairs, wrote to the British deputy high commissioner that if Canada did not get Goose Bay, then Britain would not get the financial package of war aid promised to John Maynard Keynes.[27] The British got the message, and the Canadians got Goose Bay.

Having won the fight over Goose Bay, and aware that London would be announcing constitutional changes for Newfoundland in early 1944, Canada's Department of External Affairs formulated its own policy paper on Newfoundland. It included a long list of the advantages and disadvantages of "the incorporation of Newfoundland as a tenth province of Canada." The advantages were cautiously, even reluctantly, calculated as:

a) Greater freedom in any crisis in the Atlantic.
b) Probable enhancement of our position as a world power if we maintained defence . . . commitments.
c) Possibly a better bargaining position in the matter of civil aviation.
d) Possibly more effective control . . . in export fish markets.
e) Control of iron ore deposits [Labrador] may conceivably be of future importance politically and economically.

The Canadians were more definite—even enthusiastic—about the perceived disadvantages:

a) Newfoundland would certainly be a considerable financial liability . . .

b) Newfoundland would probably be a political liability . . . . We might expect constant agitation for "better terms" . . .

(c) It would be extremely difficult to fit Newfoundland into the existing pattern of Dominion–Provincial relations . . .

(d) Canada's defence establishment would have to be considerably larger in order to maintain effective defence of her greatly extended Atlantic frontier.[28]

Nevertheless, in spite of myriad objections, in January 1944 Canadian policy makers came to the conclusion that "the United Kingdom Government should be informed that Canada is prepared to consider seriously the incorporation of Newfoundland as a tenth province if and when it should become clear that there was very general agreement among Newfoundland people to join Canada."[29]

Having declared themselves, the Canadians were at last emboldened to nudge the British with a request that they be included in the coming constitutional proposals for the Island. This request resulted in a flurry of top-secret telegrams and memos, the first on November 17, 1944, from Malcolm MacDonald, the British high commissioner in Ottawa, to his superior, Lord Cranborne, the dominions secretary:

Secret. Mr. Norman Robertson has asked me in course of conversation whether I know anything about an early proposed statement of the United Kingdom Government's future policy in Newfoundland. He said there were rumours of this here. If there is to be such a statement, he suggested that it would be an excellent thing if its contents could be communicated to the authorities here

[Ottawa] before publication. I think he was thinking of this more as a matter of courtesy than as an opportunity for consultation. Is there any news on this subject that I can give them?[30]

Lord Cranborne replied: "Secret. . . . We had already intended to discuss this matter with [the Canadian] High Commissioner on his arrival and arrangements are in hand for this."[31]

Alexander Clutterbuck at the Dominions Office in London followed through with the details:

Top Secret. My dear High Commissioner,
With reference to our discussion with you about Newfoundland, I now enclose for your personal information a copy of a note outlining our ideas. . . .
The moment for consulting the Canadians will come as soon as we have got Cabinet approval in principle for our scheme. . . .
I enclose also a copy of the note which I wrote on "The Approach to Canada," for the purpose of our discussions with the Treasury. This you saw when you were here. . . .

P.S. I enclose also a copy of a further short note given to the Treasury to-day with a view to knocking down some of their arguments on the dollar difficulty.[32]

This exchange put an end to the guessing games, and from that point forward the British and Canadians began working together on the Newfoundland agenda—without the knowledge of the Newfoundlanders.

"The Approach to Canada" was a long and comprehensive document. In it, Alexander Clutterbuck outlined with far-ranging, blunt opinions, and just a hint of exasperation, both the British government's position and

Canada's chances in Newfoundland. The writing is Clutterbuck at his best, and it gives us a fascinating glimpse of the British perspective on Canada and a vivid a picture of the political and social position of Canada in Newfoundland near the end of the war.

The Approach to Canada

The general position in relation to Canada is as follows.

Although Newfoundlanders as individuals get along well with Canadians, and large numbers of them have settled in Canada, relations between the two countries have been marred by a long background of mutual suspicion and distrust. . . . The traditional Canadian attitude towards Newfoundland has been one of detachment, condescension and even contempt. In the background there has been the conviction that Newfoundland was too small and too poor to be able to stand by herself in the modern world, and that one day, when it had tired of its struggle, the Island would fall into the Canadian lap; in the meantime, however, Canadians were in no hurry to add to their burdens by taking over the Island, with every prospect that it would prove more of a liability than an asset. Newfoundlanders on their side were well aware that this was the Canadian attitude, and the result over the years was merely to increase the jealousy and suspicion with which all Canada's actions in relation to the Island were regarded and to strengthen the determination of Newfoundlanders to hold on at all costs to their precious independence. Thus in turn a traditional attitude grew up in Newfoundland that whatever fate might hold in store for the Island, nothing could be so disastrous for Newfoundland as entry into the cold and comfortless Canadian fold.

The war has seen a marked change in the attitude of Canada; there has however been no change in the attitude of Newfoundlanders. Under the stress of war, Canadian official opinion has at last grasped what has always been evident for all to see, namely, that Newfoundland, situated as she is at the mouth of the St. Lawrence and commanding the gateway to Canada, is essential to Canada's defence, and that her full partnership is necessary not only for Canadian security but also for the proper rounding off of the Confederation, which would otherwise be incomplete. What has served to drive home this lesson has been the American entry into the Island, as a result of the grant to the U.S. Government of military, naval and air bases for 99 years. The Canadians have also been granted similar influence in Newfoundland, but they fully realise the Americans, if they wish to extend their influence in Newfoundland, can very readily outbid them. Even without any such intention on the part of the Americans the very fact that they are established in the Island will inevitably lead to closer and permanent links, commercial and otherwise, between Newfoundland and the U.S., and the lavish scale on which Americans habitually conduct their affairs coupled with the plain fact that assured entry to the huge and profitable U.S. market would revitalise Newfoundland's industries, may cause an increasing number of Newfoundlanders, notwithstanding their strong attachment to the Crown, to look upon union with the U.S. as their eventual destiny. The Canadians now realize that had they adopted a less parochial attitude towards Newfoundland in the past, there need never have been cause for the Americans to establish themselves in the Island. Now that the Americans are there, they must make the best of it; but it is not lost upon them that if the Island is not to swing into the U.S. orbit, Canadian policy must now become active instead of passive, and consciously designed to break down the old barriers of mistrust, to conciliate Newfoundland opinion and gradually to build up an atmosphere of comradeship and practical co-operation in which the union of the two countries could be seen to be in the common interest.

This, as is no doubt fully realized by the Canadians, will be a long process, for Newfoundlanders at present are as suspicions of Canada as ever. Indeed the experiences of the war have served to accentuate rather than diminish the traditional jealousies and dislikes, largely because the attitude of the Canadian forces towards the people of the Island has compared unfavourably with that of the Americans, who have proved excellent "mixers" and have won golden opinions. In this atmosphere the Canadians dare not make Newfoundland an offer, for fear that it would be rejected, as indeed it certainly would be: and they have therefore confined themselves to friendly expressions of interest, and assurances that if Newfoundlanders themselves should wish to turn to Canada they would be given a warm and sympathetic welcome. These assurances have cut no ice in Newfoundland, where indeed they have been received with something approaching derision.

The Canadian Government, who now have their own High Commissioner in the Island, will fully realise in these circumstances that there can be no prospect of Newfoundlanders, when they come to choose their course for themselves after the war, opting for political union with Canada. What would be the next best thing from the Canadian point of view? What the Canadians want is time, time to win over Newfoundland opinion and to bring home the advantages of the union of the two countries: what would suit them therefore would be something which was calculated to ensure reasonable stability in the Island until there had been opportunity for a policy of breaking down the barriers to take effect. This is exactly what our proposals are calculated to provide. . . . Moreover, in so far as the reconstruction schemes proposed would be calculated to add to the country's earning power, our proposals should be doubly welcome to the Canadians since the prospect would be that Canada, if and when she should take over Newfoundland in the future, would find herself relieved *pro tanto* of expenditure which she would then otherwise be forced to incur.

. . . We recommend that in approaching the Canadian Government we should lay all our cards on the table, explain the full scope of our proposals and the motives which have prompted them, and say we feel sure we can count on their sympathetic interest; the one difficulty we are up against is the exchange problem, and it is on this aspect particularly that we are most anxious for their advice. We could here say that the alternative to the finding of Canadian dollars for this purpose would be to give Newfoundland a new currency of its own. . . .

. . . Thus, both politically and financially, it would suit us best that we should finance the programme from our own dollars and our object, in discussing the position with the Canadians, should be to secure their acquiescence in this course.

It should be added that it would of course be necessary to keep any discussions with the Canadian on a most secret basis, since any suspicion in Newfoundland that we were in touch with the Canadians regarding our policy in the Island would have the most damaging results.[33]

Clutterbuck's description of the Canadian attitude to Newfoundland brought this "Top Secret" comment from the British ambassador in Ottawa, Malcolm MacDonald: "I do not think that the early part of the note entitled 'The Approach to Canada' is entirely fair to the Canadian point of view. But this is not a matter of great importance and I only mention it because I do not wish silence to be taken as meaning that I agree with every phrase and emphasis in that note. In general the note is true enough."[34]

The Dominions Office constitutional plans for Newfoundland were tied to a large reconstruction package, but the memorandum prepared by Turk and Tarr of the Foreign Exchange Control Board of Canada on the postwar plans of the UK exchange control foreshadowed the problems that the Dominions Office would have with that agency, and John Maynard Keynes in particular, about their ambitious schemes for Newfoundland:

> Secret. Apparently the United Kingdom Parliament is in an extremely sentimental mood about Newfoundland at the present time and a great deal of pressure is being exerted on the Government to take steps to maintain the prosperity created by American military expenditures now that those expenditures are decreasing rapidly. . . . The Dominions Office is apparently receiving information which makes it feel that there is a real danger of Newfoundland electing to link up with the United States and feels that immediate steps must be taken to prevent any tendency in this direction. The proposal which is being pressed strongly is for the United Kingdom Government to borrow $100 million in Canada to be furnished to Newfoundland for road building and other development projects.
>
> The Bank of England and the Treasury are strongly opposed to any such move because it would prejudice the post-war financial arrangements which the United Kingdom will wish to make with Canada but there is a good deal of fear that in its present mood Parliament may force the Government to take some steps of this kind.[35]

In spite of the gathering clouds at the Exchequer, Lord Cranborne remained committed to the Newfoundland strategy. On February 20, 1945, he sent a pleading letter to John Anderson, the chancellor of the exchequer:

> My dear John,
> . . . I am under increasing pressure both from Parliament and from Newfoundland itself to follow up on our main statement of policy—made, with the approval of the War Cabinet, as long ago as December, 1943—by announcing the Government's detailed

proposals [and pressure] is likely before long to reach formidable proportions . . . especially now that the new Colonial Development and Welfare Bill has been through the House of Commons.

Whatever our short-term dollar position, Parliamentary and public opinion would, I am sure, never accept a situation under which Newfoundland, alone of the dependent Empire, was to be promised no assistance for reconstruction and development—and this in spite of the special obligations which we have assumed for her welfare.[36]

But Anderson's reply was not encouraging. "I fear that when we come to talk about Newfoundland to Canada, we shall find that it will be a very difficult and delicate discussion."[37]

4

PROBLEM CHILD:
THE 1945 DEAL

In May 1944 J. Scott Macdonald was named the new Canadian high commissioner in Newfoundland to replace Charles Burchell, who at last was able to return to sunny Canberra. Burchell had established a network of prominent Newfoundlanders who were sympathetic to Confederation, and he left on good terms with British governor Humphrey Walwyn. However, Burchell was not enthusiastic about the possibility of Newfoundland entering the Canadian Confederation, and his wait-and-see attitude was marked with caution.[1]

The appointment of Scott Macdonald signalled a more aggressive approach on the part of Prime Minister Mackenzie King and the Department of External Affairs. Certainly his initial reports to the department plot a much more vigorous Canadian role in Newfoundland's affairs:

Secret. It is hardly likely that there would arise, spontaneously, a sufficient demand for federation with Canada to lead to the appointment by the proposed National Convention of a delegation to proceed to Ottawa to ascertain if the Canadian Government were willing to admit Newfoundland into Confederation, and, if so, on terms that would be acceptable. In these circumstances I have been wondering whether . . . it would be good policy to take an initiative in the matter.

The present would not . . . be a propitious moment to secure a majority for federation with Canada. We would, however, probably have to wait many years before a really propitious conjuncture of circumstances would arise, e.g.—a Government finding itself facing a depression and financially unable to carry on. Canada itself could hardly escape from the effects of any such depression and public opinion would then be adverse [sic] to accepting new commitments. Moreover, if Newfoundland is to enter Confederation there would be many advantages from our point of view in having the matter consummated during the next year or two rather than a decade hence . . .

. . . At any rate of one thing we could be reasonably sure. We would get a far more favourable and more valuable verdict through a plebiscite of the people than we would ever get through waiting for the return of Responsible Government and having the matter voted on by the Assembly. . . .

. . . It would be desirable to take means to ensure that the United Kingdom does not, in a sentimental mood, dip down into its meagre resources and provide Newfoundland with a fund for development projects that would make it economically independent and uninterested in the advantages of federation. Such a move has been mooted and may be still under consideration.

. . . It would be important that the initiative be taken by Newfoundland so that there would be no shadow of support for the opponents who assert that the "big Canadian wolf" was at last preparing to gobble up little Newfoundland. . . . A careful campaign would have to be planned to ensure that the advantages of union were made clear to the people of Newfoundland. . . . Strong teams would have to be organized under the directions of a Central Committee to see that the whole Island was covered. . . .

> ... The United Kingdom does not seem to be in any hurry to change the present system and may even be contemplating maintaining its trusteeship until questions of post-war military and civil aviation rights and the composition of the post-war sterling bloc are settled.[2]

Macdonald was obviously familiar with Turk and Tarr's memo and had accepted their argument that any thought of reconstruction in Newfoundland would be nothing but sheer sentimentality. His reference to Newfoundland's "military and civil aviation rights" was exactly the advantage that Lord Beaverbrook and others at Whitehall wished to keep, and, despite avowals to the contrary, Macdonald had deep suspicions that the British secretly wished to hold on to Newfoundland indefinitely. In spite of these perceived obstacles and the many years of bad public relations between Canada and its sister dominion, Macdonald articulated a detailed campaign, complete with "strong local teams," to bring Newfoundland into Confederation as soon as possible. As it happened, the chance that he and External Affairs were seeking to move this agenda forward came just three months later.

The Canadians and the British finally connected on Newfoundland in June 1945 at the San Francisco Conference, called to discuss the Allies' postwar policies. This meeting gave Hume Wrong, from External Affairs, the opportunity to discuss the Newfoundland situation personally with Lord Cranborne. On June 6 Wrong reported to J.E. Read, the acting under-secretary of state for external affairs:

> Dear Mr. Read,
> When sitting next Lord Cranborne at dinner last night the conversation turned from the problems of Palestine to the problems of Newfoundland. He agreed with my remark that Newfoundland was the "problem child" of the Dominions Office and said that some new steps would have to be taken without much delay. He

referred to the considerable interest in the House of Commons in the status of Newfoundland, adding that there was a strong feeling that the present system of commission government over a people of purely British stock was repugnant to a great many members.

. . . He was interested to hear that the antipathy of Newfoundland towards union with Canada seemed to be receding and I should judge that he personally feels that this would be the most satisfactory outcome from the point of view of the United Kingdom Government.

I then touched on the question of financial assistance and mentioned our unavoidable involvement in any measure of financial assistance which the United Kingdom might extend to Newfoundland in view of the existing dollar-sterling position. He said that they had had this matter under consideration in London but that it had always been their intention to discuss with us in advance any plans for new loans or subsidies between the United Kingdom and Newfoundland. I remarked that I thought it important that discussion should take place at an early stage before they had determined on a settled policy and particularly before any publicity had been given to their intentions in Newfoundland itself. He appeared to be fully in accord with this view. . . .

It would be unwise to ascribe great significance to a casual dinner table conversation. I think, however, that it would be useful for you to pass on copies of this letter to the High Commissioners in London and Newfoundland as well as to the Prime Minister.[3]

Despite Wrong's disclaimer at the end of his remarks, they had an immediate and profound effect in Whitehall, where Canadian concerns began to weigh heavily on Dominions Office plans for "little Newfoundland." Wrong had specifically linked Britain's war debt to Canada with Newfoundland's constitutional status as the subject of secret discussions to be held without the knowledge of Newfoundland.

His patronizing characterization of Newfoundland as the "problem child" of the empire suggested that grown-up Canada just might have the answer the United Kingdom was looking for—and it was entirely consistent with the Amulree tradition of demeaning and discrediting Newfoundland as a prelude to violating its rights. What Amulree began, Canada would finish. Lord Cranborne and those at the Dominions Office who still hoped that political and moral considerations would outweigh financial ones would henceforth have to deal first with the Canadian "dollar difficulty"—the nature of which Clutterbuck struggled with in his lengthy memo of August 1945, prepared for the Dominions Office and titled simply "Newfoundland":

> [Our] proposals involve the establishment by legislation here of a Newfoundland Development Fund from which grants could be made for reconstruction and development in Newfoundland up to 100 million dollars over a period of 10 years.
>
> . . . The currency of Newfoundland, however, is Canadian dollars, of which we shall, of course, be very short for many years to come, and the Treasury have felt that in these circumstances the financial objections to our proposals are overriding. The main points are:
>
> (i) During the war . . . the Canadians have made available to us at their own expense the goods which we were unable to pay for. This state of affairs will, of course, come to an end immediately the Japanese war ends, but our essential requirements from Canada will nonetheless continue after the war at a level far in excess of our possible earnings of Canadian dollars. . . . We shall have to borrow large sums from the Canadian Government and it will be essential if we are to get through our difficulties that these borrowings should be kept to an absolute minimum.
>
> (ii) In this general situation our Newfoundland proposals in practice could only be financed by increasing our borrowings from

Canada. This would merely aggravate our balance of payments difficulty and would impose an unfair burden on the British Exchequer.

Nonetheless, we have continued to press our proposals on the Treasury, pointing out that *His Majesty's Government have assumed a special responsibility for the welfare of Newfoundland and that difficult as the position may be, the one thing that is clear is that we cannot run away from this responsibility;* nor indeed will Parliament and public opinion here allow us to do so. . . .

Mr. Hume Wrong at San Francisco made an informal approach to Lord Cranborne in somewhat guarded terms which indicated that the Canadians themselves had views . . . and would welcome discussion before decisions were taken here. He implied also that the Canadian Government might take it amiss if we were, as it were, to overdo our assistance to Newfoundland and put them in so stable a financial position as to preclude any possibility of Newfoundland opinion turning in favour of confederation with Canada. . . . The interest now evidently being taken in Canadian Government circles of the Newfoundland problem is significant, and it is clear that both from the financial and also from the political point of view, early discussions with the Canadians are called for.[4]

In July 1945 Clement Attlee's Labour Party was elected to power, and Lord Addison was named secretary of state for dominions affairs. With the new government came a new resolve to settle the constitutional dilemma in Newfoundland. Clutterbuck's analysis in hand, Lord Addison wrote to Attlee on September 5, 1945:

It would, I think, be premature to give up hope of our being able to do something for Newfoundland . . . for much must depend on the outcome of the forthcoming discussions with Canada and the United States on Stage III finance. However this may be,

I think it urgent to proceed with informal talks with the Canadians on the whole Newfoundland problem as soon as possible; and, the Chancellor having agreed to this, I propose to send out Mr. Clutterbuck to Ottawa as soon as this can be arranged. I hope it may be possible for the visit to take place in the course of this month which would enable me to consult you further as to the position before Parliament reassembles.[5]

The Stage III talks mentioned here refer to the high-level and comprehensive talks among Great Britain, the United States, and Canada on postwar finance and reconstruction. In his reply to Lord Addison, Attlee agreed to the meetings with the Canadians, but he still seemed to hold out hope for the doomed reconstruction scheme in Newfoundland:

> Thank you for your note. . . . I am interested to know of the forthcomingness of the Canadians. They will have to make a very good offer to overcome the particularity and local prejudice of the Newfoundlanders, to say nothing of the vested interests of the Water Street Merchants.
>
> The late Prime Minister [Churchill] always took the line that we ought to deal generously with the Newfoundlanders, the amount required for them being a drop in the ocean of our own liabilities."[6]

It remained to be seen whether Newfoundland would get that "drop." A key moment in the fate of Newfoundland had arrived. Wrong's meeting with Lord Cranborne in San Francisco also had a stimulating effect at the Department of External Affairs in Ottawa. On September 25, 1945, Norman Robertson wrote another long memo to Scott Macdonald on the pros and cons of union. He noted with some unease that "individualism, sensitiveness to criticism from outside, and a general backwardness of outlook are, moreover, strongly marked characteristics of the

Islanders, that would not make for tractability on their easy assimilation into the Dominion."[7]

As always, the downside of the Confederation equation was the Newfoundlanders themselves. Despite these grave concerns, and after a review of Canada's defence position on the Island and the resources involved, Robertson brought himself around to Macdonald's position: "It is possible that we should take the initiative ourselves, rather than leave it to Newfoundland. . . . If the United Kingdom Government were agreeable to Union, as there is good reason to believe it would be, we might then ask that the Newfoundland people be advised accordingly and that the United Kingdom give its blessing to federation."[8]

This approach of laying the cards on the table with the Newfoundlanders and allowing them to make their choice in light of British and Canadian concerns would have been the proper procedure to follow. Certainly it would have resulted in less dissonance than the path of concealment and deception that was chosen. But Robertson's suggestion of informing the Newfoundlanders about the "solution envisaged" was too transparent for officials in London, who had little respect for Newfoundland voters and much regard for their own opinions. The high commissioner ignored that part of Robertson's memo and seized on External Affairs' approval of his more pro-active approach on the Island. He replied enthusiastically to Robertson:

> The soundest plan would be for me to be authorized, privately and on a personal basis, to suggest to leading citizens of Newfoundland, who I already know to be generally well disposed, to proceed with the formation of a Committee to advocate Union. It would be for them to work up latent public interest in the matter and ensure that, when the Convention meets to consider the future form of Government a motion would be introduced favouring the despatch of a delegation to Ottawa to ask the Canadian Government on what terms Newfoundland could unite with the Dominion.[9]

Macdonald was very excited about the process he outlined. As things turned out, he had predicted exactly what would happen. But first, events had to unfold—or at least look to unfold—in as natural a way as possible. He concluded: "It would be unfortunate, I think, if any over-zealous individual should attempt a premature crusade on his own, hoping to capture the leadership. I have, therefore, refrained from giving encouragement to anyone likely to be so minded."[10] Apparently there was no need to identify for Robertson who that over-zealous confederate might be. As they drew nearer to their goal, Robertson cautioned Macdonald: "All correspondence on our Newfoundland policy should be marked 'Confidential' since . . . it may be difficult to prevent correspondence, which might conceivably be embarrassing, from becoming public unless it is given a security marking."[11]

On September 10 Prime Minister Mackenzie King alerted Scott Macdonald in St. John's to the coming negotiations with Great Britain:

> Secret. The United Kingdom High Commissioner [in Ottawa, Malcolm MacDonald] has asked us whether we would be prepared to hold very confidential and informal discussions on matters relating to Newfoundland with Mr. Clutterbuck of the Dominions Office, who could arrive about the middle of this month. This is agreeable to us, and it would be convenient for you to time your visit to Ottawa accordingly. Ostensibly his mission would be for other purposes, and therefore this information is for you alone.[12]

The note from Lord Addison's office back to Malcolm MacDonald on September 11 is equally conspiratorial:

> Secret . . . Clutterbuck is arranging to cross by bomber 14 September arriving Montreal . . . September 15. Grateful if accommodation could be arranged for him. It is excellent that Canadian High

Commissioner in Newfoundland will be in Ottawa at the same time, but we are a little nervous that it will come out in St. John's that Newfoundland is under discussion. We trust however that Canadian authorities will have impressed on their High Commissioner [the] importance of saying nothing even in governmental quarters in Newfoundland which might disclose the object of his visit. You should know that we have been careful not to give Newfoundland Government any inkling of Clutterbuck's impending visit or its object.[13]

These top-secret memos mark the beginning of the high-level co-operation between Great Britain and Canada to bring Newfoundland into Confederation without the knowledge of the people of Newfoundland. The conspiratorial tone of these communications indicates that all parties involved were aware that they were initiating confidential negotiations that were constitutionally, politically, democratically, and morally wrong. They were certainly against the spirit and letter of everything that the British governors were telling the people of Newfoundland. They were also contrary to the vaunted Atlantic Charter, asserting the rights of all peoples to self-determination, which the British had proclaimed with such fanfare in 1941.

Yet when Clutterbuck arrived in Ottawa, he was perplexed to find that "so far from Canadians having any positive ideas to put us, there was little or no interest even in official circles and no serious consideration has been given to the problem. However we have jollied them along and they have not been unreceptive."[14] This passive-aggressive approach to union was typical of Canada's historical apathy and its desire to acquire Newfoundland by default or for as little cost as possible. Still, Clutterbuck was, as Peter Neary described in Gilbert and Sullivan terms, "the very model of the model Whitehall mandarin . . . able to reverse himself and bring the same energy and skill to one minister or policy as another. In the event, he proved as clever in negotiating the United Kingdom's exit from the administration of Newfoundland as in 1933 and 1934 he had been in negotiating her entry."[15]

By mid-October, Clutterbuck was ready with his final report to the Dominions Office on the real Canadian position. In some respects it reads like the account of a difficult and unwillingly arranged marriage, complete with arguments over the dowry:

> I arrived in Ottawa on the 15th of September . . . to compare notes with the Canadians on the Newfoundland problem. . . . Those on the Canadian side were Mr. Norman Robertson (Under-Secretary of State for External Affairs), Mr. Hume Wrong (Associate Under-Secretary of State), Mr. MacKay (Head of the Newfoundland Division of the Department of External Affairs) and Mr. Scott Macdonald (Canadian High Commissioner in Newfoundland). I, for my part, was accompanied by the Deputy High Commissioner (Mr. Holmes) and the Senior Secretary at the High Commissioner's office (Mr. Garner).
>
> As a result of an informal approach made by Mr. Hume Wrong to Lord Cranborne at San Francisco and of certain subsequent remarks made by Mr. Mackenzie King to Lord Cranborne, we had gathered the impression that the Canadians had themselves been giving a good deal of thought to the Newfoundland problem and had certain ideas which they were anxious to discuss with us before conclusions as to future policy were reached. . . . I went on to explain that we were most anxious to ensure that any new Government taking over the Island would have reasonable prospects of financial stability; with this object in view we had hoped to accompany our proposals on the constitutional side by a 10-year reconstruction programme financed by a specially created Newfoundland Development Fund. . . . Unfortunately, these hopes had now been dashed by the difficulties of our dollar position. . . . The whole Newfoundland situation would accordingly

have to be reconsidered by my Government, and it would be of the greatest help to know how the position was viewed by the Canadian authorities and what was the attitude towards the future of the Island.

To my surprise, the initial reaction of the Canadian officials to this approach was almost entirely negative. They began by explaining that there was almost complete absence of interest in Canada in Newfoundland affairs. This applied not only to the Canadian public but also to Canadian Ministers and officials. The fact was that Canadians had too many problems of their own to concern themselves with Newfoundland. . . .

Against this general background of lack of interest it would be politically out of the question for the Canadian Government to provide us with dollars necessary to finance reconstruction in Newfoundland (all the more so as any money provided for this purpose would reduce *pro tanto* the funds which would otherwise be available to us for financing United Kingdom imports from Canada); similarly there could be no question of their being able under present conditions to make any direct contribution themselves to reconstruction in the Island, since this would at once get them into trouble with their own Provinces. They much appreciated our action in consulting them, but could see no prospect in the circumstance of being able to help.

. . . I did not conceal my disappointment at this reply and pointed out that such a position would be very unsatisfactory from the Newfoundland point of view. If we on our side were unable to help her in her reconstruction measures owing to lack of dollars, while the Canadians on their side were not disposed to do so owing to lack of interest, who could be surprised if Newfoundlanders began to think seriously of turning to the United States? . . .

At this stage the Canadian officials became more helpful, and I was asked what my Government's reaction would be if the

Canadian Government were to indicate to us that they would welcome a recommendation by the proposed National Convention in favour of Newfoundland joining up with Canada. In reply I said that any such invitation would be warmly received by my Government: it had always been felt . . . that union with Canada was the Island's natural destiny. . . . It was agreed that as the next step I should have a talk with Mr. MacKay and Mr. Scott Macdonald and examine with them the financial implications of a decision by Newfoundland to enter the Canadian Confederation. . . . Canadian officials explained to me that it would be very desirable to avoid a situation in which special treatment would have to be given to Newfoundland, since this would certainly create difficulties with the Canadian Provinces and lead to undesirable controversy. Matters would be much easier from their point of view if Newfoundland could make both ends meet on the same financial terms as were applicable to the Canadian Provinces.[16]

Reporting on previous discussions between the Canadian prime minister (who was also secretary of state for external affairs at this time) and the British high commissioner, Clutterbuck noted:

The views expressed by Mr. Mackenzie King in conversation with Mr. Malcolm MacDonald were clear and decided and may be summarized as follows:

He regarded entry of Newfoundland into the Canadian Confederation as natural, desirable, and inevitable. . . .

On the other hand, it would be essential that the initiative should clearly be seen to come from them, and both we and Canada would have to be very careful to say and do nothing which might look like "bouncing" them, or give rise to suspicions that we were engaged in a conspiracy to achieve this result.

Even so . . . it was important that Newfoundlanders should take their own time and not be hurried.

At the same time . . . this would be a grand chance, which might not recur for a long time, of getting the Confederation question settled without it being made an issue in party politics in Newfoundland. Delay too might bring other dangers, such as a tendency for the Island to swing into the United States orbit, which would be very embarrassing.

I reported this very encouraging reaction to the Canadian group of officials, who were obviously much relieved and pleased. They admitted frankly that they had been drifting with no clear policy, and were delighted that they now had a definite objective to aim at.[17]

Although this description of the discussions evokes an empire in search of an emperor, Clutterbuck was probably trying to put some spine into the Attlee government's position with Ottawa on Newfoundland. Certainly it had the effect of flattering Clutterbuck's own efforts to reach an agreement. Ottawa for its part had definite ideas on how the British should proceed:

Canadian officials expressed the view that it would be very desirable to make it clear in the statement that Newfoundland should not count on receiving further financial assistance from the United Kingdom. This would accord with the realities of the position and would, they thought, assist Newfoundlanders to turn their thoughts to Canada.

It was left finally that each side would consider the position now reached, and that when our statement had been made in Parliament it might be useful to examine between us possible ways of influencing Newfoundland opinion behind the scenes. I said that the Secretary of State would no doubt wish to have a word himself with Mackenzie King on the matter while he was in London, and Mr. Norman Robertson said that he would also be at our disposal in London for a further talk whenever we should think one useful.[18]

While Clutterbuck was striking a deal over Newfoundland with the officials at External Affairs, Hugh Dalton, the new chancellor of the exchequer, was similarly engaged with officials of the Department of Finance over postwar finances. Dalton had already been to Washington and, because the United States was late in entering the war, he and Attlee had expected that the Americans would make Great Britain a gift of the war debt it owed them. Instead, the Americans extended the British a line of credit. Now in Ottawa, where Britain had more to offer—Newfoundland—the visitors hoped to achieve that same pressing goal with regard to the debt the motherland owed Canada.

The Canadians wrote off the entire $5.6 billion war debt that Great Britain owed—a magnificent "gift" in the eyes of the world. In another act of spontaneous generosity, Ottawa extended a $1.2 billion loan at 2 percent interest.[19] Canada also agreed to take over the Newfoundland sterling debt. Britain had gotten everything it wanted—and, in return, it would deliver Newfoundland to its generous Canadian partner. This arrangement satisfied both Treasury and Maynard Keynes, who wrote on December 18, "It is agreed that the right long-term solution is for Newfoundland to be taken over by Canada."[20] Only one year earlier, in June 1944, Norman Robertson had told the British high commissioner that Canada would withhold future war aid to Great Britain if Canada did not get the ninety-nine-year lease it wanted at Goose Bay. Canada got Goose Bay. Now the Canadians would forgive that war debt and take the whole country.

There would have been no need for these secret top-level talks between Britain and Canada on Newfoundland's fate if Britain had simply returned responsible government to the Island as promised by the

Newfoundland Act of 1933, but both partners were unwilling to lose their advantage by leaving it to the people of Newfoundland to decide. Both had too much to gain. Newfoundland had sacrificed her territory during the war for the "good of mankind," as Churchill implored. Now her sovereignty would be sacrificed for Canadian dollars. The Newfoundland problem was all but solved. As far as the United Kingdom and Canada were concerned, the deal was done—without any representation from the people of Newfoundland.

These irregular discussions were the ones that George Hawkins told young Jim Halley about in the hallway at Dalhousie three months later, in December 1945. A financial and a political deal had been struck between Britain and Canada, and all that remained was to play out the constitutional drama through some sort of "democratic" process. Everything would depend on the ability of Britain and the British governor in Newfoundland to control that process to assure the desired results.

The Treasury had won out over political and imperial considerations, as it was bound to do. Great Britain was bankrupt and must divest itself of its holdings. Canada was now waiting for Newfoundland, and it would help set the terms and conditions for the coming constitutional contest. The ringing words in the *Fishermen-Workers' Tribune* in 1941, when Charles Burchell was appointed to St. John's, that "the Canadian High Commissioner would now replace the British Governor as the final arbiter of Newfoundland affairs" were entirely correct, though premature.

The chastened tone in the memo from Lord Addison to the War Cabinet reflected the new reality at the Dominions Office:

> We must, I feel, adapt our policy to the changed conditions, and since we cannot now look ourselves to helping Newfoundland financially, we should now regard union with Canada as the objective to be aimed at. It would, of course, be most important that no hint that this is the solution which we envisage should be allowed to come out either here or in Newfoundland. The initiative must be

left entirely to the Newfoundlanders, and we must take care to avoid any appearances of seeking to influence them in any way. At the same time, we must say or do nothing which would conflict with this objective or make it harder to achieve.

If this view is accepted, it follows that my statement in Parliament must contain a clear warning that in all probability we shall be unable to help financially in long-term reconstruction in Newfoundland. . . . Moreover, it may be hoped that a warning on these lines would aid the swing of opinion towards Canada.[21]

Newfoundland's fate was sealed. Canada had the dollars—it was the buyer and would set the terms. Britain was the vendor and would deliver the goods—Newfoundland. The British had initially been convinced that the Confederation option could not win in any Newfoundland election, but once they discovered their penury and indebtedness to Canada, they convinced themselves of the opposite. Confederation might be made to win after all. As if to underline the agreement, three months later, in January 1946, the redoubtable Alexander Clutterbuck was knighted and appointed to Ottawa as British high commissioner to preside over the final transfer of power. The only disagreements now between the two conspirators would be on how best to execute their scheme. The first of these top-secret consultations would be about the terms of reference for the Newfoundland National Convention itself. With Canada now in a position of power, if not control, a new ease and confidence prevailed in Ottawa:

On October 18 Mackenzie King had what he described as "a most delightful and refreshing conversation" with Lord Addison [the new secretary of state for dominions affairs] at the Dominions Office. . . . In a word, the British Government are to allow the people of Newfoundland to decide on its future in some convention to be held in the coming year. . . .

The Government here would like to see Newfoundland a part
of Confederation. They do not wish to see the Island fall into the
hands of the U.S.[22]

Having concluded the secret agreement with the Canadians, Lord
Addison informed the War Cabinet in November: "I now propose, with
the approval of my colleagues, to make my proposed statement [on
Newfoundland] in the House of Lords at an early convenient opportunity. . . . [The draft statement] has also formed the subject of confidential
consultations with Canadian authorities."[23]

Nothing would go to Newfoundland now from London that was
not first reviewed by Ottawa. On December 1, in accord with their
agreement, the Canadians received an advance copy of Lord Addison's
statement on the terms of reference for the Newfoundland National
Convention:

Top Secret. It will be the duty of the [Newfoundland National]
Convention to review all the alternative courses open to the Island
and to make recommendations to His Majesty's Government as a
basis for a National Referendum. It is fitting, therefore, that it
should be given wide terms of reference and these will take the following form:

To consider and discuss amongst themselves as elected representatives of the Newfoundland people, the changes that have
taken place in the financial and economic situation of the Island
since 1934 and bearing in mind the extent to which the high
revenues of recent years have been due to wartime conditions, to
examine the position of this country and to make recommendations to His Majesty's Government as to possible forms of future
Government to be put before the people at a National Referendum.

. . . Our relations with Newfoundland have been so special
and Newfoundlanders have played such a gallant part in the war

that it would, I know, be the wish of all to assure to any new Government which may take over the Island the fairest possible start. But we must, above all, be careful not to promise what we may not be able to perform, and the special difficulties of our financial position over the next few years may well preclude us from undertaking fresh commitments. As your Lordships will understand from what I have said, the object of the procedure proposed by His Majesty's Government, is to enable the people of Newfoundland to come to a free and informed decision as soon as possible on their future form of Government. I know that this House, which has always been solicitous for the welfare of the people of the Island, will wish them well in the exercise of their choice.[24]

With this somewhat unctuous announcement, Newfoundland was effectively cut loose from the motherland after four hundred years, their "special relations" cancelled out by Britain's "special difficulties." As Norman Robertson noted in his memo of December 1 to Mackenzie King:

Top Secret. The statement is obscure and perhaps intentionally so as to whether the convention is expected to recommend a single scheme or to propose alternatives. . . . The statement warns, however, that the United Kingdom cannot make any financial commitments at the present time. This will, no doubt, disappoint many Newfoundlanders and may induce them to look for other alternatives. . . . I suggest our best course is to make certain that neither the statement itself nor the method proposed for consulting the people of Newfoundland should prejudice due consideration of confederation.[25]

For his part, Prime Minister Mackenzie King observed:

Also I thought the British Government had used "form of government" deliberately, the significant matter to be decided at present being whether the Commission form of government would continue, or a responsible government, either within the island itself or as part of some larger confederation. . . . Mr. Robertson agreed that, in the circumstances, he would not suggest [any significant] alteration of the memorandum.[26]

Vincent Massey, the Canadian high commissioner in London, was doubtful: "The words 'as to possible future forms of Government' might be held strictly to rule out the possibility of Newfoundland joining the Canadian Confederation."[27] The Dominions Office quickly allayed his fears. In a telegram marked "Important. Top Secret," Lord Addison informed Robertson that "Canadian authorities can be assured that there is no risk of any such narrow interpretation as is suggested being placed upon terms of reference."[28] Having arranged the terms of reference for the Newfoundland National Convention to Canada's satisfaction, the British government was finally ready to announce the plan to the Newfoundlanders.

A young Winston Churchill, secretary of state for air, presents John Alcock and Arthur Brown with their prize money for completing the first transatlantic flight from Lester's Field in St. John's to Ireland in 1919. The British government was keenly aware of the importance of the Air Race.

On August 14, 1941, Roosevelt and Churchill staged a dramatic wartime rendezvous in Placentia Bay, Newfoundland, to proclaim the Atlantic Charter and the right of all people to self-determination . . . except for the Newfoundlanders. Their democracy had been suspended before the war, and would not be returned during or after it.

The Big Three. William Lyon Mackenzie King, Franklin D. Roosevelt and Winston Churchill at the Quebec Conference in 1943. Roosevelt told King, "Canada ought to possess Newfoundland."

Prime Minister Mackenzie King welcomes Prime Minister Clement Attlee to Canada in November 1945, just a month after Clutterbuck had successfully completed the deal in Ottawa on Newfoundland.

Lester B. Pearson at the San Francisco Conference in 1945, where the Canadians and the British first got together to discuss the "problem child." The dapper under-secretary of state for external affairs was persuaded to set aside his scruples about the Newfoundland confederation process.

Sir Alexander Clutterbuck, the model civil servant who wrote the Amulree Royal Commission Report on Newfoundland in 1933. The Dominions Office expert on Newfoundland, he was promoted to British High Commissioner in Ottawa in 1946 to see Confederation completed.

C. J. Burchell, the first Canadian high commissioner, arrives in Gander. By 1941, with the Second World War accelerating, Canada finally felt the need for official representation in neighbouring Newfoundland.

J. Scott Macdonald, Canadian high commissioner to Newfoundland. His tenure in St. John's marked an aggressive campaign by the Department of External Affairs "to take over Newfoundland."

Jack Pickersgill in 1948. The personal secretary to Mackenzie King was very active behind the scenes promoting Newfoundland Confederation. Later he was elected a federal member of Parliament and appointed minister for Newfoundland in the Pearson government.

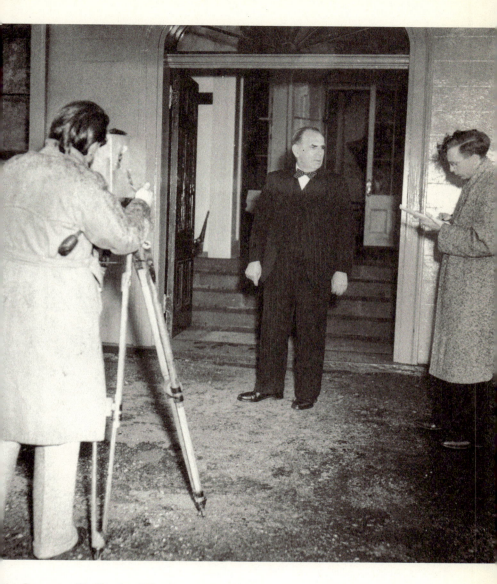

Governor Sir Gordon Macdonald speaking to a reporter outside Government House in St. John's. He was sent to Newfoundland by Prime Minister Attlee to "get the job done." His handling of the referendum process caused both resentment and suspicion.

The last Commission of Government (1947–1949) at Government House.
From left: Herman Quinton, R.L.M. James, Albert J. Walsh, Governor Sir
Gordon Macdonald, William H. Flinn, James S. Neill, Herbert L. Pottle,
and (standing) William J. Carew, the secretary of the commission. All three
Newfoundland commissioners, Walsh, Quinton and Pottle, would come out
publically in support of Confederation.

THE FAIREST POSSIBLE START:
THE NATIONAL CONVENTION

On December 11, 1945, Dominions Secretary Lord Addison, with Canadian approval, read his statement about a National Convention in Newfoundland to the House of Lords. Governor Humphrey Walwyn then announced it to the people of Newfoundland. Canadian High Commissioner Scott Macdonald immediately reported local reaction to Ottawa:

> Confidential. There was considerable excitement in St. John's yesterday when an announcement was made over the local radio that the United Kingdom Government was about to make its long deferred statement on the future government of Newfoundland. The statement itself was listened to with great attention by all classes of people and is, of course, the one topic of conversation this morning.
>
> . . . The Governor tells me that he has consulted six of the leading men on Water Street. They were rather alarmed at the prospect opened up by the British statement and were inclined to take the view that Britain had let them down.
>
> . . . The reference to Britain's inability to continue to help

them financially has, of course, not escaped them and they seem
quite ready to draw the necessary inferences.[1]

The National Convention proposed by Lord Addison was based on
a proposal initially put to the War Cabinet by A.P. Herbert after the
Goodwill Mission to Newfoundland in 1943. The Dominions Office
and Lord Addison had, however, made two fundamental changes in the
wording of the terms of reference, which would enable the UK government to override the Newfoundland Convention and do exactly as it
wished. Herbert's proposal had suggested that a "national Convention
should be set up after the war . . . and empowered to discuss and determine . . . the form of government to be recommended both to the
Newfoundland people and to the United Kingdom Government."[2] Lord
Addison's draft eliminated the word "empowered" and changed "discuss
and determine" to "consider and discuss." Newfoundland's elected delegates to the National Convention might "discuss amongst themselves" all
they wanted, but they had no power to determine anything. All they
could do was recommend to Lord Addison the course he should choose.
In other words, the National Convention had the same authority to discuss and recommend as did Governor Walwyn or Alexander Clutterbuck,
and certainly much less than Prime Minister Mackenzie King had to
recommend to the dominions secretary the course he should take. In his
Constitutional Proposal for a National Convention, Lord Addison had
given himself every power, and Newfoundland none. Not surprisingly,
the statement was loudly condemned in Newfoundland.

And there was another problem. What forms of government were
the Newfoundland delegates to consider other than a return to self-
government? What other possible forms—plural—of government were
being considered by Lord Addison and Prime Minister Attlee? Any
half-way measure of representative government and union with the
United Kingdom on the Northern Ireland model, with Newfoundland
MPs sitting in the Houses of Parliament in London, had been ruled

out. Union with the United States was not under consideration. What was left, a local monarchy or a dictatorship? As Attlee had suggested, the Newfoundland constitutional process was now open to "various possibilities." Obviously, the only other form of government acceptable was confederation with Canada. The unstated British option was implicit in the terms of reference for the National Convention and the door left open for the dominions secretary to act on it when the time came.

The announcement of the National Convention was greeted in Newfoundland with the full range of emotions, from joy to anger. The people had waited a long time for any developments on the constitutional front, and the fact that action was finally at hand was itself a cause for relief. At the same time, the potential problems presented by this National Convention and its deliberately vague terms of reference were immediately apparent to serious and thoughtful people who, along with the general population, were soon plunged into a state of confusion and doubt. In the *Daily News* Albert Perlin devoted his "Wayfarer" column to the dilemma created by the Dominions Office:

> This is a fact-finding board we have to elect and not a parliament of the people's representatives. How many realize this? Whose duty is it to see that this fact is recognized? The Convention has not the power to decide. It has power only to recommend. And there is genuine uncertainty as to its legal right to recommend in view of the limited choice set by the Amulree Report, the Joint Address, the Newfoundland Act and the Letters Patent, and yet the Convention is to be asked to recommend for inclusion on a ballot paper any form of government it may desire, regardless of the restrictions imposed by the only relevant documents. For the language of the Letters Patent and all the documents on which they are bound is that "when the Island is again self-supporting and on request of the people self-government shall be restored."

As for the Convention it may study documents, it may debate them, it may turn itself into an investigating committee with the Commission [Government] as its victim, it may divide on one very point and become a platform for demagogues, it may become a centre of operations for pressure groups, it may elevate itself into a Parliament and imagine it has parliamentary prerogatives, but whatever it does or does not do, it has power only to recommend the choices to be placed on the referendum ballot paper and even its right of full freedom in this connection is suspect. In the final analysis, it can recommend what it likes and the Dominions Office may throw out all its recommendations.[3]

Two years previously, after the return of the Goodwill Mission to London in 1943, Paul Emrys-Evans, the parliamentary under-secretary for dominions affairs, had assured the House of Commons that the Dominions Office was committed to "take steps to ascertain what machinery would be most acceptable to Newfoundland public opinion."[4] This promise was not honoured, and it is doubtful there was ever any intention of doing so. The Dominions Office was well informed by its agents on the Island, and officials there knew that the machinery now proposed of a National Convention was almost wholly abhorrent to Newfoundland public opinion. They decided to establish it anyway and "brazen it out," as they would do in Newfoundland at other critical moments.

The promise made in the British Parliament to consult the people of Newfoundland was meant for British public opinion alone. So, while one thing could be promised in the Houses of Parliament in London, the opposite could be delivered in St. John's. This dichotomy was possible in part because of the British Parliament's traditional reluctance to interfere in the Dominions Office's management of imperial affairs. As Robert Holland states: "The desire to keep imperial and colonial issues out of the parliamentary arena . . . was to be a consistent feature of official

British psychology in decolonization."[5] James Maxten, leader of the Independent Labour Party, called the Commission of Government in Newfoundland "the biggest blot" on the British democratic system, a statement that was not challenged by the House. MPs were generally relieved by Lord Addison's statement announcing the National Convention. They failed, however, to examine the fine print, where they would have discovered that this new constitutional creation was just as undemocratic as the Commission.[6] It was not lost on Perlin and other commentators that the elaborate window dressing of the National Convention was merely a framework for the entrance of Confederation onto the constitutional stage:

> Two sound views on the political situation have been expressed by Mr. C.E. Hunt and Mr. A.M. Fraser in papers read to the University Women's Club. Neither can be accused of political prejudice and their opinions on the issue of Confederation are a refreshing counterblast to those who would railroad the people into a course they might afterwards regret they had not explored in detail before taking the plunge. Mr. Hunt, apart from his general comment that there was no ground for defeatism, said that it was difficult to see how negotiations for Confederation could be opened by the National Convention. Mr. Fraser emphasized that the decision to confederate would be irrevocable and therefore necessitated patient and conscientious expert discussion and consideration. He said also that he thought union, if it were desired, would have to be sought under a sovereign government of our own choosing.
>
> These are sound views. They oppose nothing. They condemn nothing. They merely point out the gravity of the course we would follow in considering Confederation and indicate their belief that only a sovereign government of the people should conduct negotiations of so far-reaching and delicate a character."[7]

C.E. Hunt was one of the most highly regarded men in Newfoundland—a brilliant businessman and scholar, dedicated to Newfoundland—but he was not permitted to serve on the National Convention because he did not meet the new residency requirements. A two-year residency requirement for eligibility for election to office had been a pet condition of Governor Walwyn even before the Goodwill Mission in 1943, when A.P. Herbert had discussed the possibility of an elected convention with the governor in St. John's. Lord Addison had agreed with Walwyn that "this requirement would . . . suffice to secure the election of candidates who were genuinely resident in their various districts, and would effectively prevent the planting out of agents, with a view to their election, by business or other interests in St. John's or elsewhere."[8] The British were determined that Water Street merchants, mostly anti-Confederates, or their lawyers, would not dominate any elected body and control political events in Newfoundland. The principal people representing rural districts in Newfoundland, even if they were from the district, often had their main residence in St. John's.[9] There had never been a residency requirement in Newfoundland elections before the National Convention, and the result of its implementation in 1946 was to deprive the Convention of many qualified candidates.

Major Peter Cashin also failed to qualify for the residency requirement because he had lived in Montreal for several years. But in Cashin's case, Walwyn made an exception for fear of a riot. Cashin was a popular man. The son of a prominent political family and a political personality in his own right, Cashin had been minister of finance in the Squires government until he accused the prime minister of falsifying minutes in council and embezzling public money in 1929 and crossed the floor. He immediately developed a reputation as the protector of the people's rights. He was one of the few to speak out against the establishment of the Commission of Government in 1933, though, ironically, his earlier actions had unintentionally led to the end of responsible government. Cashin liked Canada, however, shortly after war's end, he returned to

Newfoundland and gave a series of broadcasts in which he condemned the plan to establish a National Convention as a violation of the terms of the Newfoundland Act. Any consideration of Confederation, Cashin insisted, was a matter for decision between Canada and an elected Newfoundland government. A fierce nationalist, Cashin became the spokesman for responsible government as factions developed out of the National Convention. These opinions brought him into immediate disfavour with Scott Macdonald. He appears in many dispatches from the high commissioner, who once described him as a "rabid and not very substantial character, although a few people with whom I have spoken regard him as an honest and outspoken champion of the common man."[10]

At the Dominions Office, Lord Addison declared himself satisfied that, "with the safeguards mentioned, it [the National Convention] should give us the results we desire."[11] Yet, officially, the department was at pains to make clear to Newfoundland and the British Parliament that it had no particular result in mind for the country. Such a preconceived outcome would be highly improper. The only men privy to the real agenda in St. John's were Governor Walwyn and Scott Macdonald

The run-up to the election for the National Convention in June 1946 was a busy time for the new Canadian high commissioner. Since his arrival in St. John's in 1944, Scott Macdonald had been exploiting the contacts made by his predecessor, Charles Burchell, and reporting on his progress to Norman Robertson at the Department of External Affairs. He identified these people in his "Very private and Confidential" memo as pro-Confederation and listed some of them:

> Mr. Justice Dunfield; Mr. Cyril Fox, K.C., one of the leading barristers in St. John's (shortly I believe to be appointed a Judge); J.B. McEvoy, who has one of the largest law practices in St. John's.

(He says no hope for Nfld. except in union with Canada and is the lawyer for practically all the Water Street merchants, all of whom are bitterly opposed to Confederation. From that point of view, he might be considered as a possible member of the Commission.); Chief Justice Horwood of the Supreme Court of Newfoundland.

All these men, and there are others, have expressed their views to me privately but would not do so publicly at the present time, but certainly would do so if a Commission were appointed to make an investigation.

I will discuss this matter more fully with you when I see you in Ottawa.[12]

J.B. McEvoy had articled in Burchell's law office in Halifax as a junior lawyer, and R.A. MacKay, the special assistant to the under-secretary of state for external affairs, had been McEvoy's political science professor at Dalhousie Law School. MacKay had already begun to court his former pupil in June 1945, looking for recruits to support Confederation in the coming campaign in the National Convention. MacKay wrote about that visit:

> Top Secret. Mr. McEvoy . . . is solicitor for most of the leading Water Street merchants and apparently also for the Bowater Pulp and Paper Company. . . . He is a forceful and effective public speaker among Newfoundland audiences. Mr. McEvoy, I should judge, has real capacity as an organizer and leader of a movement. . . . [He] would I think, be more than willing to take a stand and organize a group to lead a movement for federation. . . . Mr. McEvoy hinted that he and his friends could find enough funds for a vigorous campaign in support of federation.[13]

The announcement of the coming National Convention created a dilemma for the people of Newfoundland. At that time, most of the people qualified to serve on such a body, whether they favoured the Commission of Government, responsible government, or confederation as the solution to Newfoundland's situation, believed that any step away from sovereignty, such as entering Confederation with Canada, could be taken only by a duly elected government representing the people of Newfoundland. This group included former high commissioner Charlie Burchell. Almost no one thought it correct or legitimate to include Confederation on the ballot paper of a referendum. All the major players, with the notable exception of the delegate from Bonavista, Joseph Smallwood, believed that the return of responsible government was a necessary first step to Confederation. But even beyond that condition, the majority believed that the institution of the National Convention itself, with its dubious terms of reference and lack of real power, was an unacceptable interference in the process and constituted an abrogation of the guarantee initially made to Newfoundlanders when their local legislature was suspended.

To concerned Newfoundlanders such as C.E. Hunt, Albert Perlin, and many others on both sides of the Atlantic, Attlee's National Convention represented a fundamental breach of the Newfoundland Act of 1933, with its promise that, "as soon as the Island's difficulties are overcome and the country is again self-supporting, responsible government, on request from the people of Newfoundland, would be restored."[14] The wording of that document specified clearly that it was responsible government that would be restored, not representative or provincial or any other form of government, with the legislature in St. John's, and all the sovereignty and power that had been suspended in 1933. The only flexibility the British had was in the timing of this restoration. For Newfoundlanders awaiting the fulfillment of a contract long overdue, terms that were once clear were now unclear, and what was once guaranteed—responsible government—had now become just another option. It is fair to say that, in December 1945, Newfoundlanders felt the constitutional ground shift beneath their feet.

The extent to which these constitutional and nationalistic concerns weighed on Newfoundlanders, even those most sympathetic to Confederation, was the first and greatest obstacle to the schemers in London and Ottawa. Their anxiety is revealed in MacKay's disingenuous reply to McEvoy in February 1946: "I was . . . perturbed that you and your friends feel that the constitutional convention is the wrong procedure and . . . alarmed that you all seem unanimous against taking any part in it. I know it is rather galling to many Newfoundlanders to have the Dominions Office take such a patronizing course."[15] The Canadians knew the device of the National Convention was not so much patronizing as paternalistic, and they were anxious, even desperate, for it to be accepted by Newfoundlanders as the constitutional process. MacKay concluded his pitch to McEvoy with this plum: "Those who may show up as political leaders in the Constitutional Convention will in all probability be the leaders of Newfoundland under any new regime."[16] That new regime could only be Confederation, for what other regime would MacKay be promoting on behalf of Canada's Department of External Affairs?

No doubt promises of senatorships and other considerations of personal power moved some to accept the device of the National Convention. Everyone recognized, however, that Britain held the only legitimately constituted authority and that those who did not participate in the process already established would deny themselves any say or influence in the future direction of their country. The National Convention, though deeply flawed, was the only option. Inevitably, then, prospective delegates were persuaded to participate. As things turned out, however, participation proved to be a strategic error. In Jim Halley's words:

> That spring, in May 1946, I was approached by J.B. McEvoy with an offer. The previous summer I had worked in his law office as a student. Now he asked me to leave law school and come to work

there full time. The Governor, he said, wanted him on stand-by to run as a Delegate for the National Convention. He would be busy with the Convention, and needed help to run the office.

I knew that in McEvoy's office I would see everyone, all the major players, Gordon Bradley, Joey Smallwood and the Confederates, Ches Crosbie, Major Peter Cashin, champion of Responsible Government, the British Governor, Gordon Macdonald, and the Commissioners, and the agents for the British and Canadian governments. I would have a front row seat for this historic constitutional event. It was an offer I could not refuse.

So I said yes, and I saw it all. I saw the letters from Ottawa go across his desk from MacKay and others. I didn't read them but I saw them and his dealings with Smallwood. We knew what was going on but we didn't think they could pull it off. We thought Newfoundland would defeat them and Confederation. But we were wrong.

I was a spy in McEvoy's office so I saw how it was done, and it wasn't done right but we couldn't prove it then. We could not prove that what George Hawkins had said to us that day was true—until now. Now we can because we have the top-secret memoranda and other documents released by the Canadian Department of External Affairs and compiled by Paul Bridle, and what's not there I can tell you, and I want to before I die.[17]

Perhaps the only delegate with downright enthusiasm for the National Convention was J.R. Smallwood, the member from Bonavista, who had run openly as an advocate of Confederation with Canada. Having been resident in Gander since 1943, he also met the two-year residency requirement. Much has been said of this happy coincidence, with most scholars unwilling to take it at more than face value.

Smallwood's grandfather, David, had moved to Newfoundland from Prince Edward Island, where the family had been farmers for generations. Joey himself had a lifelong love of farming and a prejudice against the fishery, which was to prove unfortunate later in his career. He was born in Gambo, but immediately afterwards the family moved into St. John's, where he grew up. His grandfather had acquired a boot-making establishment on Water Street, and, at the entrance to St. John's Harbour, on the cliff face, he had a giant boot affixed, with the slogan "Buy Smallwood's Boots."[18] It was the first thing fishermen saw as they entered the harbour. The business was a great success, and Grandfather David became the centre of young Joe's life.

Smallwood's father, Charles, by contrast, was unreliable and an alcoholic, but with the help of his paternal uncle Fred, Joey Smallwood was educated with the privileged sons of the St. John's elite at Bishop Feild College. What little money he earned from working in the gardens belonging to his grandfather and other neighbours went to buy books and magazines, which he then rented out to classmates. He was a voracious reader but always had trouble with math. Short of stature and perpetually short of funds, Smallwood was an underdog at Feild, where he acquired an envious disdain for the affluent and ruling class. It was not in his nature to go unnoticed, however, and he led several student demonstrations. His most famous campaign was a strike against the cafeteria food. The campaign slogan, "More Treacle, Less Pudding," he lifted out of a British schoolboy comic book. At the age of thirteen Joe was already showing signs of his grandfather's brilliance at advertising.[19]

When Smallwood left school at the age of fourteen, he had already determined that one day he would be prime minister of Newfoundland. After working for a time in the newspaper business, he left Newfoundland for New York, where he threw himself into the political life of the metropolis and felt the full force of the ideological undercurrents struggling for dominance in the world. He started as a journalist, and then became a speaker for the Socialist Party. The climax of his New York political career was the election of 1924. The Socialist Party threw its support behind the Progressive Party, and Smallwood became a featured speaker. It was a remarkable education for him, but the party was annihilated at the polls. Smallwood returned to St. John's a skillful public speaker and a committed socialist. His concern for the working man and woman was genuine. However, as biographer Richard Gwyn states: "Smallwood was never a socialist in the theoretical sense, but a populist and an idealist by instinct, and a pragmatic politician and propagandist by nature."[20]

Back in St. John's, Smallwood served in the Squires government and learned a great deal from his mentor about the value of personal loyalty and party control. After the fall of responsible government, he became at different times a union organizer, cooperative organizer, journalist and author, always with exceptional energy, zeal and attention. All these qualities combined to make him famous across Newfoundland in his next incarnation as the buoyant host of *The Barrelman*, a popular radio show. An engaging mix of Newfoundland history, songs and stories, plus mail from listeners, the show made Smallwood some real money. Then, inexplicably, he abandoned his successful radio career in 1943 and, by arrangement with the British and Canadian military installed at Gander, established a large pig farm there to feed the growing number of wartime personnel at both bases.

Smallwood was certainly attracted to farming, or husbandry, and already had an unsuccessful pig farm outside St. John's on Kenmount Road, which he financed with his earnings from *The Barrelman*. Some historians have concluded that the move was the spontaneous act of a lifelong lover of pigs. But even Harold Horwood, his fellow Confederate and biographer, allowed that "by all rules of common sense Joey should have stayed with *The Barrelman* until he was ready to step out into politics, but common sense was not his strong point."[21]

However that may be, most commentators on Smallwood, whether for or against him, seem to agree on one point—the man was single-minded and driven in search of his destiny. And that destiny lay in politics, not in pig farming. Smallwood never wavered in that pursuit. The idea that Smallwood would leave St. John's, the centre of all political activity, as well as a lucrative and high-profile broadcasting career, just before the big constitutional issues of Newfoundland's political destiny were to be decided, is psychologically unconvincing—unless that move was part of some greater political strategy.

Some writers have asserted that Smallwood could not possibly have known of the residency requirement for elections as early as 1943. But that is not necessarily the case. As Jim Halley recalled:

> Smallwood was a "familiar" in the office of Charlie Burchell, the Canadian High Commissioner. We saw him going in and out all the time. I say "we," but I mean Grace Sparks, who lived across the street from Burchell on Circular Road and watched Joey going back and forth there. Grace worked for the Responsible Government League later on and went around the Island campaigning for the league during the referendum. So we presumed Joey was Burchell's man, or one of them. And of course Burchell talked with Governor Walwyn regularly. Burchell knew about Walwyn's insistence on a residency requirement for any elections, and he knew about the idea of a National Convention since at least the summer of 1943. But whether there was to be a National Convention or some other elected body, there was going to be a residency requirement because Walwyn was insisting on that to break the hold of the Water Street merchants and their lawyers over Newfoundland politics. There was a clash of elites there between the British and the local. The Canadians wanted the same thing as Walwyn. Like the British, they blamed the Water Street merchants for all of Newfoundland's problems, especially for keeping Newfoundland out of Confederation in 1895.

Joe would have known all that from Burchell. As a possible

player on the Canadian team that Burchell was putting together, he surely would have been given any relevant information, such as a possible residency requirement, for any coming local elections. Charlie Burchell set him up out in Gander with the Canadian military and the British buying his pigs. It was a perfect match for Joe—he could kill two birds with one stone. And if the National Convention had been elected when it was originally scheduled in '45, then Joe would just have qualified. But the Convention was postponed a year because the war in Europe dragged on and so he had to wait it out in Gander for another year before he got back to town.[22]

The announcement for the election of the National Convention found Smallwood ideally situated outside anti-Confederate St. John's in the district of Bonavista Centre, where he was already well known for his union and co-op work, not to mention *The Barrelman*. He campaigned with his usual single-minded determination more fiercely than any other delegate. During his residency in Gander he had become an expert on Canadian federalism, especially the benefits of the new social programs supported by Ottawa, and his campaign was an unabashed cry for Confederation. So far as Scott Macdonald and the Department of External Affairs were concerned, Smallwood was a valuable asset as a proselytizer and a salesman for Confederation, but not as the leader of the campaign. To them, he lacked the gravitas necessary for that role. They considered Gordon Bradley, the last leader of the Liberal Party in Newfoundland, a more suitable candidate, and he personally distrusted Smallwood. In 1935, when he was the magistrate in Bonavista, he had written to the Commission of Government:

> If the government has any intention of giving financial assistance to a co-operative movement in Bonavista (and I heartily support the idea) both its policy and its funds should be wholly free from

the control or even the influence of Mr. Smallwood. I think he might be quite useful as a propagandist to travel about the country teaching the idea of co-operation, but as a business executive he is hopeless. No reliance is to be placed upon him where steady work or sound judgment is required. He is not stable.[23]

Eventually, Bradley, McEvoy and their friends were all persuaded to set aside their constitutional scruples and stand for election. Smallwood had no such hesitation.

On June 21, 1946, thirty-four delegates were elected to the National Convention, which convened on September 11 that same year. Several weeks later Albert Perlin gave this account of their progress:

> The National Convention is a hard working body. Anyone aware of the immense amount of patient effort that is going into committee work will not need to be told that. Day after day committees are meeting for hours, discussing the particular problems before them, seeking expert evidence that will help them to marshal a full array of facts to guide them in their ultimate decisions.
>
> They are working under a handicap. There are no statistics worth very much. The Chadwick-Jones report summarized most of what there is and one had only to glance over that document to see what little exists in the way of reliable and basic information.
>
> It was thought at the beginning that there would be a great volume of highly technical and detailed information, carefully prepared and submitted by the Government. Nothing of the sort has happened.
>
> Its [the Convention's] committees have no power to summon witnesses and have no funds out of which to retain counsel to assist in gathering and marshalling the facts produced by witnesses. . . .

The Convention has none of these advantages or facilities. Nevertheless it is expected to produce reports on the basis of which the destiny of the Country may be decided.

The thing is absurd. It was absurd from the beginning. One wonders if it were ever intended to be anything else.[24]

On October 28, exactly as Scott Macdonald had feared, Smallwood suddenly proposed that the Convention send a fact-finding delegation to Ottawa: "Resolved that the appropriate authorities be advised that the Convention desires to inform the Government of Canada of the Convention's wish to learn the Government's attitude on the question of Federal Union with Canada and further wishes to ascertain the terms and conditions on the basis of which the Government of Canada consider that such a Federal Union might be effected."

Smallwood accompanied his proposal with a passionate plea for Confederation in which he painted a very bleak picture of Newfoundland:

The people view the future now with more dread than they felt a century ago. . . . We live more poorly, more shabbily, more meanly. Our life is more of a struggle. Our struggle is tougher, more naked, more hopeless. . . .

We are so used to our railway and our coastal boats that we scarcely see them; so used to our settlements and roads and homes and schools and hospitals and hotels and everything else that we do not even see their inadequacy, their backwardness, their seaminess.

We can of course persist in isolation, a dot on the shore of North America, the Funks of the North American continent struggling vainly to support ourselves and our greatly expanded public services. . . . By our isolation from the throbbing vitality and expansion of the continent, we have been left far behind by the march of time, the "sport of historic misfortune," the "Cinderella of Empire." Our choice now is to continue in blighting isolation or seize an opportunity that may beckon us to the wider horizons and the higher standards of unity with the progressive mainland of America . . . . I insist that as a constituent part of the [Canadian] federation we should continue to be quite free to hold to our love of our own dear land.[25]

This characterization of Newfoundland and Newfoundlanders was so reminiscent of the hated Amulree Report of 1933 that it caused an uproar in the Convention. After a long and heated debate the motion was deemed premature, and even those delegates who supported the idea in principle strove to distance themselves from Smallwood's pejorative comments about Newfoundland.

Scott Macdonald was furious:

The reason for premature introduction of motion to send a delegation to Ottawa was that Mr. Smallwood, without any good reason, became apprehensive that someone, other than himself, might get the publicity that would be attached to introducing such a motion and rushed in with one of his own.

There is no doubt that Smallwood's indiscreet action has dealt a heavy blow to the cause of Confederation here. The motion was deplorably ill-timed, being put forward before reports had been received from various Committees studying the economic and financial position of the country. It was tactlessly presented, for instead of merely setting forth desirability of securing information on what conditions Canada might be prepared to offer, he made an impassioned plea for Confederation, in the course of which he painted a very dark picture of Newfoundlanders and their position. Moreover, one of the oldest and most respected members who is also President of the Fishermen's Union, collapsed while making protest against Smallwood's tactics, adding a dramatic touch to the Opposition's stand.[26]

The commentary by Albert Perlin in the *Daily News* did little to calm the high commissioner's anxiety:

> Mr. Smallwood has allowed his zeal to outrun his discretion. . . . In defiance of the understanding that all delegates should work objectively towards the end the Convention was set up to attain, he has buttonholed members and others for private lessons in the virtues of Union with Canada, he has held meetings of groups of members at the Newfoundland Hotel to discourse them on the same subject, and what Mr. Harrington and Mr. Hollett said about promises of a free trip to Ottawa and a senatorship in the same city has been related by others with variations on the original theme. . . . Mr. Smallwood alleges he is the apparent victim of the conspiracy. But charges such as those made by Mr. Harrington and Mr. Hollett are not lightly made, and if Mr. Smallwood is the victim, it is of his own impatience.[27]

Major Peter Cashin declared that the Convention had only two legitimate options to consider—responsible government or a continuation of the Commission of Government. In his view, the Convention might as well pass a resolution "to get a delegation to go to Moscow and ask Joseph Stalin what kind of government or terms he would give us."[28] In the end, Smallwood's resolution was defeated 29 to 17. However, on November 4 Gordon Bradley introduced an amendment which stated that the Convention had the right and authority to ask Canada its position on Newfoundland joining Confederation. This amendment passed, signalling that a delegation to Ottawa was merely postponed. Scott Macdonald was thereupon moved to qualify his initial condemnation of Smallwood in his next "Top Secret" memo to Robertson: "While Mr. Smallwood's initiative was clearly both premature and tactless, his failure has had the effect of bringing the Hon. Gordon Bradley and the group of which he is the leading spirit, to take a public stand on the Confederation issue."[29]

The Convention was off to a dramatic start. It was Kenneth Brown, the delegate from King's Cove and president of the Fishermen's Union, who collapsed during his impassioned condemnation of Smallwood's unpopular resolution. Shortly afterwards, on November 16, Judge Cyril Fox, the chairman of the Convention, died suddenly. At the request of the delegates, Fox was replaced by Gordon Bradley, who had the most parliamentary experience of them all in the old House of Assembly. He was the third pro-Confederate chairman of the Convention, indicating that Scott Macdonald's "highly organized team" was already well out of the gate.

Ottawa was shifting into high gear in its effort "to take over Newfoundland," as Prime Minister Mackenzie King had put it in 1940 to O.D. Skelton at External Affairs. Increasing resources were now devoted to the project. The Second Political Division at the department was already overseeing the Newfoundland operation under the leadership of Escott Reid. In the summer of 1946 King set up the Interdepartmental Committee on Canada-Newfoundland Relations; the committee consisted of senior government ministers and bureaucrats, with Louis St. Laurent, the new secretary of state for external affairs, as chairman. On November 7 that same year, Lester Pearson, the new under-secretary of state for external affairs, prepared a top-secret memo for the committee which focused on the fundamental constitutional problem with the scheme to take over Newfoundland:

> A serious difficulty in dealing with a delegation from the Constitutional Convention would be that they could have no authority to negotiate terms of Union since they would not be representing a government. . . .
>
> An "offer" from Canada to a delegation from the Constitutional Convention might, however, be misinterpreted in Newfoundland as indicating a strong desire on Canada's part to annex Newfoundland

and possibly as an attempt to take advantage of the present situation when Newfoundland has no responsible government which could negotiate terms.[30]

Taking advantage of the situation in Newfoundland was, however, exactly what some key officials in External Affairs hoped to do. Pearson himself, and others within the department, did not approve of this approach and instead favoured negotiations with an elected Newfoundland government. This became the central problem that baffled and bothered almost everyone from Ottawa to St. John's to London who took the time to consider the situation. It was the subject of long discussions between Clutterbuck and Pearson in Ottawa as they grappled with the question of how the unavoidable negotiating process might work:

Top Secret. . . . Sir Alexander asked if we had given thought to the question of procedure. Mr. Pearson said that we had and that we wish to avoid a situation in which, on the one hand, a Newfoundland delegation would come to Canada making positive demands which could only lead to an inappropriate sort of bargaining or in which, on the other hand, we would present the Newfoundland delegation with a cut-and-dried offer which might give the impression that we are over-anxious to bring them in. . . . There is, he continued, the fundamental difficulty that a delegation from Newfoundland would not be representing a government and would have no power to negotiate. We might expect at least to be able to provide the Newfoundland delegation with the information which they would consider sufficient for the purposes of the Convention. . . .

Sir Alexander said it was this part of the process which he himself found difficult to envisage very clearly. He said that, in arranging for the establishment of the National Convention, the Dominions Office had felt that their only acceptable course was to set up machinery which would enable Newfoundland . . . to determine its choice in accordance with the will of its people. In doing so they did not lose sight of the possibility that Confederation might be one of the alternatives which the National Convention might wish to consider. They had found it impossible, however, to foresee at all clearly how the issue might arise. He feels, he said, that it would be well to arrive at as definitely agreed terms as possible before the question is submitted to the people. However, he finds it difficult to see how this could be done unless the Commission of Government were brought into the discussions at some stage.[31]

Clearly there were very serious constitutional problems with the process being improvised by the British in Newfoundland. However, despite all the difficulties the situation presented for them and the Canadians, not to mention the disadvantages for Newfoundland, the UK government never once considered employing the constitutionally correct procedure. It resisted all calls to return Newfoundland to the pre-1934 constitutional status and, instead, created the National Convention—to facilitate the transfer of Newfoundland's sovereignty to Canada. Now, having constructed their constitutional golem, Clutterbuck and the British were at a loss just how to bring it to life and make it appear to negotiate.

Political blocs began to form early on in the National Convention, largely in response to Smallwood's passionate partisan appeals on behalf of Confederation. To counter the sudden formation of the Confederate Bloc, the Responsible Government League was formed in December under the direction of F.M. O'Leary, a leading businessman and the sponsor of Smallwood's radio show, *The Barrelman*. The League included many prominent Water Street merchants—the Bowrings, the Bairds, the Ayres—and professional men such as C.E. Hunt and Gordon Higgins.

However, Major Peter Cashin, the spokesman for responsible government in the Convention, was not at first among them. He was as much distrusted by his fellow responsible government supporters as Smallwood was by his Confederates. His melodramatic style and histrionics reminded them of the old-style politics of the 1920s from which they were trying to distance themselves. As the time drew close to the referendum, however, they were compelled to join forces against the growing Confederate threat, but such divisions did not make for a strong, coordinated campaign from the League.

Following the defeat of his first motion of October 1946 to send a delegation to Ottawa, Smallwood organized a second resolution in early 1947 asking the governor to canvas Newfoundland's options on several fronts: possible economic ties with the United States, financial guarantees for responsible government or the Commission of Government from Great Britain, and more details about the terms for union with Canada. He arranged this package request with R.B. Job, an important fish merchant and a supporter of economic union with the United States. According to the deal between them, if Job supported Smallwood's request to go to Ottawa, then Smallwood would support Job's request to go to Washington. It seemed reasonable, but it was a trap set by Smallwood. Sir Gordon Macdonald, the British governor, would allow inquiries to Ottawa, but not to Washington. Cashin and Malcolm Hollett, another delegate for responsible government, knew well what would happen, so they voted against the resolution. It passed anyway. The governor, as expected, then informed the Convention that, as far as Job's proposal went, any overtures to the United States were a "matter for negotiations between governments through regular diplomatic channels." The jurisdiction of the Convention would extend only as far as Ottawa, where such negotiations might be as irregular as they could be.

Both Smallwood and Scott Macdonald were naturally concerned about the formation of the Responsible Government League and, despite their initial disagreement about timing and tactics, they were closely allied at this point. It now seemed likely that the Convention would form two delegations, sending one to London to ascertain British financial commitments, if any, to a responsible government or to a continued Commission of Government; and the other to Ottawa to investigate the conditions that might be offered for Confederation with Canada. Both delegations were completely ignorant of the understandings, financial and otherwise, reached between the Canadians and British officials in October 1945. The strategic deployment of these two delegations was of the utmost concern to Prime Minister Mackenzie King and the Department of External Affairs, and on January 8, 1947 Macdonald sent a secret dispatch to King, outlining his recent conversation with Smallwood:

> Secret. Sir, I have the honour to report that, in conformity with your instructions, I had an informal conversation, on my return from Canada last evening, with the Honourable Gordon Bradley, K.C., Chairman of the National Convention, and with Mr. J.R. Smallwood, member for Bonavista Centre, the advocate in the Convention of Confederation with Canada. . . .
>
> Later in the evening I had a further and more extended conversation with Mr. Smallwood. . . . I suggested to him that, from his point of view, there would be a good deal to be gained if the dispatch of a delegation, assuming that the Convention will agree to it, could be postponed for three or four months. Mr. Smallwood was disappointed but apparently not very much surprised. . . . He stated that he would use all his influence to prolong the present discussions and postpone raising the question of sending a delegation to Canada. At the same time he pointed out that the feeling among the members of the Convention . . . was very definitely in favour of pushing on and coming to a conclusion. . . . Some extension might . . . be secured by raising points that had not hitherto been covered. . . . He also agreed with my suggestion that the task of correlating the economic and financial information contained in

the various reports was a very important and intricate one and might well . . . keep the discussion going in the Convention until perhaps the beginning of March, though that would be the best that could be hoped for in the circumstances. A Resolution might then be put forward that an enquiry be addressed to the Government of the United Kingdom to ascertain whether, and if so to what extent, that Government might be prepared to continue to make itself responsible for the finances of Newfoundland in the event that the country retained the Commission form of Government, or, alternatively, adopted Responsible Government. If it could be arranged that nothing be done pending a decision on this basic question, a further period could be gained and perhaps the matter of sending a delegation to Ottawa postponed till after Easter. He did, however, feel that it would be most difficult to keep members of the Convention from forcing the pace and coming to definitive decisions before that date and in this I must say that, knowing something of the present feeling of members, I share his apprehension.[32]

If Smallwood was not taking his marching orders from Charles Burchell, Canada's high commissioner in 1943, he certainly was from Scott Macdonald at the beginning of 1947. This incidence of Canadian attempts to manipulate the agenda of the Newfoundland National Convention is noteworthy because of its success. Macdonald and the Canadians wanted the delegation to go to London first, to gain Ottawa more time, and a nervous Macdonald sent this note to Lester Pearson in Ottawa, who relayed it to Robertson in London: "The important thing at this stage is that the United Kingdom Government agree to receive a delegation and not head them off by an offer to reply to any questions . . . by correspondence . . . anything that could be done to ensure this result would be worthwhile."[33] Macdonald had reason for alarm. Eric Machtig at the Dominions Office and Alexander Clutterbuck, the British high commissioner in Ottawa, did not want any delegation from Newfoundland in London at all. Now that Britain had "run away from this responsibility" and had nothing for Newfoundland in the way of support, it had withdrawn psychologically as well, causing a complete turnaround in attitude at Whitehall.

On March 4, 1947, Norman Robertson, now the Canadian high commissioner in London, wrote to Pearson regarding his conversation with Machtig:

> The Dominions Office fear that the presence of a Newfoundland delegation in London might provoke a demand from both sides of the House of Commons for assurances of assistance and support for Newfoundland comparable to the Colonial Development Fund Scheme, which might be difficult to resist.
>
> For reasons such as these, Machtig is inclined to argue . . . that our ultimate interest might be better served if the delegation went first to Canada.
>
> . . . Machtig fully appreciates that his Government will have to consider procedure in respect to Newfoundland developments in close concert with ours and take Canadian advice before determining what further instructions are to be given to the Governor [of Newfoundland].[34]

"Canadian advice" was quick in coming. On March 13 Macdonald sent this vehement telegram to Pearson:

> Immediate. Secret. . . . The weakness in the programme they advocate is that it disregards the facts of the situation. The decision of the National Convention taken on February 28 is that a delegation should go to the United Kingdom first to ascertain what financial and other assistance they may hope to receive in the future from the United Kingdom and that no delegation shall go to Ottawa until delegation from United Kingdom has returned and reported

its findings to the Convention. . . . The logic of the whole position is that a delegation go to the United Kingdom first and, in any case, any attempt to exercise pressure in the other direction would only defeat its object. . . .

Years or decades hence a further opportunity may arise to bring Newfoundland into the Dominion. But it is not likely. For reasons I have outlined many times—the growth of further vested interests; the development of Labrador; the increase of American influence . . . make union with Canada yearly more difficult. . . . There is no likelihood that I can foresee of Canada and Newfoundland growing gradually closer together over the years and, in any case, Newfoundland could not be secured on more favourable terms later than it can now.

In my view, the setting has been arranged in a way that gives us the greatest possible prospect of success and nothing should be done to disturb it.[35]

Lord Addison ultimately accepted Scott Macdonald's advice. The Newfoundland Commission of Government, it seemed, now had a Canadian commissioner in addition to the three British commissioners, three Newfoundland commissioners, and the British governor. Smallwood, for his part, delayed the introduction of his resolution to send a delegation to Ottawa until March, after an assiduous examination of all committee reports. The week before, on February 28, by prior arrangement, Malcolm Hollett had introduced a resolution to send a delegation to London. Both resolutions passed.

On April 1, 1947, Gordon Bradley, the chairman of the Convention, read out Canada's reply to the Convention's request to send a delegation to Ottawa:

His Excellency the Governor has been informed by the High Commissioner for Canada in Newfoundland that the Canadian

Government will be happy to receive a delegation from the National Convention of Newfoundland at a mutually convenient date. The Canadian Government is of the opinion that the questions to be discussed with the delegation are of such complexity and of such significance for both countries that it is essential to have a complete and comprehensive exchange of information and a full and careful argument by both parties of all issues involved so that an accurate appreciation of the position may be gained on each side. The Canadian Government is confident that the friendship and cooperation which have marked the relations of our two countries should provide a firm basis for the discussions. The delegation from the National Convention will be warmly welcomed in Ottawa.

The following delegates were elected to constitute, with the Chairman, the delegation that will proceed in due course to Ottawa: G.F. Higgins, T.G.W. Ashbourne, J.R. Smallwood, R.B. Job, Reverend Lester Burry and C.H. Ballam.[36]

The fundamental problems presented by a Newfoundland delegation to Ottawa—the same issues that had so bedevilled Clutterbuck and Pearson—were immediately the subject of great concern in St. John's as well. Analyzing press reaction to Canada's acceptance of a Newfoundland delegation, Scott Macdonald noted with some discomfort:

The *Daily News* . . . says that . . . it is evident from the terms of the reply that the Canadian government is prepared to treat the delegation as a body authorized to discuss in detail all questions arising out of a possible political relationship between Newfoundland and Canada. This, it says, is an astonishing position.

It expresses surprise that Canada, unlike the United Kingdom in its reply to the Convention, "sets no restrictions on the subjects to be discussed, asks for no specific topics and requests no explanatory memoranda."[37]

The *Evening Telegram* was in favour of Confederation, and its opinion carried more weight but provided no more comfort for the Department of External Affairs. While it endorsed the idea of a delegation to Ottawa, it stated:

> "The terms of such a union would have eventually to be determined by negotiation between the constituted governments of the two countries. . . .
>
> The Canadian authorities must be credited with the elementary knowledge that any such issue as Confederation could only be discussed with a duly constituted Government of Newfoundland."[38]

Although Gordon Bradley had already ruled the motion for a US delegation out of order on May 22, 1947, D.I. Jackman, the president of the Wabana Mines Union, proposed to the Convention "that this National Convention appoint a delegation of some six members, or less, forthwith to proceed to Washington—if and when arrangements can be made—for general trade discussions and other relevant matters affecting the future economy of Newfoundland with the Government of the United States of America."[39] The Convention passed the Jackman resolution unanimously. But as Paul Bridle, now attached to the Canadian High Commissioner's Office in St. John's, noted with unease:

> The Commission of Government has subsequently informed the Convention that it regards the conduct of trade discussions as beyond the scope of the Convention.
>
> The High Commissioner feels that the attitude of the Commission of Government in this matter, while altogether correct, will be regarded in many quarters as further evidence that there is a conspiracy afoot to shepherd Newfoundland into the Dominion of Canada.[40]

Jim Halley relates:

> I was the one who wrote up the proposal with Jackman at the Newfoundland Hotel where most of the delegates were staying. Jackman, although a powerful and influential Union leader, was not literate. So I was there to draft it with him. We wanted the Convention to put Union with America on the ballot and if not that, then at least to keep Confederation off. Jackman's resolution was passed unanimously by the Convention. Joey supported it heartily, knowing that the Governor, on orders from Whitehall, would say no and that our request to talk to the U.S. was "beyond the scope of the Convention," but not the one to Ottawa.[41]

When the UK government set up the National Convention, it sent Kenneth Wheare out to St. John's as the constitutional expert to assist the delegates. Wheare took exception to Governor Macdonald's ruling and advised that the Convention did have the authority and jurisdiction to talk to the Americans. He was immediately recalled to London.

Once it was determined that a delegation could go to London before the second delegation was sent to Ottawa, the Canadian officials had one lingering concern—that London should offer no hope of any financial or economic assistance at all to Newfoundland. There was much heated debate on this topic, especially in St. John's between Canadian High Commissioner Scott Macdonald and British Governor Gordon Macdonald.

COLD SHOULDER:
THE NEWFOUNDLAND DELEGATION TO LONDON

In January 1946 Humphrey Walwyn had completed his term as governor of Newfoundland. A large crowd waved him and Lady Walwyn off to the strains of "Auld Lang Syne." He had arrived in 1936 on a passenger liner out of Liverpool, and he departed aboard an American bomber from Harmon Air Force Base in Stephenville after a leisurely train ride across the Island in the comfort of the vice-regal carriage, the "Terra Nova," attached to the Newfoundland Railway Express. The new governor, the recently knighted Welsh MP Sir Gordon Macdonald, was Clement Attlee's friend. Sir Gordon's arrival, like that of his counterpart Scott Macdonald, the Canadian high commissioner, signalled a more aggressive approach to getting the planned job done in Newfoundland.

Attlee had been prime minister in Britain for six months, and it was time for a new team in Newfoundland. There seemed little likelihood now of Newfoundland's getting that "drop in the ocean" Winston Churchill had mentioned. Churchill, Beaverbrook and now Walwyn were gone. There was a new wind blowing into Newfoundland from England, and it had even less warmth than the last one. Despite criticism of the Commission of Government, Sir Humphrey Walwyn had been a popular governor. Sir Gordon was not. In St. John's it was widely and rightly believed that he had been sent by Attlee specifically to put the Island into confederation with Canada. The mission shared by the two Macdonalds now in charge of Newfoundland should have fostered a close working relationship between them, but it did not. The Canadian high commissioner, Scott Macdonald, was a hard-drinking, hard-talking pragmatist, while the equally strong-minded new governor was a tee-totalling, self-righteous evangelist who even took to the pulpit in local churches to deliver fiery speeches. They did not get along. The Canadian was suspicious of the British appointee and believed that he wanted the Commission to hang on in Newfoundland for his own purposes. On March 22, 1947, he wrote to Louis St. Laurent:

> Secret. . . . The Governor may be planning to try to induce the Dominions Office to agree to extend its present commitments with respect to guaranteeing the service of the national debt and to meet any deficits that may occur. . . . For some months past, as I have already indicated, I have sensed the development of some such general idea in the Governor's mind. I am inclined to believe that his views are now crystallized and that, as appetite comes with eating, he has persuaded himself that if he were given control of Newfoundland for five years he could revivify the Commission and could promise, by using the surplus, to avoid any cost to the Treasury of the United Kingdom and at the same time give the country a more progressive government.
>
> In this connection I think I should report that [Gordon Bradley,] the Chairman of the [London] delegation and Mr. Smallwood came to my room in the hotel and stressed the danger that would arise if the United Kingdom authorities should listen to advice of this kind. They strongly urged me to bring the situation to the attention of the Government in Ottawa in the hope that they would take steps to prevent it developing unfavourably.

...I feel convinced in my own mind...that if the Government of the United Kingdom extends financial aid to Newfoundland there would be no point in considering further the question of encouraging the country to enter the Dominion or even of permitting the question of federation to appear on the ballot.[1]

It is clear from the tone of this ultimatum just how tenuous the Canadians considered their position in Newfoundland to be. As much as they downplayed their desire to annex the Island, it would be a serious blow to their national pride if Confederation with Canada were to be rejected in a referendum. Clearly, from Macdonald's comments, Smallwood and Bradley were aware of the ongoing communication between Canada and Great Britain on the subject of Newfoundland. For some time, in fact, Smallwood had been Macdonald's chief lieutenant and the de facto leader of the Confederation movement. He now felt it necessary to write directly to St. Laurent himself with this extraordinary plea: "The fairest thing they [Great Britain] could do would be to say frankly that even under a continued Commission Government they could not give us any financial help."[2]

With the exception of Bradley, Smallwood was almost certainly the only delegate from the Newfoundland Convention to demand that Newfoundland "alone of the dependent Empire...be promised no assistance for reconstruction and development." His political reasons were clear enough. If Newfoundland was financially isolated, Confederation would become a more attractive alternative. The absence of the promised British backing would reduce Newfoundland's options and perhaps even its stability. Smallwood had persuaded himself that his own political needs and the needs of the country were one and the same. It was a dangerous game: if the Canadians got cold feet again and pulled out, as they had in 1933, Newfoundland would be stranded. In the end, not even the British could support such drastic positions as Smallwood and Scott Macdonald demanded.

On April 16, 1947, Major Peter Cashin presented the long-awaited Report of the Finance Committee on the Economic Position of Newfoundland to the Convention. It was a detailed and comprehensive analysis of Newfoundland's financial history in the first half of the twentieth century. Among the highlights, Cashin noted that in 1909 Newfoundland's budget was balanced and the total public debt only $27 million. The First World War imposed a public debt of $45 million on the Island, and it was that debt, combined with the cost of veterans' pensions, the building of the railway, and the Great Depression, not mismanagement, that was the real cause of Newfoundland's financial troubles in the late 1920s and '30s. Cashin further emphasized that while the United Kingdom appeared to be helping Newfoundland in 1933, it was doing little more than helping itself, and that the grants-in-aid, as well as allocations from the Colonial Development Fund, were just sufficient to pay the interest on the debt to the United Kingdom bondholders.

At the end of the fiscal year of March 31, 1946, however, the report showed that "the total revenue collected amounted to $37,247,132, the highest ever collected in the history of Newfoundland. . . . Expenditure during the year amounted to $37,141,138, leaving a surplus of revenue over expenditure of $105,994. . . . The total accumulated cash surplus . . . amounted to $32,000,000."[3] By April 1947 Newfoundland stood in the strongest financial position in its history. In short, the report concluded, the main condition for the return of responsible government had been met.

After the financial report was unanimously accepted by the Convention, the delegation to London—consisting of Gordon Bradley, Peter Cashin, Ches Crosbie, A.B. Butt, Malcolm Hollett, W.J. Keough and Pierce Fudge—was free to leave. In the meantime the Dominions Office had presented yet more conditions. It now wanted Governor Macdonald and Albert Walsh, the commissioner of justice, to come along to help Lord Addison answer any awkward questions from the delegation and to keep the members within certain limits.

The defensive, almost hostile British attitude towards any demands from the Newfoundland National Convention was becoming a cause of indignant comment in both the Convention and the press. Albert Perlin wrote in the *Daily News*:

> The British government is the government of Newfoundland. . . .
> The curious thing is that it is necessary to send a delegation to
> obtain information that ought to have been proffered to the con-
> vention when it first assembled. . . . The generous Cranborne plan
> [of $100,000,000 for reconstruction] has been consigned to obliv-
> ion. We ask no favours in its place. But the people of the island do
> want to know if Commission Government would be continued at
> their request and under what conditions, they want to know what
> commitments have been made in their name and how these may
> affect their future, and they require information on a number of
> other matters that are highly pertinent to the determination of our
> true situation.[4]

On the eve of the delegation's departure for London and after long discussions, passionate dispatches and top-secret memos between the Canadians and the British on exactly what Newfoundland's true situation would be, Scott Macdonald reported in a secret memo on a more satisfactory meeting he had with the new governor, Gordon Macdonald:

> The Governor reaffirmed the view that both he and the
> Commissioners consider it is "almost indecent" for the Convention
> to make any request to the United Kingdom, either for the can-
> cellation of the sterling debt or for the payment of interest on
> the monies Newfoundland loaned to the United Kingdom during
> the war. They will also take a strong stand against the view of the

delegation that tariff or other concessions should be sought from the United States in return for the grant of the bases. . . . In all these matters, therefore, the Governor and the Commission are taking a stand, very favourable from our point of view, against the United Kingdom being asked to grant further assistance to Newfoundland.[5]

High Commissioner Alexander Clutterbuck in Ottawa even passed over to Lester Pearson a copy of the list of questions that the Newfoundland delegation had for Lord Addison, the dominions secretary, in London. The Canadians also wanted the United Kingdom to discontinue guaranteeing the principal and interest on the Newfoundland debt, but the British government refused, fearing a general loss of face along with support in Parliament. Canada obviously felt it had to isolate and even punish Newfoundland before Confederation would be found palatable on the Island.

Hemmed in by their friends in the Canadian dominion and the British empire, the luckless Newfoundland delegation left from Gander for London on April 25. They had been asked by the British to bring their own towels, but there was a mix-up when they arrived and no accommodation was available. A hotel was finally found and, after a three-day wait, they were received with chilly formality by Lord Addison and his battery of advisers—including, to their surprise, Governor Macdonald and Albert Walsh. Lord Addison assured the delegates that the UK government had "no pre-conceived ideas" as to the future government of Newfoundland. That was a deliberate lie to both the delegates and the Convention, as he had already decided on Confederation for Newfoundland as the official Dominions Office policy. Because this policy was secret, however, and carried Lord Addison's personal warning that "no hint that this [Confederation] is the solution envisaged should be allowed to come out here or in Newfoundland," the delegates were reassured with carefully worded deceptions and indignant denials.

After four very stiff meetings with Lord Addison, where written answers were proffered for the written questions requested, the delegation returned to St. John's largely dissatisfied, except for Gordon Bradley and Malcolm Hollett. A.A. Butt, a staunch imperialist, was traumatized by the event: "to be treated with a coldness I had never experienced in my life, that is, an individual coldness . . . it was unbelievable!"[6] The *London Daily Express* was equally indignant:

> How cold, graceless, ungenerous and chuckleheaded is the attitude of the Government towards Newfoundlanders. . . . It tells the Newfoundlanders harshly that, if they vote away the present Commission, Britain will no longer guarantee the interest on Newfoundland's loan of $71 million. Is this the way to talk to kith and kin? When Newfoundland made Britain an interest free loan of £2.5 million for the war effort, she did not extract a promise in return. Newfoundland sent her young men to fight alongside us, sent her sailors to defy the U-boats, she provided bases, she begrudged nothing. The statement made to the Newfoundland delegation by a Government which has poured out millions in dollars to succor strangers from China to Czechoslovakia in the last two years is contemptible."[7]

Having already given away the shop, the British were understandably frightened and angry at being asked for an accounting of their fourteen-year occupation. They had little left to offer—no hospitality and not even fair play. However, the disgraceful reception by their hosts at the Dominions Office was all good news to the Confederates, as Smallwood's biographer Harold Horwood remembers. "This is what Joey had expected and hoped for—bare justice and a cold shoulder."[8] Lord Beaverbrook, observing the delegation's progress in London, was moved to charge that "our rulers spoke for Britain with the voice of a shark lawyer."[9]

Shortly before his departure for London, Gordon Bradley, who was chairman of the delegation, had a long and confidential conversation with his friend Charles Granger in which he declared passionately: "Over my dead body will we go into Confederation without having responsible government first." While in England Bradley had a secret nighttime meeting with Prime Minister Clement Attlee, which was discovered by another delegate, Ches Crosbie. Bradley refused to disclose the substance of his discussions with Attlee; however, after the private audience, he ceased to demand the return of responsible government as a precondition for Confederation and returned to St. John's a committed Confederate partner with Smallwood on Scott Macdonald's "team" in the National Convention.[10]

Standing again before the National Convention in St. John's on May 19, Major Peter Cashin presented his report on the London talks. He had seen clearly through Addison's denials and was in no doubt about the British government's secret agenda. As usual with Cashin, it was plain talk and high drama:

> I say to you there is in operation at the present time a conspiracy to sell, and I use the word "sell" advisedly, this country to the Dominion of Canada. . . . Some people may think I am talking wildly, but I would ask them to remember that long before this I made statements in this House which were regarded at the time as wild prophesies, but time proved that I was right.
>
> At present our country is nothing more than an international pawn, and is being used by the U.K. government for the purpose of making international deals both with the U.S. and Canada. . . . This visit [has] shown that they had long ago finalized their plans concerning us.
>
> Listen to the flowery sales talk . . . telling Newfoundlanders they are a lost people, that our only hope, our only solution, lies in following a new Moses into the promised land across the Cabot Strait.[11]

Speaking of the planned delegation to Ottawa, Cashin predicted: "The joy bells will ring out when they arrive."[12]

As for Smallwood's performance in the National Convention, Paul Bridle, the secretary to the high commissioner, sent this appraisal to Ottawa:

> Mr. J.R. Smallwood attempted to undermine the value of the U.K. Government's assurance that it would continue to be responsible for Newfoundland's financial stability. He painted Britain's plight in hopeless terms and drew a dark picture of Newfoundland's fate under her continued tutelage. . . .
>
> He apparently ran up against his fellow members' pro-British instincts. He received practically no applause when he sat down.[13]

Had Cashin been privy to the top-secret correspondence between the Department of External Affairs and the Dominions Office, he would have been able to substantiate his assertions. But his assessment, although shrewd and accurate, was not taken seriously in the patriotic, "pro-British" climate existing after the war, where the only information available came in the form of vague, official statements crafted in carefully ambiguous Oxbridge English by the mandarins of Whitehall and Ottawa. In this stultifying political climate it was left to commentators like Albert Perlin to interpret the official signals for the public:

> The attitude of the Dominions Office as represented by Lord Addison appears to have been wholly defensive, almost as if the delegation had come to raid a diminished treasure chest rather than to seek enlightenment on matters of grave consequence to the people of this island.
>
> . . . Remember that the Convention has been charged with the task of formulating an opinion on the financial and economic prospects of the country as a first step to the consideration of forms

of government. Our affairs have been administered by the Dominions Office through agents in Newfoundland who were dignified by the collective title of Commission of Government. That has been the situation for fourteen years. In those fourteen years the people got what information the Commission was willing to give and not a jot more. That same Commission has been deaf to all appeals to reason in connection with fiscal policy. It had returned no answer to reasoned statements that debt reduction was logical and necessary. It has taxed how it pleased, when it pleased, and even when it was not necessary. It has taken small interest in urging our trade requirements. It could give none of the answers to the questions asked by the Convention which had at length to send a delegation to London to find them.

Now this London delegation was not like the delegation that will go to Canada. It was not going to ask how much value was placed on Newfoundland's assets as the first stage in selling our national identity to Canada and our industries to the domination of Ontario and Quebec. It went as representatives of Britain's oldest colony to talk with representatives of the Mother country, kin to kin, and even then it went only to ask questions that should have been answered long before. It was not received in that spirit, by all accounts, and we prefer to take the opinion of the majority of five to that of the minority of two. For this the British people are not to blame even if the Dominions Office is. There seemed to be a predominating feeling on the Dominions Office side that this upstart delegation should be put in its place and sent home as soon as possible. May 31, 1947.[14]

At this time the war had been over for barely two years. Newfoundland's contribution to the Second World War was equally as generous and heroic as it had been during the Great War. Once again in 1939 it had sacrificed its young men and donated large amounts of money—and had done so more quickly than any other territory of the empire. The valour of the Newfoundland soldiers in battle was legendary, and in 1940 King George VI was "pleased to assume the Honorary Colonelcy of the Newfoundland Regiments . . . the King's appointment . . . also to apply to any other Newfoundland Heavy Regiment that may subsequently be formed."[15] When the first contingent of the Newfoundland Royal Artillery arrived in England for training, Sir Anthony Eden, the secretary of state for dominions affairs, welcomed them with these words:

> Newfoundland, whose sons have fought side by side with Englishmen since the days of the Tudors, responded at once to the call that echoed around the world last September. It was a call to your own hearts, a call for voluntary service in a noble cause, and your answer has been clear and firm. You may be sure that the spirit of Newfoundland, both as represented by those who have come across the Atlantic and by those who have remained at home, is not forgotten.[16]

To Newfoundlanders who had given so much and so willingly to fight for Britain, it was unimaginable that the British government would deal in any manner other than honourably and fairly with their constitutional issues after the war. The British depended on that.

Lord Addison had offered Newfoundland the minimum, but it was too much for Scott Macdonald, who was now convinced that the governor was trying to give the Commission of Government the advantage. The British had no such intention; rather, they believed that the modest guarantees the Dominions Office gave the Commission of Government would take votes away from the choice of responsible government in the referendum. It was unlikely that any one option would receive enough overall votes to win outright, so the three-way split would result in a second referendum between the top two options. In setting up the conditions for a run-off vote on Newfoundland's sovereignty, many felt that the British had abandoned all sense of constitutional decorum. It was also felt that the second chance would favour Confederation, not least by providing more time to campaign. Scott Macdonald did not see it that way, however, and even indicated that Canada had been betrayed by the British. This concern, or paranoia, underlay the escalating conflict between the Canadian high commissioner and the British governor over the wording of the Newfoundland referendum ballot:

> This morning, in the course of a general talk on the arrangements for the holding of the referendum on the future form of Government for Newfoundland, Sir Gordon Macdonald, the Governor, told me confidentially that during his visit to London it was agreed that the electors would not be asked to approve the retention of the Commission of Government indefinitely but for a term of five years only. In reply to my question . . . he stated that the Chairman of the delegation, Mr. Gordon F. Bradley, was not aware of the arrangement. . . .
>
> This is, of course, a decision of basic importance, more particularly when it is viewed in combination with the United Kingdom's offer, already announced, to be responsible, as hitherto, for the financial stability of Newfoundland if the people of Newfoundland vote to retain the Commission for a further period. Newfoundlanders can hardly be expected to take so irrevocable a step as Confederation, with all the uncertainties and readjustments that it would involve, when they are presented with so favourable an alternative by the British Government. No one, of course, can forecast with complete assurance, least of all here where the physical means of contacting the elector and of gauging the trend of opinion is so limited, how an electorate will exercise its franchise. I feel convinced, however, as I pointed out in my despatches No. 106 of February 28th, No. 151 of March 22nd and on other occasions before the British Government's

plans were formulated, that with the scales weighted so heavily in favour of the Commission, there is not sufficient likelihood of Confederation winning a majority to justify the government engaging the prestige of Canada by entering the contest under these conditions.[17]

For the second time, an indignant Scott Macdonald had issued this particular ultimatum. Escott Reid, the head of the Second Political Division in Ottawa, relayed Macdonald's alarm to Lester Pearson:

Secret. . . . It is evident, as we have long believed, that the Governor hopes to see the Commission of Government continued and appears to be taking definite steps to foster such a development. I find it a little difficult to understand why he has been so frank in telling Mr. Macdonald about his plans and I am wondering if he may not wish to make the difficulties in the way of Confederation appear as formidable as possible in order that our own government might be discouraged from entering in a forthright manner into a contest in which its chances would not be particularly good.

Whether this is so or not it strikes me that if, as the Governor states, there is an arrangement between himself and Lord Addison regarding Commission of Government being placed on the ballot for a specified period of five years, the United Kingdom's attitude on the question of Newfoundland's political future must be rather different from that which we have hitherto understood it to be. I would suggest, therefore, that after you have talked to Mr. Macdonald you might wish to discuss the matter with Sir Alexander Clutterbuck.[18]

Peter Cashin was convinced that the British wanted to hang on in Newfoundland to get their hands on the cash surplus of between $30 and $40 million: when the surplus ran dry after about five years, they would hand the Island over to the Canadians. So rumours build and spread when motives are not apparent.

As Scott Macdonald brooded over the five-year limit or extension for the Commission of Government, he again gathered with his Confederate forces to plan a strategy to undermine the perceived British agenda and turn it to their advantage:

> Secret. I have the honour to report that I had an informal discussion last evening with the Chairman, the Honourable Gordon Bradley, and the Secretary, Mr. J. R. Smallwood of the Newfoundland delegation to Ottawa, on a number of points respecting the forthcoming meetings. . . .
>
> On the substance of the discussions I found that they were deeply disappointed at the reply of the British Government, which we recognize places the projected campaign for Confederation under a tremendous handicap. They feel that it is now essential for them to delay the referendum and that, instead of trying to finish the discussions quickly and meet the timetable the Governor prefers, they should proceed with the discussions as leisurely as possible, adjourning from time to time to permit full exploration of particular subjects. . . . The general objective would be, without appearing to do so, to postpone the referendum till next year.
>
> Undoubtedly anything that would delay the holding of the referendum would be advantageous from the viewpoint of federation with Canada, for on so vital an issue people make up their minds very slowly and in this country the facilities for influencing opinion are so backward that the process takes longer than it would in a more highly developed community.[19]

Macdonald, with the help of his Confederate team, continually sought to manipulate the proceedings of the National Convention for Canada's advantage. In this case they succeeded in delaying the referendum until

1948—and the return of democracy to Newfoundland by a full year.

Aside from keeping Newfoundland financially isolated and creating more time to sell Confederation, the other constant concern of the Inter-Departmental Committee on Canada-Newfoundland Relations as it contemplated the arrival of a Newfoundland delegation was once again, as Pearson had pointed out in his memo of November 7, 1946, the impediment of the peculiar legal hurdles they would have to overcome in their effort to draft Newfoundland into Confederation while its constitution was suspended. On June 11, 1947, the Legal Sub-Committee reported to the Department of External Affairs:

> Secret.... Unless an elected legislature is restored in Newfoundland, an Act of the United Kingdom Parliament will be required for the admission of Newfoundland into Confederation....
>
> If it is deemed desirable that elected representatives of the Newfoundland people participate in the detailed negotiations with the United Kingdom and Canada as to the terms of federation and the provincial constitution subsequent to the referendum, the Newfoundland Statute providing for the referendum could continue the National Convention to act as the voice of Newfoundland in such negotiations.
>
> Another method of giving the people a voice in such negotiations would be to restore the former constitution of Newfoundland and to have a legislature elected thereunder.[20]

This last alternative would obviously be the most correct and the simplest way forward—and the Canadian negotiators were determined to avoid it.

As the Committee on Newfoundland considered the arrival of a delegation from the National Convention in St. John's and what its own proposals might be, in June 1947 it produced another exhaustive account of the merits and demerits of association, *Benefits from Union with Newfoundland*, which was as usual preoccupied with Labrador, the United States, and the cost of the Island:

1. The Dominion would be enlarged by about 163,000 square miles, an area larger than Sweden and three times the size of the Maritime Provinces. The population of Canada would be increased by about 321,000 people of English and Irish extraction with a relatively high birth rate.

2. Newfoundland has always imported a wide range of Canadian goods. It ranks eighth on Canada's list of customers (countries ranking higher are, in the main, countries presently in receipt of large credits from Canada). Newfoundland's imports from Canada rose from almost $10,000,000 before the war to about $40,000,000 annually at present. . . .

8. On the other hand, should Newfoundland turn to the United States, the economic concession in which it is most interested would be entry of Newfoundland fish into the U.S. market. . . . If Newfoundland were successful in obtaining a substantial market for its fish in the United States, there is little doubt that it would hit very hard the market there for Canadian fish, resulting in perhaps a loss of as much as $20,000,000 annually to Canada, the burden of which would fall entirely upon the Maritime Provinces and Eastern Quebec. . . .

10. In Labrador . . . a very large deposit of high-grade ore has been found which, in view of approaching exhaustion of present U.S. sources of supply, may in future prove to be of very great importance and, if proven and developed, might yield the government as much as $2,000,000 in revenues. In addition, a substantial amount of waterpower is available in Labrador, the largest single undeveloped site at Grand Falls being capable

of over one million continuous horsepower, which would compare favourably with horsepower currently developed by the
Ontario Hydro Electric Commission at Niagara. . . .

13. Should Newfoundland remain outside Canada, the present
United States ascendancy in the Newfoundland-Labrador
region will almost certainly increase and might very well lead
to a virtual withdrawal from the area by Canada in favour of
the United States. Although it may be argued that Canada
would have little to lose by such a development from the point
of view of defence, this would inevitably point to absorption of
Canada within the United States orbit. This absorption might
hamper Canadian air communication with the United Kingdom
and Europe and would certainly make Canada's freedom of
action on her north-eastern borders almost entirely dependent
on the goodwill of the United States.[21]

On the financial cost to Canada of union, J.R. Baldwin, the secretary
for the Interdepartmental Committee on Canada-Newfoundland
Relations, concluded in a secret memo:

1. . . . The federal government could collect in Newfoundland
enough revenue to cover the cost of extending ordinary federal
services to Newfoundland. This cost has been estimated at
about $19,700,000 while probable federal revenue is $20,200,000.

This amount proved to be a gross underestimation of revenues from the
Island:

1. . . . Assuming no debt, no capital expenditures, present levels
of services and no railway costs in the provincial budget, the
remaining deficit in the provincial budget . . . might run as low
as $300,000 and as high as $3,500,000 depending on the extent

and speed with which the provincial government developed new sources of revenue. In the early years it would almost be certainly closer to the latter figure.[22]

Even at this early stage it was apparent to the Canadians that the new Province of Newfoundland would run deficits. But they seemed satisfied that a stripped-down provincial government could manage, while they would secure more than adequate revenue to cover the cost of federal services. Their minds were filled with dreams of Labrador, the pot of ore at the end of the rainbow after the constitutional storm was over.

While the bureaucrats in Ottawa brought the expertise of their various departments to bear on Canada's concerns, C.E. Hunt in St. John's, in a special feature in the *Daily News* on the eve of the delegates' departure, looked at the presumed benefits to Newfoundland and found that:

Confederation would not increase our commerce. Our remoteness from the centre of Canada would be to our disadvantage. Undoubtedly many of our industries would wither, thereby creating much unemployment. Not even the argument that, being then Canadians, we could have access to the mainland would be sufficient solace to those who do not wish to be compelled by adverse conditions to leave this island.

. . . Not so long ago Senator James P. McIntyre stated in the Canadian Senate: "The idea of Confederation was initiated in Ontario and Quebec. The Maritime Provinces had established a satisfactory trade among themselves; their market was close at hand and easy of access and traffic with that market was mainly by sea. Certain inducements were held out to the Maritimes to consent to Confederation. The New England market would be lost but a better and more profitable market—that of the central provinces— might be substituted therefor. The coal of Nova Scotia was to find a market in Toronto; the fish, lumber and agricultural products were to find a market in Quebec and Montreal. As time went on, it turned out that the coal of Nova Scotia did not find a market in Toronto and the fish, lumber and agricultural products did not find a market in Montreal. In the meantime the New England market had been lost.[23]

WARM WELCOME:
THE NEWFOUNDLAND DELEGATION TO OTTAWA

On June 24, 1947, the Newfoundland delegation arrived in Ottawa. Gordon Bradley, the chairman of the Convention, was again leader of the group, with J.R. Smallwood as secretary. Scott Macdonald had high hopes for this mission and wrote to Louis St. Laurent with clear enthusiasm: "This is an excellent delegation. . . . If we desire to take advantage of it, we have in this delegation the best opportunity we have ever had to bring Newfoundland into the Dominion."[1]

Major Peter Cashin's predictions of a warm welcome were fully realized. The reception in Ottawa was in every respect the opposite of the poor treatment meted out to the Newfoundland delegation in London:

> On the evening of June 24th the Prime Minister, the Right Honourable W.L. Mackenzie King, gave a dinner at the Country Club in honour of the Delegation from the National Convention of Newfoundland which arrived in Ottawa earlier the same day to commence discussions with the Canadian Government regarding the possibility of federal union of Canada and Newfoundland. The guests at the dinner included the Right Honourable L.S. St. Laurent, Secretary of State for External Affairs, and other

members of the Cabinet who will meet with the Newfoundland Delegation, the leader of the Opposition in the Senate, the leaders of the Opposition parties in the House of Commons, the High Commissioner of the Commonwealth countries and a number of Government officials.

. . . Mr. Bradley thanked the Prime Minister most sincerely for the warm welcome which he and his associates had extended to the Newfoundland Delegation and he said that ever since the delegation had arrived on Canadian soil they had been greatly impressed with the friendliness and goodwill of the Canadian people.[2]

The dinner was a grand affair, almost worthy of visiting royalty, and all for "little Newfoundland," which until six years earlier had not even rated a diplomat. The next day, as the discussions began, there were more speeches and another line-up of top Canadian officials led by the prime minister and including top cabinet ministers Louis St. Laurent (External Affairs), J.L. Isley (Justice), Dr. J.J. McCann (National Revenue), Douglas Abbott (Finance) and Frank Bridges (Fisheries). Scott Macdonald, the high commissioner to Newfoundland, was present, as well as Lester Pearson, R.A. MacKay, Paul Bridle, Mitchell Sharp, Dr. Hugh Keenleyside and numerous other Canadian officials. On the Newfoundland side, besides Gordon Bradley and J.R. Smallwood, the Newfoundland delegation included Gordon Higgins, Charles Ballam, the Rev. Lester Burry, T.G. Ashbourne and F.W. Crummey.

The huge imbalance in expertise, resources and authority between these two official groups immediately created a fundamental problem with the process. This ad hoc group of delegates from the Convention, whom Smallwood called "clod-hoppers" compared to the Canadian officials, were supposedly there to inquire, to ask questions only. They specifically had no power to negotiate. Yet unofficially they were there to negotiate the Terms of Union that Canada would offer to the governor in Newfoundland. These terms would then be voted on in a referendum.

Officially the terms of 1947 remained unnegotiated, a simple spontaneous offer from Canada which kept the Newfoundland delegation in Ottawa for over three months as they asked questions that were carefully framed not to appear as negotiations. Facing this compromised group from Newfoundland was the seasoned government of Canada, with all the resources of its departments and institutions behind it. The Canadian officials had all the authority they required to negotiate and deal; the delegation from Newfoundland had none. As Albert Perlin had written, "The thing is absurd. It was absurd from the beginning. One wonders if it were ever intended to be anything else."

The British knew the process was seriously flawed. Just four months earlier Sir Alexander Clutterbuck, the high commissioner in Ottawa, had written in a secret memo to Lester Pearson: "The Dominions Office is very anxious that no Delegation from the Convention should assume the stature of a negotiating body."[3] They reserved that right for themselves until it suited them otherwise. Clearly, the group that should have been sitting down with the Canadians in the summer of 1947 was a delegation from the responsible government of Newfoundland, elected by the people of Newfoundland, and with all proper authority to negotiate with the Canadians on an equal basis.

In Ottawa, all the departments of the government of Canada were thrown open to the delegates from Newfoundland. It was a long way from the cold shoulder in London that April. And it was to prove a much more drawn-out affair. Paul Bridle reported to Pearson on recent conversations with Clutterbuck, who was in constant contact with External Affairs officials in the capital:

> We have some reason to believe that the Newfoundland delegation are in no hurry to conclude their discussions at an early date and that one reason for this may be that certain members of the delegation feel that it would be to the advantage of the confederation group if the referendum were delayed until next spring.

Sir Alexander said that he thought that there might be something to be said for this. The time-table presently in the mind of the Newfoundland Government (i.e., having the Convention's recommendations in the hands of the United Kingdom Government by August 1st) seems to him to be crowding the whole business to some extent. He thinks there might be risk in presenting the question for decision at an early date because this would mean a snap judgment which might easily be an unfavourable one.[4]

Clutterbuck was now on board to promote the new timetable devised by Scott Macdonald and J.R. Smallwood. This wily Newfoundlander had emerged as the master salesman for Confederation, and he knew he required more time to make the deal with the people of Newfoundland. In the middle of a very hot July, with talks going nowhere and the Newfoundlanders waiting on Canada's pleasure, Lester Pearson gave this candid and undiplomatic assessment of the status of the delegation to the press corps on Parliament Hill: "The Newfoundland delegation has no power to agree or promise anything." Then he dropped the bombshell: "Canada would prefer to negotiate with an elected government to forestall any possibility of future complaints by Newfoundlanders that they had no voice in the actual negotiation of terms."[5]

Pearson's remarks were reprinted in the St. John's *Daily News*. Scott Macdonald was furious. Bradley threatened to return home over the slight to the delegation, and Smallwood had to employ all his powers of persuasion to keep him in the Canadian capital and prevent a total breakdown of the process. Pearson had expressed the deep divisions within the government over policy on Newfoundland. It was the last time he would do so. St. Laurent, Howe and Pickersgill swung into action, and Mackenzie King recorded in his diary on July 18 that St. Laurent had reminded him "of the value it would be to my name and to the future to have Newfoundland come into Confederation while I am still P.M."[6]

St. Laurent's appeal to vanity, glory and posterity had the desired effect. At a special Cabinet meeting to deal with the crisis, King agreed that the talks should take on the status of negotiations and ultimately produce concrete terms of union. But that was not permitted by the terms of reference for the National Convention. No one seemed to be clear about the muddled process, largely because the participants were again improvising and defining the parameters of the "discussions" and "negotiations" as they progressed. The unlawful "negotiations" were conducted in an atmosphere of official denial entirely inappropriate for the scale and importance of the issues involved.

The sudden death of Minister of Fisheries Bridges caused the federal government to delay formulating its final offer of terms to the delegation. Mackenzie King feared a possible reaction in all three Maritime provinces—Nova Scotia, Prince Edward Island and New Brunswick—to any terms being offered to Newfoundland, especially now that Bridges, the Liberal government's direct link to the New Brunswick premier, had gone. They feared that if the terms offered were known, they would become the subject of political debate during the New Brunswick by-election. So the delegates waited in Ottawa over the summer as the prime minister arranged a hasty by-election in New Brunswick.

Smallwood was pleased with the delay, but the Convention and the local papers back in St. John's were becoming restive and suspicious as to what kinds of discussions or even forbidden negotiations were taking the delegates so long. They seemed to have been swallowed up by Ottawa. The High Commission office in Newfoundland reported nervously to External Affairs:

The St. John's *Daily News*, the *Grand Falls Advertiser* and the St. John's *Observer's Weekly* continue their attacks on confederation and on the discussions now taking place in Ottawa. The *Daily News* repeats its charge that the pro-confederate members of the delegation now in Ottawa are deliberately endeavouring to prevent a referendum this fall to "railroad" confederation through in a referendum next year, thus avoiding the danger of placing the issue in the hands of a duly elected Newfoundland government.

. . . The *Grand Falls Advertiser* also refers to an address which Major Cashin apparently made in Grand Falls recently and endorses a number of statements said to have been made by him, among them "that there is a plot afoot to stall the referendum and place the country on the auction block with the U.K., Canadian and Commission Governments in cahoots" and that the people should ignore the convention and present a National Petition to the British Government demanding the "fulfillment of 1933 pledge"—restoration of Responsible Government.[7]

In spite of the problems that the delay was causing the Convention in St. John's, the Canadian government felt it had no choice but to suspend talks and hold the delegates until, as External Affairs stated, "the Cabinet included an elected representative of the Province of New Brunswick. Meanwhile, this would permit the minister of finance to discuss, during his forthcoming visit to the United Kingdom, the disposition of Newfoundland's sterling debt with the U.K."[8]

And so the summer continued, with significant allegations and threats as the Newfoundland delegates continued to wait on the Canadian government's agenda and its further secret negotiations with the British. In St. John's the remaining delegates demanded that Bradley, as chairman, reconvene the Convention so they could continue with business, but he refused. As August gave way to September a group of delegates from the Convention sent an angry telegram to the delegation in Ottawa, charging that members had exceeded their terms of reference by participating in detailed negotiations and demanding that they return home. Bradley replied that they had kept discussions within the terms of reference laid out, and the delegation sat tight. Bradley was pushing his authority to the limit and, by refusing to reconvene the Convention, he was probably overstepping it.

Newfoundlanders were not the only ones who were suspicious of the real motives behind Canada's moves towards Newfoundland. Russell Cunningham, the CCF opposition leader in Nova Scotia, alleged that "vested interests" favoured Confederation because it would "eliminate" a dispute that he felt was imminent between Newfoundland and Quebec over ownership of the iron-ore deposits on the boundary between Labrador and Quebec.[9] It was generally understood in Canada and Newfoundland, as well as in Great Britain, that Canada wanted Newfoundland for Labrador, and that if it could get Labrador without taking Newfoundland it would. As Julian Harrington, Lester Pearson's friend at the US Embassy in Ottawa, noted: "Newfoundland as a tenth province without Labrador and its iron ore would have little political or economic sex appeal to Canadians."[10] The position of the Quebec government was well known:

> Premier Duplessis predicted the annexation of Newfoundland would result in everlasting squabbles because half the people on the island were not agreeable to joining Canada. . . . He compared the entry of Newfoundland into Confederation to the admission of a new member into the household without consulting the members who built the house. The Federal Government was paying millions for the 10th Province whose people would benefit without cost from social legislation, transportation services and so on, at the expense of the other nine provinces."[11]

By then the Newfoundland constitutional situation had drawn notice from the American press as well. The *Chicago Tribune* charged that 80 percent of Newfoundlanders wanted to join the United States but that the Newfoundland National Convention was being prevented by Britain from seeking terms of union from the south. The citizens of

Newfoundland, it said, would do well to vote for responsible government and then sue for statehood with the United States.

G.L. Magann at the Canadian Embassy in Washington drew Ottawa's attention to this item from the U.S. Congress:

> The Preliminary Report Ten of the House Select Committee on Foreign Aid (The Herter Committee) contains a suggestion that "some participation in Labrador iron ore deposits might be allocated as security against any U.S. loan to Britain. It is further suggested that present deliberations regarding Newfoundland's political future might be made the basis of negotiations in this respect. It clearly assumes that Newfoundland, which owns Labrador, is "a colony of Britain and not a Dominion."[12]

Britain, however, had already agreed to turn Labrador and Newfoundland over to Canada as a way to settle its war debt:

> Mr. Magann concludes his letter by pointing out that the Herter Report, which speaks of the "astonishing results" in terms of possibilities of repayment which might be produced by a systematic review of world resources on the above basis. Mr. Magann says he would think that this proposal with regard to Labrador's resources would excite other and more lasting emotions than astonishment on the part of Newfoundlanders.[13]

For a while in September it had looked as if the delegation to Ottawa would return to St. John's empty-handed. Still deeply conflicted, Mackenzie King was relieved at the prospect and mused in his diary: "It may be infinitely better to have nothing done until Newfoundland has a responsible government of its own."[14] The prime minister had expressed this wish before—and he would again. By then, however, Smallwood, working round the clock with Pickersgill, had come up with terms that seemed acceptable to both sides. He was now the lead man of all the committees, having demonstrated the prodigious knowledge of the Canadian federal system he had acquired on jaunts to Ottawa while still farming pigs in Gander. Finally by October, with the by-election in New Brunswick over and another Liberal MP from there safely seated in Ottawa, the discussions were concluded and the delegates were free to return home. The proposed terms were sent on later to the governor, who was and remained the government of Newfoundland up to the moment the Canadians took over.

The Convention reconvened in St. John's on October 10. A resolution to censure Gordon Bradley and the delegation to Ottawa for their overlong sojourn had been planned, but Bradley anticipated their action and, after a dramatic speech denouncing "certain members," he suddenly announced: "This Convention is now without a Chairman."[15] Harold Horwood, Smallwood's old confederate partner, described the scene: "Pandemonium broke loose, led by Joey himself, who tossed papers into the air and kept shouting across the floor that the Convention was no longer in session. To emphasize the point he lit a cigarette and started to blow smoke around the hallowed chamber."[16]

Reports of the unruly behaviour in the Convention convinced many that it would be unwise to "turn our government over to that crowd," and some began to look more favourably on Confederation. Ironically, it was Smallwood who was the ringleader of the bad behaviour that turned the Convention into a farce, and it would be his group that, through Confederation, would take over the government of the new province. The *Daily News* concluded that the whole business of the National Convention was futile:

> To make matters worse the persistence of one member of the Convention diverted it from its main purpose so that for the last year it has seemed as if the whole reason for the Convention's existence had been to examine the complex issue of union with

Canada which it is wholly incompetent to do on a proper basis because of its limited powers of enquiry and its lack of authority to negotiate. In the spate of political dissension thereby created, to which aggressive tactics of the delegate from Bonavista Centre contributed, it has become impossible to give objective study to anything.[17]

In the aftermath of the debacle at the Convention, John B. McEvoy, Jim Halley's law partner and another Confederate, was appointed by Governor Gordon Macdonald as chairman to replace Bradley. Scott Macdonald was pleased and reported the news to St. Laurent. On October 29, 1947, Mackenzie King finally sent Canada's proposed Terms for Union with Newfoundland to the governor:

> My dear Governor . . . I am now in a position to advise you regarding the arrangements [terms] which the Government would be prepared to recommend to Parliament as a basis for union. . . .
>
> I feel I must emphasize that as far as the financial aspects of the proposed arrangements for union are concerned, the Government of Canada believes that the arrangements go as far as the Government can go under the circumstances. . . .
>
> The Government of Canada would not wish in any way to influence the National Convention nor the decision of the people, should they be requested to decide the issue of confederation. Should the people of Newfoundland indicate *clearly and beyond all possibility of misunderstanding their will that Newfoundland should become a province of Canada on the basis of the proposed arrangements*, the Canadian Government, subject to the approval of Parliament, would for its part be prepared to take the necessary constitutional steps to make the union effective at the earliest practicable date.[18]

Sir Alexander Clutterbuck's report to the Dominions Office on the delegation's visit to Ottawa and the "negotiations" there was very enthusiastic:

> Some difficulty was naturally encountered owing to the fact that the Delegation was empowered only to seek information and had neither the authority, nor indeed the qualifications, to enter into negotiations with the Canadian Government. This difficulty would no doubt have been felt more acutely if the Canadian Government had adopted a less forthcoming attitude; as matters turned out, however, it cannot be said that the interests of Newfoundland suffered in any way on this account. . . . In sum the terms proposed amount to a very generous offer.[19]

In no way would Sir Alexander have been so sanguine and trusting of the constitutional arrangements and their outcome if his own country had been sitting at the table to decide its destiny with "neither the authority nor indeed the qualifications to enter into negotiations."

As the Convention drew close to debate on Canada's Terms of Union, J.R. Baldwin from the Department of External Affairs held discussions with Norman Robertson, now the Canadian high commissioner in London, and Sir Eric Machtig at the Commonwealth Relations Office (the renamed Dominions Office) on possible constitutional procedures to be followed during the period after the referendum and before Newfoundland officially became a province of Canada. They were ahead of the game and in agreement on two main points. Baldwin reported in a confidential memo to St. Laurent:

> That in some fashion, representatives from Newfoundland should be associated with the final drafting and other detailed work required between the referendum and the required date of the union; and . . .

. . . [the] Commission of Government might be maintained until after the effective date of union; that during this period a representative group of Newfoundlanders might be called upon to cooperate with the Canadian and U.K. governments in any further drafting of terms of union."[20]

It was becoming difficult to find a place for Newfoundlanders in the new Newfoundland. With only a ceremonial role at best in drafting the final terms of union, they would have no meaningful say over Newfoundland's political arrangements if they co-operated, and even less if they did not.

On November 25, 1947, Scott Macdonald and J.R. Smallwood were shocked by a sudden turn of events. As Macdonald informed St. Laurent:

The local political scene was enlivened a bit yesterday by the launching, through an advertisement in the *Daily News*, of a new party, to be known as the "Union with America Party," with the object of securing terms of union from Washington and having them submitted to the people in the forthcoming referendum. It is stated that 112 group heads have been chosen in various parts of Newfoundland and that a drive for membership, which will be open to all Newfoundlanders twenty-one years of age or over, will shortly be launched.

So far as I can ascertain, no one of any prominence is connected with the movement. It has already provoked a strong editorial in today's *Evening Telegram*, a copy of which I enclose herewith for your information, together with a copy of the advertisement under reference.[21]

Announcing. Newfoundland Party for Economic Union with America to be known as the "Union With America Party"

1. Membership open to any man or woman in Newfoundland over 21.

2. A membership drive will be started shortly and will be announced in the local press.

3. A group of 15 local leaders with 112 group heads in various Newfoundland outports are now forming plans; other group heads are required.

4. The terms from Washington must be obtained as were the terms from Ottawa.

5. The American Republican Party will be asked to support the aims of the NEWFOUNDLAND UNION WITH AMERICA PARTY....

6. If the PEOPLE of this country do desire to find out the terms of U.S. Union then why is it not being put on the ballot paper? GIVE THE PEOPLE ALL THE FACTS—WE WANT THE AMERICAN TERMS. ALL NEWFOUNDLANDERS ARE ASKED TO JOIN THIS PARTY. NEWFOUNDLANDERS, WAKE UP TO YOUR DESTINY ... BECOME A MEMBER OF "THE UNION WITH AMERICA PARTY."[22]

Of all the threats to Confederation, the possible union of Newfoundland with the United States was the greatest. There were hundreds of thousands of Newfoundlanders living and working in New York and Boston, more than there were in Newfoundland itself. In 1895 the large Newfoundland-Boston community of some 30,000 had been outspoken against Newfoundland joining Canada, and all for her coming in with the United States.[23] Now, with thousands of American service personnel in Newfoundland, the threat was even more immediate. The Canadians might harass the British to eliminate the Commission of Government as a choice on the referendum ballot and insist that it and the responsible government option be stripped of any financial backing whatsoever, but what they feared most was to have union with America on the ballot in any form. If the Union With America Party could successfully link responsible government and Newfoundland independence with a political union or economic link to the United States, then Smallwood and company feared that Confederation would be finished.

The Canadian terms were finally delivered to Convention chairman McEvoy on November 6, 1947, in the middle of the debate on the report on the Island's economic condition. Scott Macdonald's memo on Smallwood's speech is worth reading for what it reveals about the perils of propaganda. The report found, as expected, that Newfoundland was in excellent economic condition with a large cash surplus, none of which suited the Confederate cause or the Confederate candidate:

> Unfortunately Mr. Smallwood . . . leaves the impression that he is deliberately and for his own purposes endeavouring to paint conditions as darker than they really are. . . .
>
> Mr. Hollett (Grand Falls), who opened the debate, scored neatly at the expense of Mr. Smallwood. Referring to his attack on Major Cashin the previous day he quoted very effectively from Mr. Smallwood's book on Newfoundland written in 1930 in the same period when Mr. Cashin was Minister of Finance.
>
> "The Newfoundland note, then, is distinctly one of hope. The country has put its worse behind it. The future is most promising. This march to industrialism is no flash in the pan. Newfoundland is round the corner. Much remains to be done to make conditions ideal, it is true, but the encouraging fact is that much of it is being done. And after all, when all is said, where is the other country in which life is so comparatively free and easy, where men live so easily in health and happiness as in Newfoundland? One has only to witness the bread-lines in front of hospitals and various charitable institutions, and see the vast crowds of hungry unemployed men in New York and other American and Canadian cities, and read of the same terrible conditions in every country of Europe, to appreciate just how well off we really are in Newfoundland. . . . Those of us who are interested in the great changes that are coming

over Newfoundland, and who have also some contact with the industrial life of the United States and Canada, have one fervent hope, and that is that, with the coming of modern industrialism to Newfoundland, we may never lose the fresh bloom of that wholesome life which constitutes much of the charm of our country."

Macdonald concluded with some amusement, if not pleasure: "Rarely can a man have been more neatly hoist with his own petard."[24]

But Smallwood would not be put off by history, his own or anyone else's, and he was now out to prove the opposite true. He positioned himself in front of one of the microphones in the Convention Chamber and made full use of it. He always timed his major speeches for prime-time radio listening and dominated sessions with a steady stream of propaganda for Confederation. When the Convention finally turned to a discussion of the Canadian Terms of Union, Smallwood took to the floor to sell them, not to the delegates in the Convention but to the Newfoundlanders listening at home—the voters in the coming referendum. Scott Macdonald was suitably impressed by his performance and, in several dispatches, reported the goings-on in the chamber to Pearson:

The Convention and the country have been treated for a full week to the amazing spectacle of one man without any formal position or authority, dominating by sheer force of personality and a wide and accurate knowledge of Dominion-Provincial relations, the whole discussion. The debate was broadcast and the generally good expositions, interspersed with entertainment in the form of heated verbal duels, must have been of very considerable propaganda value. Indeed at times when interest flagged, Mr. Smallwood appeared deliberately to stir up controversy for this purpose. On one occasion, for example, he threw the Convention into an uproar through deliberately refusing to answer a question put to him by Mr. Higgins, and going so far as even to defy the Chair. He argued, in defence of his stand, that he had already answered the question the previous day, implying that Mr. Higgins hadn't been listening attentively and pointing out that in any case Mr. Higgins was, equally with himself, a member of the delegation and it was ridiculous to have to coach him on matters he should have learned at Ottawa. Newfoundland is accustomed to violent, personal abuse of the kind common in Canadian politics half a century ago and such attacks still appear to be good tactics here. . . .

I have to report that the remainder of the week was taken up with a running criticism of Mr. Smallwood's hypothetical Provincial budget.[25]

Mr. Hollett argued that Mr. Smallwood's estimate of revenue and expenditure was altogether irresponsible and misleading. . . .[26]

. . . Mr. Hickman . . . took the floor and expressed the view that Mr. Smallwood's estimate of expenditure was far too low—half a million short in Education; a million short in Public Health; two and one-half million short in Reconstruction and that revenues would fall considerably short of Mr. Smallwood's optimistic estimate. The new Province, he asserted, would face a deficit of between five and six million per annum in the first four-year period and when the time came for a review of the financial position, would find itself insolvent and forced to dispose of Labrador to Canada.[27]

Major Cashin . . . got in some of his oft-repeated assertions respecting the enormous size of the Canadian national debt and the interest charges on it. He claimed, also, that in return for taking over the very small Newfoundland debt Canada would be getting very valuable public utilities. The Major continued by repeating once again his oft-reiterated assertion that when Newfoundland went off the gold standard to save the Canadian Chartered Banks in 1931 the Banks had made some twenty millions of dollars and that in World War II the Bank of Canada had the advantage of using hundreds of millions of U.S. dollars spent in

Newfoundland and it was estimated the Bank had made $150,000,000 from this source.[28]

The only reason Canada wants Newfoundland, said the Major, is for the iron ore and the fifty or sixty million cords of wood in Labrador. By the inclusion of Newfoundland into the federation Canada would be in the position of controlling the entire steel industry of the North American Continent. He then compared the present situation to the sale of Alaska by Russia to the United States for a mere pittance.[29]

Once again Cashin spoke the truth, but without the proof. Gordon Higgins, one of the delegates to Ottawa, followed Cashin in the debate and was more deferential:

> He stated that every courtesy and assistance was extended to the delegation while in Ottawa and that he had nothing but the greatest praise and kindliest feelings for all those he had come into contact with from the Prime Minister down. He felt, however, that the Newfoundland delegation was seriously handicapped in the discussions by lack of knowledge of the many and intricate problems bound up with Confederation. The Canadian representatives, he pointed out, were assisted by some of the top men in the Civil Service of Canada who had had the question under active study since October, 1946, and, in a general way, had been studying it for some years past. The proper approach, he said, was that a complete study of the Canadian system should be made by the various Department heads of the Newfoundland Civil Service to advise on the effect Union would have on Newfoundland and that these experts should confer with a delegation which should have full power to negotiate.
>
> A further point, which he emphasized strongly and which is bound to create a considerable impression here, is that while the

offer received appears to be a fair one he is confident that a delegation properly informed, assisted by competent advisers and with the power to negotiate, would receive a better offer from Canada than the one they were now considering. The facts brought back by the present delegation would, he argued, be a good basis for future negotiations and he assured his hearers that if the present offer from Canada is not accepted it will not lapse unless world economic conditions greatly change. He therefore concluded that the proper course for Newfoundland was to return to Responsible Government and if later on they desire to consider Confederation further it could be brought up again under more favourable conditions from Newfoundland's point of view.[30]

It was the most passionate debate of the Convention, and, on January 28, Scott Macdonald reported the final results to St. Laurent:

> It was 5 o'clock this morning before Mr. Smallwood completed his rebuttal bringing the debate to a close. The roll was called and the motion to place the Canadian terms of Union before the electorate at the forthcoming Referendum was defeated by twenty-nine votes to sixteen.
>
> I attach, herewith, to complete the record, a list of members who voted for the motion and those that opposed it.
>
> While the terms offered are the minimum terms that would enable Newfoundland to carry on as a Canadian Province, they are, fairly considered, so advantageous from Newfoundland's point of view that it is disappointing to find that they have not attracted a greater following in the Convention.[31]

The Canadian high commissioner was evidently surprised and even offended that the Newfoundlanders would reject terms from Canada which would barely allow the Island to survive. Smallwood was suitably outraged and called the majority who had voted to keep Confederation off the ballot the "29 Dictators." But in truth the result was not unexpected by the Canadians or by Smallwood, and they were not overly concerned by it. Norman Robertson in London already had Prime Minister Clement Attlee's personal assurance that it meant nothing:

> Secret and Personal. . . . Mr. Attlee's feeling was that it would be unjust and unreasonable to exclude the Confederation option from the referendum simply because a majority within the Convention, made up of the supporters of Responsible and Commission Government, were able to combine to vote down advocates of Confederation. Macdonald assumes that the report of the Convention will at least refer to the substantial minority vote in favor of adding Confederation to the ballot. . . .
>
> United Kingdom Government would not, repeat not, of course put Confederation on ballot against wishes of Canadian Government.[32]

The UK government would not put Confederation on the ballot if the Canadians did not wish it but would, however, do so whether the Newfoundlanders wished it or not. Usually in a democratic contest it is a majority opinion that prevails, especially if it is a substantial majority. In this case the Commonwealth Relations Office chose to play by different rules and accepted the minority vote as conclusive. Lord Addison was particularly bitter about the Convention's failure to "give us the result *we* desire," as he had written to Attlee optimistically in November 1945. His memo to the prime minister in February 1948 bristles with imperial pique:

> When it was decided to set up the Convention, it was hoped that this would consist of a body of responsible people who would look at the various possible forms of government dispassionately and clarify the issues to be put to the Newfoundland people for their

decision. Actually this hope has not been realized. The Convention has consisted of political aspirants who have dealt with the matter on bitter party lines, and they have in fact tried to anticipate the decision which it was intended should be left to the people as a whole at the referendum. In spite of having received very generous terms, which the Canadian Government have indicated that they would be prepared to recommend to the Canadian Parliament as a basis for union between Canada and Newfoundland, the Convention so conducted their operations as to endeavour to prevent this issue being put before the people.

It is clearly open to the United Kingdom Government to decide that Confederation with Canada as well as the other two courses should be placed on the referendum paper, since it was not the intention that the Convention should in effect be able to decide the issue, and it would be intolerable if the opponents of Confederation in the Convention were successful in a manoeuvre which would prevent the matter being submitted to the people of Newfoundland. On the other hand, the tactics require some consideration. . . .

The term "responsible government" should be defined as Responsible Government as it existed in 1933 before the institution of Commission of Government. There would be no question at present of the adoption by Newfoundland of the Statute of Westminster or of it assuming full Dominion status on the Canadian model.[33]

Lord Addison's tone is that of a controlling Victorian father indignant at his daughter's refusal of the marriage arranged for her. The punishments for Newfoundland's defiance of the Commonwealth Relations Office were heavy indeed, and certainly a long way from Lord Beaverbrook's plan to rearm the country with dominion status—a point on which Lord Addison seems to be confused. Newfoundland enjoyed full dominion status when its parliament was suspended in 1933 and it was expected to resume that status when its parliament was reinstated. That was Churchill's understanding and also Lord Beaverbrook's, whose memo to the War Cabinet in November 1943 demanded that Newfoundland be offered "the right to resume Dominion status." As for political aspirants attempting to hijack the agenda of the National Convention, the delegate who most fit that description had to be their own agent, Joe Smallwood.

The National Convention had made its move. In a final attempt to limit the referendum to the original terms of the agreement in the Newfoundland Act of 1933 and control events, it recommended that only two choices be given on the ballot—a continuance of the Commission of Government or the restoration of responsible government. As Jim Halley remembered the moment:

> We rejoiced when the National Convention rejected Confederation as a choice on the ballot paper and recommended just the two, responsible government or Commission of Government. We thought we'd won and shown Great Britain that Newfoundland didn't want Confederation, or at least not through a referendum run by the British and the Canadians. The Canadian government's terms had been debated thoroughly in the National Convention and found to be seriously inadequate, which became obvious to everyone later on. The Convention therefore wisely decided not to submit Confederation on the basis of those terms to the general public in a simple referendum. It was the correct thing to do to protect Newfoundland's interests, especially its power to negotiate terms with Canada for itself.
>
> So we were jubilant. We didn't think the UK government would go against the recommendations of the National Convention which they themselves had set up, and we had all participated and gone through a year of this Convention and its importance. . . . England still had enormous prestige after the war. Not everyone

trusted them, of course. The more Irish you were, and the more familiar with the recent Irish history, the more unwilling you were to take anything the British said or did at face value. Trusting the English was not something the Irish could do. But we all got a shock. It's one thing to suspect something and another to have it happen.[34]

On January 29, 1948, the National Convention dissolved, and Wainwright Abbott, the American consul in St. John's, reviewed its performance:

By no stretch of the imagination can it be credited with having achieved with distinction and success its appointed task of considering possible future forms of government and objectively weighing their advantages and disadvantages. With the introduction of the Confederation issue, the Convention was split from the beginning with the issue dominating the debates to the extent of their revolving principally about it and nothing else; their usefulness suffered proportionally. If the Convention has served no other purpose, it has aroused political interest in this country which for 14 years has lived in a political vacuum. It is generally expected that a bitterly partisan campaign will now commence and be waged in preparation for the coming referendum.[35]

8

WORDS, WORDS, WORDS:
THE REFERENDUM BALLOT

Shortly after the National Convention dissolved in January 1948, thirty-two members of the Law Society of Newfoundland representing the cream of the country's legal community petitioned Lord Addison to uphold the Convention's decision and return responsible government to Newfoundland. Only three lawyers abstained:

Lawyers Protest to British Government

Maintain No Irrevocable Decision to Union with Canada Should Be Made Until Free Negotiation Is Conducted at Government Level

"The undersigned members of the Bar of Newfoundland are of the considered opinion and firmly maintain that . . . the Newfoundland Act of 1933 enacted by the British Parliament provided specifically that Newfoundland's constitution would be merely suspended and would be restored to the people at their request when the country again became self-supporting. As the National Convention has decided that Newfoundland is self-supporting, therefore only two forms of government can be considered and submitted to the people in the referendum, namely

Responsible Government and Commission Government. The issue of Confederation can be properly decided in the usual constitutional manner at a general election. [The] Canadian Government has presented unilateral proposals only and we consider that no irrevocable decision as to Union with Canada should be made without prior full examination by a Newfoundland Government and its financial and economic advisers and after detailed and exhaustive negotiations between governments."[1]

Once again the UK government received a clear and unambiguous request to fulfill the terms of the Newfoundland Act of 1933. Newfoundland had already met the financial requirement set out in that Act. Britain had established the National Convention ostensibly to give body and voice to the vaguely phrased condition "on request from the people of Newfoundland," and the Convention had been elected along lines specifically laid down by the Dominions Office to achieve the greatest and fairest possible representation of the Newfoundland people. A two-year residency requirement had been introduced to keep the influence of Water St. merchants to a minimum. The Convention was as representative and cooperative a body of Newfoundlanders as London could hope for. At the close of the Convention's meetings, Judge Gordon Higgins proposed a resolution that the people of Newfoundland be asked at the earliest possible time their choice between "Responsible Government as it existed in Newfoundland prior to 1934" and the existing form of government—the Commission of Government. This motion passed unanimously.[2] The conditions had been met, but would responsible government be returned?

In 1943 Lord Beaverbrook had declared the terms of the Newfoundland Act to be fulfilled and the UK government to be in an illegal position in Newfoundland. Ten years earlier, during the debate on the Act in the British Parliament, Lord Snell had observed: "What is now proposed will clearly indicate that in as short a time as possible responsible government will again be in operation."[3] And D.H. Thomas, the dominions secretary at the time, had assured the House that "'Temporary' is written all over this bill."[4] It was now 1948, over fourteen years later, and the fulfillment of that promise was long overdue.

While the members of the Law Society and the rest of Newfoundland waited for the decision on the choice the United Kingdom would give them, Lord Addison entered into detailed negotiations with Canadian officials on the all-important wording of the options on the Newfoundland ballot paper. He took care to conceal these discussions just as Lester Pearson nervously reminded everyone at the Department of External Affairs of the need for absolute secrecy. The considerable tension within the department over the underhanded path being taken to acquire Newfoundland came to a climax in early February 1948. On the eve of their secret negotiations with Great Britain, a fierce battle erupted in Mackenzie King's Cabinet over the procedure. Norman Robertson demanded non-interference and argued forcefully against the inclusion of Confederation on the ballot paper. Mackenzie King supported this position and recorded in his diary:

> Robertson pointed out quite emphatically that what they [Newfoundlanders] should do is to decide between responsible governments and other governments, and when they had found responsible governments, come to negotiate with them [the Canadians]. That is the position I have taken from the beginning. . . .
>
> St. Laurent was inclined to feel that all that had been done up to the present should not have been attempted if that was the view taken. In this, I think, he is quite wrong. . . . I could see St. Laurent was unwilling to do other than press the matter . . . seeing this I left the discussion to other members of the cabinet particularly Wishart, Robertson, McCann, Abbot—all of whom thought it would be wrong for Canada to express any opinion on what . . . Britain should do.[5]

Once the prime minister quit the field, the decision belonged to St. Laurent and the powerful C.D. Howe, along with R.A. MacKay, Jack Pickersgill, and Scott Macdonald—all ardent supporters for acquiring Newfoundland and Labrador while they were still under British control. Pickersgill, MacKenzie King's executive assistant, kept him buoyed along towards a more active policy on Newfoundland. He believed that the "whole future of Canada" depended on Newfoundland and that, if the United States took over in Newfoundland, reaching into the east coast of Canada as Alaska did on the west coast, Canada would be "strangled not physically but spiritually."[6] St. Laurent was equally persuaded and, along with C.D. Howe, also anxious to acquire Labrador's valuable mineral assets. If the Cabinet and External Affairs could not agree on the right way to proceed with Newfoundland's entry into Confederation, however, they could unite on one key point. On February 13 the federal Cabinet issued a statement that, "in the Canadian view, the addition of Union with the United States on the ballot in the forthcoming referendum would be undesirable."[7] The statement was a perfect expression of "defensive expansionism" in play. "Each phase of expansion in Canada has been a tactical move designed to forestall, counteract or restrain the northward expansion of American economic and political influence."[8] Above all else, the Canadians did not want to be put into competition with the Americans.

The next series of top-secret memoranda between Ottawa and London is marked with no less tension than that within the Department of External Affairs, and, although Canada did not get all the concessions it wanted, the shift in the centre of gravity in Newfoundland affairs from London to Ottawa is clear. On February 14, 1948, Sir Eric Machtig at the Commonwealth Relations Office opened up the dialogue with a telegram to High Commissioner Alexander Clutterbuck in Ottawa:

Secret. . . . We are . . . sending you a separate official telegram asking you to advise Canadian Government what we propose. This should be done informally and confidentially as it might well be embarrassing to the Canadian Government if it could be said that they had been formally consulted by us [on the Newfoundland referendum]. . . . We should of course like to know as quickly as possible whether they have anything to say, since the Governor of Newfoundland is anxious that he should be able to make an announcement on the subject early in March. . . . We would let you have an advance copy of this despatch.[9]

Clutterbuck in turn outlined the Canadian position for Sir Eric:

Important. Secret. Your telegram No 151. Newfoundland. I saw Pearson about this yesterday and had further word with him today.

Officially Canadian attitude is that they are grateful to us for informing them in advance of announcement but that they do not wish to be consulted and are quite content that we should proceed as we think best. They are anxious to be able to say, if questions are asked in Parliament here after announcement, that the Canadian Government were not repeat not consulted, that there was no reason why they should have been consulted and that the matter was purely one for United Kingdom decision in light of the local circumstances.

Unofficially however, while greatly welcoming decision to place confederation on ballot paper and also proposal for second referendum if necessary, Pearson expressed some concern on following three points:

(1) They feel that if Commission of Government is placed on ballot paper with suggested limitation to five years, there would be strong temptation for people of Newfoundland to vote for this course and scales would be unduly weighted against confederation . . .

(2) As regards continuation of Commission of Government they wondered also whether we had it in mind to explain to Newfoundland people before voting takes place the financial implications of this course . . . viz. that in view of the United Kingdom's own dollar difficulties it would be impossible for the United Kingdom Government to help them much in the future as they had done in the past.

(3) In connection with the placing of Confederation on ballot paper . . . Canadians were anxious . . . for it to be made clear by United Kingdom Government in proposed announcement that in the event of vote being in favour of confederation, means would be provided to enable final details of proposed terms and arrangements for constitution of Newfoundland as a province of Canada to be discussed and settled officially between the two countries. . . .

(5) As regards (3) Pearson at first suggested . . . that it might perhaps be improved by addition of words "whether by the formation of a provisional government or otherwise" after the words "means would be provided." Point in mind is that it would presumably be for responsible Newfoundlanders (possibly with our assistance) to settle matters finally with Canadian Government.[10]

Unofficially the Canadians had quite a shopping list for the British. Pearson's phrase "means would be provided" begged more questions than it answered. What "means," and "provided" by whom and for whom? It was exactly the sort of high-sounding, fuzzy ambiguity the British relished. In the end it would allow some ad hoc groups of co-operative Newfoundlanders to be picked by the governor to ratify the whole deal.

In London Lord Addison, having accommodated as many of Pearson's suggestions as he felt possible, advised Governor Gordon Macdonald in St. John's:

> Immediate. Personal and Secret. . . . In drafting the despatch we
> have had the advantage of assistance of Clutterbuck who has just
> arrived here and has advised us of the confidential discussions he
> had with Canadian authorities on receipt of our telegram referred
> to in my No 43. Wording of second sentence of paragraph 7 of the
> despatch has in particular been adopted to meet observations made
> to him by Canadian authorities.[11]

The second sentence of paragraph 7 read as follows: "In the event of the
vote being in favour of confederation, means would be provided to enable
final details of the proposed terms and arrangements for the constitution
of Newfoundland as a province of Canada to be discussed and agreed
between representatives of Newfoundland and Canada."[12]

MacKay and Bridle replied from Ottawa that this phrasing was not
satisfactory and that some mention of Canada's terms must be included
in the statement. Clutterbuck wrote to Machtig and Addison and, after
a great deal of back-and-forth, St. Laurent weighed in with this decision
to Norman Robertson, the high commissioner in London:

> Immediate. Secret. . . . The essential point in our suggestion was
> that a qualification such as "on the basis of the Canadian
> Government's offer" should be inserted in the sentence. So long as
> some such phrase is included, we are not disposed to object to
> insertion of the words "the full" before the "terms," or to the sub-
> stitution of "settled" for "discussed and agreed," although the latter
> seems preferable since it would tend to give Newfoundland people
> a clearer impression of active participation by Newfoundland rep-
> resentatives in the working out of the final terms.[13]

The Canadians were at pains to stay as close as possible to the unilateral terms of 1947 while also creating the "impression of active participation by Newfoundland representatives" in negotiating the final terms.

In St. John's, Governor Sir Gordon Macdonald told Canadian High Commissioner Scott Macdonald of Lord Addison's final decision and, on March 3, 1948, the high commissioner broke the "bad news" to St. Laurent.

> Confidential. His Excellency the Governor was good enough to receive me for an hour this morning and to outline his conversations with Prime Minister Attlee and members of the Government on the form of the ballot in the forthcoming referendum.
>
> It has been agreed during the discussions in London and Lake Success, he stated, that three questions would be placed on the ballot, namely, Responsible Government as it existed prior to 1934; Commission of Government for a period of five years; and Confederation with Canada. With respect to the latter question the electorate would be asked to vote merely on the question of principle, leaving the terms to be discussed and agreed between the Commission of Government and the Government of Canada.
>
> I asked him if the Government of Canada was aware that such proposals were contemplated. He assured me that they had been communicated to the Canadian Government through the British High Commissioner in Ottawa and that Mr. Robertson, the Canadian High Commissioner in London, had recently been in Canada for consultations on them. In this connection he pointed out that there was some difference of opinion as to the conditions under which the Commission of Government would negotiate terms of union with Canada and stated that the formula proposed by the Canadian Government, namely, the substitution of "settled" for "discussed and agreed" would not be acceptable to him as it took for granted there could be no negotiation on matters of substance. As I was not aware of these discussions I did not feel it wise to pursue the matter further. . . .
>
> The Governor, who was very friendly, continued to express the hope that Newfoundland might someday become a part of the

Dominion. As his sentiments appeared to be genuine, I refrained from pointing out that a third defeat for Confederation—the likely result of a referendum carried out under the conditions he had mentioned—would make it a good deal more difficult than it would be in a fair contest now.[14]

Scott Macdonald did not try to conceal his bitterness. He thought "discussed and agreed" sounded too much like real negotiations. Lord Addison's compromise reflected not only the high commissioner's concerns but the pressure he was feeling from both Macdonalds in St. John's. After extensive talks with Clutterbuck and Robertson, Addison advised the acting British high commissioner in Ottawa: "Important. Secret and personal. We have considered very fully [the] wording. . . . If Canadian authorities should still feel difficulty, Clutterbuck will be able to explain position to them more fully on his return to Ottawa at beginning of next week."[15]

The Canadians did still continue to "feel difficulty," and even panic, about the possibility of further negotiations over Newfoundland. St. Laurent telegraphed MacDonald: "We do not feel we can agree to this wording since it seems to open much wider consideration than the Prime Minister's letter to the Governor covering the proposed terms."[16] Nevertheless, on March 10 Lord Addison released the final version of the Newfoundland Referendum Ballot:

The questions to be put before the people at the National Referendum will therefore be:

(a) Commission of Government for a further period of five years.
(b) Responsible Government as it existed in 1933 prior to the establishment of Commission of Government.
(c) Confederation with Canada.[17]

The Commonwealth Relations Office had completely ignored the wishes of the National Convention—the voice of the people. The National Convention had not been set up to ascertain the wishes of the people in the first place but only to introduce Confederation on the ballot. The ballot paper was the ultimate place to direct the Newfoundland voter to the new choice both Britain and Canada wanted them to make—Confederation. The wording was therefore crucial, and a great deal of thought and effort went into it on both sides of the Atlantic. In the final version, the Commission of Government was presented first but for only "a period of five years," which immediately gave it a limited future and more uncertainty. Next, responsible government was presented, but qualified with the phrase "as it existed in 1933"—in other words, with the negative association of the Great Depression. Finally came Confederation with Canada—clean, simple, without qualification or further uncertainty.

The Canadians had wanted a definite qualification attached to the Confederation option—"on the basis of the Canadian government offer." That wording would have given voters as much pause as the conditions on the other two choices, but the British understood the psychological implications and, to shorten the odds, left out the reference to Canadian terms. With every constitutional advantage at their disposal, British officials felt confident they could control the final negotiation process and manage Canadian anxiety over better terms for the Newfoundlanders. They could take these calculated risks because they were not Canadians. They therefore cleverly positioned Commission Government with the unsatisfactory present, responsible government with the past, and Confederation with the future. Lord Addison had given Confederation as much psychological advantage as he dared—and it was considerable.

Scott Macdonald did not appreciate the psychological subtleties and vented his displeasure to St. Laurent and Mackenzie King:

> Confederation will not be put to the people specifically on the terms offered by Canada. Indeed it will be put before them in

ambiguous and equivocal terms. Voters are to be left in the dark as to whether they would be voting for Confederation, if they should so vote, on the terms set forth by the Canadian Government as modified in discussions with representatives of Commission of Government or on different terms. Moreover the provision in the penultimate paragraph that the final terms of settlement must be left to the Commission of Government (in whom, by the very fact of voting for Confederation, the voter will have expressed lack of confidence) is, to say the least, a requirement that will give rise to considerable misgiving.[18]

Gordon Bradley, the president of the Confederate Association, was of exactly the same mind as Macdonald. If these two informed and senior political leaders were confused about what the Newfoundland electorate was being asked to vote on, ordinary voters would surely be doubly confused. Yet the matter was important. It was the first issue on which the people of Newfoundland had been permitted to vote in fourteen years, and they would be making the complex and irrevocable choice of whether to transfer their sovereignty. The Canadians wanted the matter clarified for the voters; the British did not, preferring to keep the Newfoundland electorate confused and to fudge their way to the end.

R.A. MacKay in Ottawa was equally displeased. On March 12 he wrote back to Macdonald:

Secret and Personal. . . . As you know, our proposed amendment to the last sentence in the second-last paragraph of the despatch to the Governor was not accepted by United Kingdom authorities. Clutterbuck was instructed to come in and see us and explain why. He was in Tuesday and again Wednesday last. On Wednesday, Escott Reid and I had about twenty minutes with him on the Newfoundland statement. He was considerably on the defensive, explaining that the United Kingdom had wanted to assure the

Newfoundland people just as we did that they would have some
voice in arranging the final details of union and drafting their
own constitution. . . .

It was quite evident from Clutterbuck's statement that the
real pressure was coming from the Governor and possibly the
Commission of Government who Clutterbuck seemed to think
had been consulted. Considered in the light of your dispatch
No. 106 of March 3rd, I am not at all sure that the Governor does
not hope, in the event of a favourable vote for confederation, to
re-canvass the whole basis of confederation. Clutterbuck said,
however, that it had been made clear to the Governor that the
Canadian Government meant what was said in the Prime
Minister's letter of October 29th about finance.[19]

The Canadians were indignant that the British had not completely
followed their orders in Newfoundland. Clutterbuck smoothed feathers
and fears in Ottawa about the possibility of any Newfoundland participation in the negotiations, and Governor Gordon Macdonald was left to
reassure the high commissioner in St. John's. On March 15, 1948, Scott
Macdonald reported to MacKay:

Secret and Personal. . . . Having won his point, the Governor
seemed to be more conciliatory now. In an interview I had with
him yesterday, in which I emphasized again our position with
respect to financial terms, he assured me that . . . in the event that
Confederation should win a majority in the forthcoming referendum, there would be no disposition on the part of the Newfoundland
representatives to reopen the financial aspects of the proposed
basis of the union. . . . The Newfoundland representatives should
not be allowed to defeat the expressed will of the people by stubborn insistence on conditions the Canadian Government may not
be prepared to accept.[20]

Scott Macdonald was still unconvinced and, in a closely following dispatch, he canvassed the issue once again with the governor:

> I further . . . expressed the view that it would be most unfortunate if, after a favourable vote, settlement could be deferred indefinitely, through the recalcitrance of the delegation that might be chosen. Sir Gordon stated, however, that there was no reason to fear any such outcome. . . . He would do his utmost to see that the representatives chosen were men who would understand that their duty was to see that the will of the people was carried out rather than men who might use their position to prevent full agreement being reached.[21]

Sir Gordon was the head of the government of Newfoundland. Yet he is here giving entirely improper assurances to the government of Canada that the delegation from Newfoundland will be chosen to sign whatever terms Canada chose to offer, and that the negotiation process will be but a ceremonial show to legitimize what the British and the Canadians had already agreed on. If it was not treason in London, it certainly was in St. John's. In any context it was a conflict of criminal dimensions and a fundamental breach of faith. A quite different slant was given to the Newfoundlanders. The governor's words, however, were meant for Canadian ears only, and they had an immediate ameliorating effect. It was clear to Scott Macdonald that Sir Gordon felt himself to be in the driver's seat for the referendum ride and, further, that he was confident of winning. And so the two conspirators patched up their differences and the referendum campaign finally began.

9

LIMITLESS FUNDS:
THE FIRST REFERENDUM CAMPAIGN

It was very discouraging for us when Great Britain went against
the decision of the National Convention on the Referendum. We
realized then that the fix was in and that Britain and Canada were
going to do everything in their power to make Confederation
happen whether it was fair or not.

All that time I was working in McEvoy's office but it was
becoming awkward. He was clearly working for the Confederates
and I clearly was not. No one really knew at first who had put the
advertisement in the *Daily News* announcing the formation of the
Union with America Party. Scott Macdonald was the one who found
out.[1]

On February 5, 1948, Canadian High Commissioner Scott Macdonald
sent a dispatch to Lester Pearson:

I have the honour to refer to my dispatch No. 548 of November
26th, 1947, respecting the formation of the Union with America
party. It has now been ascertained that the two moving spirits in
the party are Mr. James Halley, a local lawyer who is the partner

of Mr. J.B. McEvoy, Chairman of the National Convention, and Mr. Geoffrey Sterling, Editor of the tabloid newspaper the *Sunday Herald*, which has a large and rapidly-growing circulation in Newfoundland.

It is understood that the promoters of the new party have been putting considerable effort into organizing local groups and trying to outline a plan of campaign. . . . Mr. Jackman and one or two other members of the National Convention are sympathetic. . . .

But while the Union with America party is not in a position to do anything worthwhile in the present campaign, there is no doubt of the very large latent interest in union with the United States as the best solution of Newfoundland's difficulties. I feel certain that, if the Commission of Government is retained for a further period, it will be quite impossible to prevent this question being fully explored when the time arrives to set up an alternative form of Government. I doubt that the United Kingdom Government is fully aware of this situation or of the repercussions it could have. A new Administration in Washington might not discourage advances from Newfoundland and once Newfoundland began to negotiate terms of union with the United States, the question would very soon become a live issue in the British West Indies, British Honduras and British Guiana, more particularly as the officials and leading citizens in all of these possessions are much less to the Left than the Government of the United Kingdom. This is the danger involved in a further period of office for the Commission of Government. By its nature it cannot be more than a temporary expedient but its continuation now could raise problems of succession that could easily prove unmanageable.[2]

Much was at stake in the game now being played out in Newfoundland. The fear of American influence always had a focusing effect on the mind of the high commissioner. He now informed Governor Gordon

Macdonald that it was Jim Halley who had taken out the advertisement for the Union with America Party (also called the Economic Union Party) in the papers—and the governor passed the word on to Halley's law partner, John McEvoy. "I stayed as long as I could," said Halley, "to get as much information as I could, of course, but after the referendum was called I left McEvoy's office and went to work on the campaign full time with Geoff Sterling and D.I. Jackman. Our greatest achievement was getting Ches Crosbie to lead the party. Ches Crosbie gave Scott Macdonald a lot to worry about."[3]

Faced with this first real threat to Confederation, Scott Macdonald carefully sized up his new enemy. On March 22 he reported:

> Mr. Chesley A. Crosbie, former member of the National Convention and prominent Newfoundland fish producer, announced on March 20th in a radio address that he has decided to lead "the Party for economic union with the United States." Mr. D.I. Jackman, the former head of the Party, has given his allegiance to Mr. Crosbie....
>
> Mr. Crosbie says that he believes that economic union with the U.S. would effect a fundamental solution for Newfoundland's economic problem by developing two-way trade with Newfoundland's largest potential market—particularly for fresh fish....
>
> Mr. Crosbie is aggressive, ambitious and a man of means, willing to spend it in the pursuit of political power. He presents himself to the people as a man engaged in the fishing industry who is anxious to see all others engaged in the same industry enjoy the just fruits of their labours. In the elections to the National Convention he headed the polls in the district of St. John's City West and secured the largest number of votes cast for any single candidate. In spite of the flimsy basis upon which Mr. Crosbie has launched his campaign, his words will almost certainly possess powerful appeal for uninformed fishermen who constitute the bulk of the electorate. The morning after his radio announcement about

one thousand people called at his headquarters in St. John's to sign on as members of his party and a considerable volume of telegrams is flowing in from outlying settlements.[4]

There was no doubt that Ches Crosbie had caught the attention of the Canadians. Paul Bridle, now attached to Canadian High Commission in St. John's, followed up with another dispatch on the Economic Union Party the following week: "It is claimed that 40,000 people have expressed the desire to join the party advocating economic union with the United States. This figure is almost certainly exaggerated."[5] "Mr. C.A. Crosbie . . . and Mr. D. Jamieson, his campaign manager, have recently given radio addresses. Mr. Crosbie developed his thesis that Confederation would jeopardize Newfoundland fisheries. The High Commissioner feels that Confederation is vulnerable on this score."[6] The fishery was the main concern of Newfoundlanders. It was the country's chief employer and the source of its largest export. If "Confederation would jeopardize Newfoundland fisheries," then it would jeopardize Newfoundland's ability to survive. Bridle continued: "He also thinks that Mr. Crosbie's program for economic union with the U.S. will gain many adherents among 'gullible fisherfolk' if it cannot be shown to be wishful thinking."

It was to these same "gullible fisherfolk" that Macdonald and Bridle hoped to sell Confederation, even if it threatened their livelihood. Bridle concluded on a more positive note from the Confederate camp:

Mr. Gordon Bradley, leader of the Confederation movement, also spoke over the radio recently. He argued the futility of Newfoundland endeavouring to secure economic union with the U.S. He said that it is contrary to established United States commercial policy, which is of a non-discriminatory character; that there would be strong opposition to such a move on the part of U.S. fishermen; and that the U.S. would be unwilling, merely to please Newfoundland, to discriminate against countries such as Canada which buy vastly more U.S. products than does Newfoundland.[7]

The *Evening Telegram* described economic union with the United States as "wishful thinking," though the *Daily News* thought that a trade agreement with the southern giant was inevitable. Still, Crosbie and his new party did have legitimate reasons to believe that some form of economic union with the United States was possible. When, at the beginning of the war, the Leased Bases Agreement was signed, giving large tracts of territory and jurisdiction in Newfoundland over to the United States "free of all consideration," Cordell Hull, the US secretary of state, had released a statement to the *Evening Telegram* in St. John's:

> There is one message to Newfoundland which I am definitely authorized to give. It is that: when the present emergency is over, the United States will be disposed to consider sympathetically the commercial relationship between Newfoundland and herself with the view to the development of mutual trade. The Newfoundland Government of the day will be very willing, I feel assured, to co-operate in that study. . . . We are assured that the United States desires closer economic relations with Newfoundland and we hope the day may not be far distant when this prospect will be realized.[8]
>
> And in 1941 John D. Hickerson, the US expert on Newfoundland (and also assistant chief of the State Department's European Affairs division and secretary of the American Joint Board on Defense), reiterated that "the Bases Agreement did constitute a ground for expecting closer economic relations between the two countries."[9]

By now the relationship between the Canadian high commissioner in St. John's and the British governor had deteriorated to the point that

Ottawa felt a fresh face would be better able to deal with the governor on the tricky issues arising out of the referendum process and the constitutional manoeuvring that followed. Scott Macdonald's continuing belief that the governor wanted to stay on in Newfoundland for another five to ten years had brought the two men into several divisive arguments. The intense and bitter haggling over the wording of the ballot paper had used up the last reserves of good will between them, and Governor Macdonald let it be known to Whitehall that he found the attitude of the Canadian high commissioner threatening. A word is often sufficient to the diplomatically sensitive if not wise, and the Canadians, who enjoyed the upper hand but had no desire to offend the British in any way that might jeopardize their goal in Newfoundland, or indeed their own relationship with the motherland, thereupon appointed Paul Bridle as acting high commissioner to replace Scott Macdonald.

Bridle was already in St. John's as secretary to the High Commissioner's Office. Scott Macdonald had done a superb job working with Smallwood to create a strong Confederate organization around the Island. But he was both too vocal and too visible for Lester Pearson, who worried that Macdonald's outspoken manner and hands-on management of the Confederate campaign with Smallwood would become public and embarrass Canada—which had often declared publicly that it had no wish to interfere or influence the Newfoundland referendum process. Bridle, able and expert though he was, did not have the same seniority to preside over the final takeover of power. In due time the ever-cautious Mackenzie King called Charles Burchell back yet again from Australia to secure the Newfoundland deal.

Scott Macdonald never forgave Pearson and St. Laurent for his transfer. On May 12, 1948, seven weeks before the referendum vote, he sent this last defiant dispatch to External Affairs:

The outlook in general is good. In leaving Newfoundland to take up my new post in Brazil, I see no reason the revise the forecast in my Despatch No. 210 of May 6th that Confederation, barring some unforeseen development, will head the poll.

During the week the Commission of Government announced the extension to the 1948 season of the arrangement adopted last year to convert dollars to sterling obtained by the fish sales in Europe. It is emphasized that the arrangement is designed to safeguard the position of the fishermen and to avoid the need for heavy expenditure on relief. The announcement, a copy of which is attached, emphasizes that this arrangement will apply only to the 1948 production and that it will not be possible in subsequent years. This blunt warning will go a long way to show Newfoundlanders the inability of the Commission to ensure financial stability and support and, though tardy and adventitious, is a fairly effective substitute for the statement of its inability to provide further financial assistance which I have frequently urged should be made by the British Government.

Another question is the difficulty of establishing a satisfactory Provincial Budget that will enable Newfoundland to carry on the services devolving on it as a Province. The discussions . . . revealed a weakness in the terms themselves that was not generally appreciated when they were formulated."[10]

The debate on the Canadian terms in the National Convention had in fact revealed that these conditions were financially unsound, and the Convention was correct in refusing to allow Confederation to appear on the ballot on the basis of those terms. Scott Macdonald had been truculent about the Convention's rejection and had characterized the delegates as ungrateful. Lord Addison and Alexander Clutterbuck had both declared the terms to be "exceptionally generous," but, ultimately, everyone would have to agree that they were in fact unworkable. Back in Ottawa the high commissioner was debriefed by the prime minister on May 19: ". . . had a talk of some length with Scott Macdonald who thinks

Newfoundland almost certain to come into Confederation but agrees with me it is going to be a source of trouble for some time to come. The only thing to do to save the Island from drifting into the hands of Americans. Specially important to Canada."[11]

Newfoundland would certainly be a "source of trouble" under the terms proposed. Nevertheless, and despite their penurious offering, King was beginning to style Canada as the "Saviour" of the island, though not from poverty but from the threat of American prosperity.

On May 21, less than two weeks before the vote, the *Western Star* in Corner Brook published a "Report on the Proposed Arrangements for the Entry of Newfoundland into Confederation," prepared by McDonald, Currie and Co. of Montreal. It was commissioned by Crosbie and the Economic Union Party and represented the first expert, outside appraisal of the terms offered by Canada. The local press was quick to advertise its conclusions, as Bridle wrote to External Affairs:

> The St. John's *Daily News* and speakers on the radio favouring Responsible Government have played up the Report's prediction of a $4,468,000 provincial deficit and have emphasized its statements regarding more people having to pay income taxes and per capita debt being vastly increased. . . . The Report confirms its own view that "too little is known about the impact of union to permit a valid decision of a final nature."[12]

Given these misgivings about Confederation, it was becoming clear that any decision about Confederation in a referendum was not only inappropriate but potentially damaging to Newfoundland.

The referendum campaign was vigorously waged by all parties with the exception of the Commission of Government, which had no one to speak for it save the governor. The Responsible Government League

campaigned across the country. Peter Cashin began to talk about economic union with the United States, but not until late in the game. The
Confederates had strong, well-organized teams, and the ubiquitous Joe
Smallwood—the St. Paul of Confederation—waged a tireless, relent-
less, and inspired campaign as he walked across the island to preach the
new gospel.

Smallwood even tried to convert the new leader of the Union With
America Party. According to Harold Horwood: "He went to see Crosbie,
a thing easily arranged since they were old acquaintances who had shared
many small business ventures in the past, and offered to make him
Premier of Newfoundland if he would discover that the U.S. wasn't interested in Economic Union with Newfoundland after all, and if, following
this discovery, he'd swear allegiance to Confederation instead."[13] Crosbie
wasn't interested in Smallwood's offer, but they parted on good terms,
according to Jim Halley:

> The Economic Union Party put on a strong campaign. Geoff
> Sterling had article after article in the *Sunday Herald* and produced
> 50 Senators who were sympathetic to Newfoundland joining up
> with the U.S., including Senators Taft and Wagner and other pow-
> erful figures. The *Christian Science Monitor* said that the U.S. could
> do worse than cultivate Newfoundland for Statehood. Jamieson
> was a good speaker, and T.I. Jackman and myself, but we were no
> match for the Confederate Campaign or their Canadian money."[14]

Horwood provides a colourful, inside account of the financing of the
Confederate campaign in his biography of Smallwood:

> C.D. Howe [minister of reconstruction and supply in King's gov-
> ernment] supplied Ray Petten with a letter of introduction to be
> used among his friends in the Canadian business community, and
> sent him off to Senator Gordon Fogo, who was head bag man for

the Liberal Party of Canada. Joey, fearing a wire tap, would never mention those names in phone conversations. Talking by phone to Bradley, for instance, Howe became "the man who knows how it's done." The senator was simply "the man from Fogo."

Gordon Fogo gave Petten a copy of the Liberal party's hit list: corporations that could be readily tapped for funds at election time. Many of those corporations turned out to be one branch or another of the liquor business. They were merchandisers, brewers, vintners and distillers. With a little prodding by way of Howe's letter, they coughed up surprising amounts of cash. No one knows just how much, since no records were kept. . . . For example, I myself received a single donation of $3000 in cash, and spent it in cash: half the amount on printing bills and half on travelling expenses.

. . . Altogether the Confederate campaign must have cost about a quarter of a million dollars . . . so we got the money, and Mr. Petten got his senatorship and a profitable string of liquor agencies as a sort of bonus.

With seemingly limitless funds now at his disposal, Joey put on the most dazzling campaign in Newfoundland history: flags, music, guns, bands marching, blizzards of campaign literature—it seemed less like an election campaign than a national triumph.

It was perfectly obvious to everyone that we were outspending the Responsible Government League by a factor of at least two or three to one, and there were loud demands from our opponents to know where the money was coming from. . . . Obviously, they said, Joey must be a patsy of powerful foreign interests that had designs on Newfoundland, probably just a puppet playing out a script hatched in London and Ottawa.

. . . We were forced to invent fictitious sources of funds, and that's how the story got around that scores of fishermen were sending in their one-dollar bills and two-dollar bills (and even a few four-dollar bills saved from the nineteenth century when there really were such things in Newfoundland), each with a little note pinned on, saying something like, "God bless you, Mr. Smallwood, for what you're doing for we poor people. We're praying for you."[15]

The referendum was held on June 3, 1948. In the early hours of the vote, with responsible government leading, Mackenzie King confessed once again: "Personally I would prefer to see responsible government carry and then an agreement made between a [Newfoundland] government that was responsible with the Canadian Government."[16] The Responsible Government League and the Economic Union with America parties wished for no less, as did Major Cashin and Albert Perlin. But, in the struggle between principles and politics, King's politics ultimately proved to be more powerful.

On June 8, Paul Bridle reported the results of the referendum to the Department of External Affairs:

Returns are now virtually complete, only Labrador remaining to report its final count. . . . Subject to confirmation in writing of returns received by telegraph, the present totals may be taken as substantially representing the final standing of the three forms of government. These totals are:

Commission of Government for a period of five years . . . 21,944
Confederation with Canada 63,110
Responsible Government as it existed in 1933 . . . . 69,230.[17]

Responsible government had come first in the referendum by more than 6,000 votes, but without a sufficient overall majority to carry the election. The third-place group, the Commission of Government, would therefore be eliminated, and a second referendum was scheduled for

July 22. As the British had calculated, Confederation would now have a good second chance at winning. The referendum results nevertheless proved that Newfoundlanders were eager to take back control of their country's political affairs.

It was a disappointing result for the Economic Union Party, which had hoped for a responsible government victory on the first ballot. Members feared that the Commission of Government supporters, who had chosen the security of British backing and fair play, would now choose Canadian backing and fair play instead of independence.

Bridle's assessment of this first referendum result was sober. As he reported back to Ottawa:

> The blunt fact remains, of course, that Confederation received fewer votes than Responsible Government did; moreover, it appears unlikely on the face of it that either Confederation or Responsible Government will obtain a really large numerical majority at the second poll.
>
> The . . . special factor which contributed to the success of Responsible Government at the polls was, of course, the appeal of the proposal that a responsible government should endeavour to negotiate economic union with the United States. As you know, the advocates of this plan ran a rather theatrical campaign replete with advertising-agency techniques which certainly must have impressed not an inconsiderable number of voters. Nor should one overlook the political force of Mr. Chesley A. Crosbie, whose sincerity appears to be so taken for granted that a substantial body of people are prepared, as he puts it, "to give him a chance."[18]

Jim Halley had his own explanatory postscript to the referendum results:

> Crosbie became discouraged before the final vote and after he read

the results he quietly disbanded the Party and let everyone go their own way. Joey and the Governor had been working on Crosbie, and Joe told him that the Commission of Government or a new Provincial Government could call in the loans that Crosbie's businesses had from the Government and force him into bankruptcy. On the other hand if Crosbie would go along and not fight the second Referendum he would be eligible for contracts from the new Government on a cost-plus basis. So Crosbie and his construction company built the new wing of the Waterford Hospital and the new Memorial University buildings and he became a wealthy man.[19]

With the second referendum at hand and the possibility of a Confederate victory, J.B. McEvoy sent a letter to R.A. MacKay at External Affairs, setting out the political manoeuvrings afoot on the Island. MacKay in turn passed it on to Paul Bridle in St. John's:

(a) Attached are copies of personal letters from Mr. J.B. McEvoy, formerly Chairman of the National Convention and a prominent member of the Newfoundland Bar. As the letters indicate, Mr. McEvoy has been asked to take the leadership of the Confederate Party, I gather by Mr. Smallwood and others who have been disappointed by Mr. Bradley's lack of aggressiveness. Mr. McEvoy would certainly bring the Confederate Party considerable prestige and would undoubtedly make a dynamic leader. He has advised me by telephone that two of the Commission of Government (presumably Mr. Walsh, Commissioner of Justice and Defence, and Mr. Quinton, Commissioner of Education and Home Affairs) and Mr. W.S. Monroe, the only surviving prime minister of

Newfoundland and a prominent businessman on Water Street, will come out publicly if he (McEvoy) assumes the leadership. I think Mr. McEvoy has already decided to accept but he said he has business to clear up before any public announcement is made.[20]

Halley had this to say about these negotiations: "Joey asked McEvoy, probably with Bradley's approval, to become Party leader, as a sop to his vanity and to keep him out of the running for the premiership of the new province."[21]

Smallwood wanted several other things from McEvoy as well. Lester Pearson, who was extremely nervous that the extent of the Canadian involvement in the Newfoundland referendum process would become known, was stonewalling Smallwood's constant requests for more detailed information about federal departments. Smallwood hoped that McEvoy's close personal friendship with MacKay would, however, open up a channel for this information at External Affairs—and he was right. McEvoy was also on close personal terms with the governor, Sir Gordon Macdonald, and the members of the Commission of Government—all of whom could prove useful to Smallwood. As the lawyer and confidante of the Water Street merchants, McEvoy was in a unique position to persuade some of those eminent gentlemen to come over to the Confederate cause and give it an air of respectability. In due time, Smallwood's calculations proved fruitful on all counts.

Up to that point, McEvoy had managed to appear more or less neutral. As Don Jamieson records: "McEvoy had never publically disclosed his political leanings and, given his mercurial temperament and massive ego, it was in character for him to play both ends against the middle."[22] Before he took the plunge, however, McEvoy sought reassurances from MacKay. As MacKay reported to Bridle:

Mr. McEvoy asks for information or opinions on a number of

points, among them the following:

(a) Whether the existing Canadian terms are final and unalterable, especially in financial matters;

(b) Whether the Canadian Government is merely luke warm or indifferent to unity;

(c) Whether the present Newfoundland system of controlling fish exports would be wrecked by Confederation;

(d) Clarification of the statement in the Prime Minister's letter to Governor: "Should the people of Newfoundland indicate clearly and beyond all possibility of misunderstanding their will that Newfoundland should become a Province of Canada. . . ." —Mr. McEvoy asks whether a bare majority would be considered sufficient.[23]

These same questions were vital not only to McEvoy, as the new leader of the Confederation Campaign, but also to most Newfoundlanders as they pondered the option of Confederation in the forthcoming second referendum. The Canadians and the British did not want to answer them, however. Instead, they would set the rules of the game to their own advantage for as long as they could.

A POOR MAJORITY:
THE SECOND REFERENDUM CAMPAIGN

In late June 1948, during the tense period between the first and the second referendum, Commonwealth Secretary Philip Noel-Baker recalled Governor Gordon Macdonald to London to determine the constitutional steps that would be taken between the final vote and the handover of power to Ottawa. The contingency plan—the return of responsible government—was a simple and straightforward matter. The 1934 letters patent would be revoked and a general election held for the new government to take over on January 1, 1949.[1] The other path led through murky and uncharted constitutional territory where they must blaze their own trail. These top-secret meetings also included Sir Eric Machtig from the Commonwealth Relations Office; Albert Walsh, the commissioner of justice in Newfoundland; Norman Robertson, the Canadian high commissioner to London; and M.H. Wershof of the Canadian High Commission Office in St. John's.

Having brushed aside the return of responsible government, the British North America Act and all legal means at hand for Newfoundland to join Canada, the two conspiring countries were again faced with the tricky, still unresolved question of how exactly they could accomplish the union in the absence of a Newfoundland government. As Robertson thought about several issues under consideration, he wrote in a telegram marked "Secret" to External Affairs in Ottawa: "The next question is, by what legal process is union to be accomplished. The Commonwealth Relations Office said . . . the United Kingdom Government would be most anxious to avoid putting the terms of union through the Parliament of the United Kingdom once there has been a satisfactory vote for con-federation [and that] the terms of union are . . . of no concern to the United Kingdom."[2]

Although the terms of union were of primary concern to Newfoundland, the Islanders would not be permitted to debate or negoti-ate them. As Robertson continued: "The solution, the Commonwealth Relations Office and the Governor think . . . is to amend S.146 of the B.N.A. Act to provide that the Commission of Government of Newfoundland, fortified by the result of a referendum, *should be competent* to make the address to His Majesty which, as S.146 now reads *must be made* by the non-existent "Legislature of Newfoundland."[3] Even though earlier in the telegram he insisted that "the Commission of Government has been rejected by the voters, [and] the sooner it is ended the better,"[4] he now suggested that the outgoing administration should still be asked to perform one final constitutional convolution. Even a defeated dictator-ship "should be competent" to assume the authority of a "non-existent legislature," it seemed. The request to amend section 146, and dispense with the need for a Newfoundland government would have to come from the Canadian government, the other party in the negotiations—and offi-cials there were only too happy to oblige.

In this way, in the shady underworld of international intrigue, the Anglo-Canadian plot progressed to rob Newfoundlanders of their right to represent themselves in any union with Canada. That left only the problem of the referendum to sort out—and the plotters felt less confi-dent in this area: "The Governor of Newfoundland and the Commissioner of Justice [Albert Walsh] said that in their view there is no chance of a big majority for confederation, certainly not more than three thousand

(3,000) and very probably much less."[5] Governor Macdonald was fearful that "a decision to proceed with Confederation in [the] face of a very narrow majority might indeed lead to disturbances in Newfoundland and particularly in St. John's, where a large majority of the population strongly favours Responsible Government." He insisted that, "in view of the political conditions in Newfoundland, there should be no undue delay in establishing a new government."[6] Commissioner Walsh cautiously attempted to slow the machinery: "If the majority is very small," he warned, "it would not be wise to base upon it an irrevocable constitutional change."[7]

Two years earlier, in the spring of 1946, after one of his many meetings with Governor Gordon Macdonald, Scott Macdonald had reported to External Affairs that the governor had informed him "that both Prime Minister Attlee and the Secretary of State for Dominions Affairs had told him confidentially that they regarded Union with Canada as the best thing that could happen to Newfoundland and would be happy if it could be brought about with a large majority of the people."[8] In fact, Governor Macdonald had stated that a two-thirds majority would be necessary to transfer sovereignty, and the Canadians, especially Prime Minister Mackenzie King, felt the same way. But in July 1948, as they prepared for the possibility of a small majority in the second referendum, the British and the Canadian officials had to decide exactly how small that majority could be and which of them would make that decision. It was a "hot potato" neither of them wanted to handle. As External Affairs put it: "Secret. . . . Should any question arise as to the size of the majority for union which would be required by the Canadian Government, the U.K. Government should be informed that this was primarily a matter for decision by the U.K Government."[9] And from London, Norman Robertson wrote to St. Laurent on July 2: "Secret. . . . On the United Kingdom side it has been made clear that they would regard any majority for confederation, however small, as binding and that, if the decision were solely for them, they would arrange for confederation, even though the majority were as small as one."[10]

It was certainly a long way from Attlee and Addison's "large majority" to a "majority as small as one," but the British felt confident of bridging the gap. The voters in Newfoundland had no inkling of this change in attitude. But the British had only a few cards left to play. They could see the end of their responsibilities to Newfoundland, and they were determined to get out at all costs.

On July 16, a diffident Lester Pearson responded to Robertson in London:

> Important. Secret. . . . It would appear that in the event of the majority being too small to justify proceeding with Confederation, the United Kingdom would like to place full responsibility for the decision on the Canadian Government. We should like if possible to avoid this since it might well prejudice any later chances of Confederation. If you have an opportunity, would you please stress with the C.R.O. that, while we appreciate their view that Canada should have the deciding voice as to whether Newfoundland should be accepted in the event of a very small majority, we hope that if circumstances require that this course be taken, the United Kingdom will appreciate the desirability of at least endorsing Canada's position in the matter.[11]

The Canadians required the backing of the United Kingdom to carry off this constitutional coup. Both empires would put their credibility on the line, hold their noses if need be, and sign off on the deal. On July 12, after Governor Macdonald had returned to St. John's from his secret meetings in London, Noel-Baker drafted a dispatch to confirm that "the London meetings were designed to ensure as far as possible that you and I were in agreement as to the action which will have to be taken."[12] The following day, a nervous Sir Gordon replied to Noel-Baker: "It would be advisable to have within a day's outing of St. John's a Cruiser or Destroyer on Friday night July 23rd [the day after the vote]. We should need to know how to contact the ship to inform the Commander, as soon as possible, as to whether it was necessary for him to sail into St. John's Harbour. I am sorry that one is unable to be more definite, but you know the difficulty, especially as the whole matter is to be kept top secret."[13] For the moment at least, Governor Macdonald's accustomed bluster and air of invincibility wavered before the spectre of the crowd's fury at the outcome he was to announce. Tensions were running high in both British and Canadian camps as they approached their final play—one they now knew full well would not be a clear victory "beyond all possibility of misunderstanding."

The Canadians were optimistic, perhaps overly so, because they continued to ignore the major financial difficulties for Newfoundland as the tenth province of Canada. R.L. James, the finance commissioner for the Commission of Government, was well aware of the problems, however, and discussed them with Paul Bridle, who was still the acting Canadian high commissioner in St. John's. On June 21 Bridle wrote to MacKay as the secret meetings in London were getting under way:

Secret and Personal. The points mentioned by Mr. James were as follows: . . .

It appears that the Newfoundland provincial government will be unable from the outset to balance its budget. The gap between revenue and expenditure is difficult to estimate, but in Mr. James' opinion, it is likely to be considerable. . . .

I told Mr. James that I was rather surprised to find he anticipates a substantial provincial deficit at the outset [and that] we had ourselves anticipated that the provincial budget would come very close to balancing in the first three years of the union. . . .

. . . He also made the point that the Newfoundland Provincial Government, unlike the existing provincial governments, would have to meet the cost of such essential and expensive services as education, public health and road construction almost entirely unaided by local government. . . .

. . . Mr James' main point is that, no matter how much one may reduce expenditures, a certain number such as those he mentioned would inevitably have to be carried on by any Newfoundland Government, be it an independent government or a provincial government. . . .

Mr. James' fundamental assumption regarding the provincial budget is so similar to that of those critics of Confederation who would be the first to demand better terms that I felt in talking to him I must defend our position. . . . It seemed that . . . his appraisal of the budgetary aspects of the terms would inevitably reinforce any predisposition on the part of Newfoundland representatives to seek better terms. . . .

The rather nice question of the degree of control which the Newfoundland Government [the British Commission of Government] would have over the delegation arises here of course. . . . At the same time, it is relevant here to recall that some two weeks ago the Governor remarked to me that there would be no difficulty at all in appointing suitable representatives and finalizing the terms.[14]

The high commissioner answered his own key question about the degree of control the Commission of Government would have over the Newfoundland delegates. Less than a fortnight later Norman Robertson, in London, after his talks with Governor Macdonald, confirmed in a "secret" telegram with External Affairs: "The Governor has already decided whom he would ask to be on the Newfoundland delegation which would go to Ottawa to discuss and settle with the Canadian Government the full terms and arrangements. The anti-confederation people would be represented on it but most of its members (5 out of 7) would be pro-confederation."[15]

The Canadians were concerned not with the considerable financial shortfall for the new province, but only with selecting a delegation from Newfoundland to accept the deal. The governor's control over this delegation was crucial. Governor Gordon Macdonald used his constitutional authority and position as head of government in Newfoundland to guarantee Newfoundland's acceptance of Canada's Terms of Union before they were negotiated or even voted on. This abuse of office by an appointed official of a government freshly defeated at the polls constitutes a serious offense against the people of Newfoundland and casts grave doubt on the legality of the final constitutional arrangements between Newfoundland and Canada.

Earlier that year, on February 9, in response to a question posed by the *Evening Telegram* on how the actual union of Canada and Newfoundland should be effected in the event of a Confederate victory in the coming referendum, J.B. McEvoy, the past chairman of the National Convention and new leader of the Confederate Party, had written:

> If the Office of Commonwealth Relations decides that Confederation is to go on the referendum ballot paper, it should go on only in principle and not on the basis of the present terms which are unnegotiated.
>
> If the people favour Confederation in principle, this would mean that the question of Responsible Government would be erased, and the Commission of Government would be retained temporarily and empowered to negotiate final terms of Confederation with the Canadian Government.
>
> The result of these negotiations would be submitted to the people, who would then vote for or against union on the basis of the new negotiated terms.
>
> In effect, this would mean two referendums.
>
> The present terms of Confederation were received by a delegation hampered by their lack of power, and the people should not

be asked to make an irrevocable decision based on the unnegotiated terms which this delegation received.[16]

McEvoy naturally presumed that the Newfoundland public would
have the right to vote on and ratify the Terms of Union after they were
negotiated, not before. But in the *Alice in Wonderland* world of the constitutional process created by the British in Newfoundland, it took
McEvoy some time to realize that up was actually down, and he later
apologized for his too logical assumption. After the first referendum vote
and a lengthy talk with the Canadian high commissioner, he came to an
entirely different opinion. As Bridle reported to St. Laurent on July 17:

> [Mr. McEvoy] said that in February of this year he had stated in
> an interview with a newspaper reporter that he felt that
> Newfoundlanders should vote in the referendum on Confederation
> in principle only, a final decision being postponed until a later date.
> When, however, the British Government decided otherwise, he
> applied himself to a study of Confederation and of the terms
> offered in the same way that he had investigated the proposal for
> economic union with the United States. He arrived at the conclu-
> sion that Confederation is the best course for Newfoundland and
> that, even though the terms have not been negotiated, it would be
> impossible to effect any material change in them."[17]

While now adopting Canada's novel position and its terms of union,
McEvoy still acknowledged fully that those terms had never been negotiated and that the elected delegates from the National Convention had
never possessed the mandate in their terms of reference to negotiate anything. McEvoy's apology was accepted, but the damage to his future
political ambitions had been done.

On June 21, the same day that Bridle informed MacKay of the bad
news in R.L. James's report, Smallwood and Bradley wrote to C.D. Howe

about a significant "new group of Confederates." McEvoy had been able to poach Commissioners Herman Quinton and Herbert Pottle from the Commission of Government, but the most significant catch were several of the hated and much-vilified Water Street merchants, in particular Sir Eric Bowring, Sir Leonard Outerbridge, and the Monroes, senior and junior. These men, Smallwood noted, "would bring to the cause what it has hitherto lacked, namely the respectable element of society." The result, he predicted, would be "a comfortable majority for Confederation." Following immediately on this positive message, he informed Howe that the Confederate side needed "at least another $20,000. We need it *quickly*."[18]

The second referendum was more desperately engaged and dirtier than the first. Smallwood had got through to Ches Crosbie, Geoff Sterling and others and effectively neutralized the Economic Union Party. Jim Halley, C.E. Hunt, D.I. Jackman and the rest carried on, but the party was no longer a major force behind the Responsible Government League.

The League itself redoubled its efforts, sending out teams to canvas across the Island. However, these workers did not have nearly the reach of the Confederates, who already had well-organized teams in place and enough money to hire Confederate agents in every district. That was significant because many illiterate voters had to indicate to the returning officer or the poll clerk which way they wished to vote. Polls with only Confederate officers—and there were many—played a decisive role in delivering a Confederate vote. One shocked voter wrote to F.M. O'Leary of the Responsible Government League on July 29:

> Honestly, I believe this referendum crooked in strong Confederate centres where illiteracy is great. I may be wrong, but I have a feeling votes were illegally marked in stations where poll officials were both Confederates and where no Responsible Government agent was present. . . . Cannot understand why Magistrate was not allowed to

open ballots [in] my presence [so] that I could check count and compare with that reported by message from various stations. This [is all] most undemocratic[,] and I vehemently protest conduct and procedure of this referendum. . . . There was nothing [to] prevent an ardent Confederate deputy [from] mark[ing] illiterate ballots for Confederation where we had no agent.[19]

Responsible Government League voters in Champney East and other outports later complained that their votes had not been counted in their community totals.[20] The Responsible Government League also worked without any external support, while the Confederates enjoyed not only tactical support from the Canadians, the Commission of Government and the British but even more Canadian money, this time augmented by contributions from local businessmen shopping for senatorships. On orders from Smallwood, no receipts were kept.

The religious card had been played with some apparent success in the first referendum. The Confederates condemned the power of Rome in St. John's in the person of Archbishop Roche, who presumed to require a return to self-rule before there could be any consideration of Confederation. In his opinion, the population was not sufficiently informed of the implications of Confederation to make an irrevocable decision in a plebiscite.[21]

Both the Economic Union Party and the Responsible Government League refused to capitalize on sectarian divisions. Wick Collins, the secretary of the Responsible Government League, wrote that the league "had neither the intention nor the talent to engage in a war of deceit, vilification or ridicule."[22] Smallwood and the Confederates, in contrast, eagerly exploited religious bias as well as regional rivalries and class hatred in their all-out attempt to divide town from outport, Protestant from Catholic, and rich from poor. As Harold Horwood of the Confederate Party recorded: "The Religious divide in particular was considered as a split we could use to great profit."[23]

At this point Governor Gordon Macdonald himself mounted the pulpits at St. Andrew's Presbyterian Church and at Gower Street United Church in St. John's to lend his moral and constitutional authority to the Protestant Confederate forces. At a Methodist Convention in the city he declared: "There is one denomination here [the Roman Catholics] which played a big part in the last referendum. It is time that the Protestant bodies should unite."[24] In the opinion of American Consul General Wainwright Abbott, the governor's performance served only to inflame the Responsible Government League and "proved conclusively their charge that the British, at the instigation of Canada, had connived to 'railroad' Newfoundland into union with Canada."[25]

Many people were distressed at the reopening of old sectarian rivalries. A.B. Butt, a Convention delegate, felt that during the second referendum campaign Newfoundland came closer to civil war than at any time in its history. The Catholics felt isolated by the political establishment and several prominent people told him before the vote that Newfoundland would be going into Confederation regardless, and that they had to do what they had to do.[26]

In an appeal to pro-British and Protestant sentiments on the Avalon Peninsula, Smallwood devised a new slogan, "British Union with Canada," which he hoped would siphon off the Commission vote from the first referendum. The basic appeal of the second Confederate campaign, however, remained the same as the first—Canada's new social programs, the Family Allowance and the Old Age Pension.

In the latter days of the race, Smallwood campaigned extensively by airplane in the remotest regions, bursting through the clouds to proclaim the new Gospel of Confederation through a loudspeaker.[27] In many places the campaign took on Messianic overtones as Smallwood cheerfully delivered his message in biblical terms. Against this onslaught the Responsible Government League fought valiantly, but it failed to articulate a clear and compelling vision of Newfoundland under a renewed responsible government.

Paul Bridle continued to provide Ottawa with detailed accounts of the various campaigns right up to the last moment before the vote. In his long dispatch on July 19, he reported on C.C. Pratt, a prominent Newfoundland businessman and brother of Canadian poet and professor E.J. Pratt. In a passionate radio broadcast in favour of responsible government, Pratt had claimed: "If we vote ourselves into Confederation at this stage we have not got one vestige of bargaining power left. We shall be placed in the humiliating position of first having made a deal and then with our hands out ask Canada to adjust our difficulties as a favour and not as a right. As I see it, that is a position which a self-respecting people should avoid at all costs."[28]

Writing in the *Evening Telegram* on behalf of the Economic Union Party, D.I. Jackman, its former leader, warned:

It seems as if speed is not needed at present in a hurried attempt at Confederation. If Newfoundland will first appoint their legal representatives, the present terms or even new ones will be considered in the future after a period of cooling off and a serious meditation on where Newfoundland's best interests will be. There is no incompatibility in adjusting her best interests with those of Canada and the United States with a government of her own people, first.[29]

All the time, Joey Smallwood plied the airwaves and, in Bridle's assessment, "once again showed his extraordinary capacity to appeal in a direct and simple manner to the common sense of the average person. In the latter part of his address, he demonstrated his equal skill as an uninhibited propagandist."[30] Besides enlisting the open support of Commissioners Pottle and Quinton in return for positions in the new provincial government, Smallwood, with McEvoy's help, now recruited the third Newfoundland commissioner, Albert Walsh—all of whom provided a connection with the outgoing government and gave the Confederate cause added status, if not inevitability. When Governor

Gordon Macdonald came out for Confederation and against responsible government, the veneer of impartiality was stripped away as the most powerful institutions and individuals—the Commission of Government, Joey Smallwood, and High Commissioner Charles Burchell, in addition to the governor—all united in support of Confederation.

Nevertheless, in Ottawa, two days before the vote in the second referendum, Mackenzie King and even Louis St. Laurent expressed serious misgivings about the prospects ahead. As the prime minister wrote in his diary: St. Laurent "personally feels, and I agree, that unless there is something more than a poor majority, we should not take the Province into Confederation . . . The estimate the Department [of External Affairs] have is that Confederation will carry, but with a very small majority."[31]

The second referendum was held on July 22, 1948. Paul Bridle reported the final count:

Responsible Government . . . . 71,464 votes
Confederation with Canada . . . . 77,869 votes.[32]

Confederation secured 52 percent of the vote, with a little over 6,000 votes more than responsible government. The voter turnout was 150,000 out of a possible 176,000, some 5,000 voters fewer than in the first referendum.

US consul general Wainwright Abbott wrote to the State Department on August 2:

Had it not been for the success of the governor in obtaining the aid of the United Church, the Orangemen, two of the Commissioners and a few other prominent citizens [Walsh and Outerbridge] at the last moment, the result would probably have been different. Mr. Joseph Smallwood attracted a large following with his promises of family allowances; but he repelled a great many of the more substantial class by his extreme claims and by his injection of class hatred and regional differences into the campaign. The new men who came out at the last moment reassured more conservative voters and cast an aura of respectability about the Confederate party which had been lacking before. Having made use of Smallwood's undoubted organizing and demagogic talents, these new accessions to Confederation are now faced with the problem of how to get rid of him, which they privately state they wish and intend to do. He is reported to have an almost hypnotic influence over the audiences which he addresses, and the more conservative elements may well find that it is easier to release a genie from a bottle than to persuade him to return.[33]

In the somber atmosphere in St. John's following the final results, Bridle wrote to St. Laurent: "I am convinced that something of the meaning of Confederation has entered the minds of the mass of the people of Newfoundland. . . . If one were to single out one Newfoundlander more responsible than others for this development, one would name Mr. J.R. Smallwood. He is known in this country as the 'Apostle of Confederation.'"[34]

The Canadians had reluctantly recognized their saviour. There were no riots in St. John's, but nerves were still on edge at Government House. Frank Graham of Imperial Oil, a friend of the vice-regal family, said that the governor and his wife lived in dread of attack.[35] As for the destroyer Governor Macdonald had requested be sent to St. John's, "if only because the safety of the Governor and Commissioners may come into question,"[36] Lord Hall of the Admiralty informed Noel-Baker that no destroyer was near enough to answer the call in time. It is perhaps unfortunate the destroyer was not available to sit in St. John's harbour so that the populace who had contributed so magnificently to the recent war could see the guns pointed at them and obtain a clearer perspective of their place in the events unfolding around them. If this was the shotgun that was thought necessary to enforce the union, it was not required. All the newspapers, including the *Sunday Herald*, called on the people to unite and work together for the success of the new Province of Newfoundland.

The Responsible Government League immediately went on record to oppose the procedures as unconstitutional. On July 25, three days after the vote, the secretary of the league wrote directly to Mackenzie King:

> Personal. Responsible Government League, speaking with the force and backing of more than 70,000 voters representing 48 percent of those voting in the July 22nd Referendum, vigorously protest any procedure other than negotiation conducted through properly elected government for inclusion Newfoundland in Canadian Federation. . . . We dispute constitutional right commission government to determine what is satisfactory majority because commission was totally repudiated in first referendum and has subsequently prejudiced its position as impartial arbiter this vital matter through intervention by two of its members [Pottle and Quniton] as spokesmen for confederate cause. . . . Consummation of confederation before negotiation of terms or understanding of financial and economic impact on Newfoundland people and industry is neither sound nor just and creates source of bitter controversy in future.[37]

On July 30, in his response to a request from the league to send a delegation to Ottawa, Mackenzie King felt compelled once again to state: "The Canadian Government has at no time intervened in any way in the determination of the procedure to be followed in Newfoundland."[38] Aside from such denials, Canada, now confronted with the reality of the "poor majority," said nothing at first. Observing Canada's silence, Sir Eric Machtig at the Commonwealth Relations Office in London wrote an agitated note to High Commissioner Alexander Clutterbuck in Ottawa:

Immediate. Secret and Personal. . . . I have today received private letter from Gordon Macdonald dated July 23rd. He asks that this should be treated as very private mainly, of course, because he does not wish anyone in Newfoundland to know that he has written in this way. . . .

The result of the referendum would give Confederation at least five thousand majority. . . . I consider it a fine achievement. . . .

In my personal opinion there is only one course for the Canadian authorities, namely, to accept the decision and to ask for a delegation of authorised representatives [to] be appointed, and to state that such a delegation would be received at an early date. . . .

There must be no hesitation on the part of the Canadian authorities. Any sign whatever of hesitation will be fatal.[39]

The vote was five thousand times better than a majority of one, and certainly good enough for the British to brazen it out, but the Canadians were unused to such bold action. Mackenzie King remained doubtful about the "fine achievement" and questioned whether a majority of barely 52 percent would be accepted as enough to transfer sovereignty. Jack Pickersgill, who would later become Newfoundland's federal minister in Ottawa during the Smallwood administration, was prepared for these doubts. He reminded King that in the last two federal elections, the prime minister had won his own seat by an even smaller majority. That argument proved sufficient to convince King and, on July 30, he declared in a statement: "The result of the plebiscite in favour of union between the two countries is 'clear and beyond possibility of misunderstanding.'"[40] He then repeated for the third time that "this result was attained without any trace of influence or pressure from Canada."[41]

THE RIGHT SORT OF PEOPLE:
THE SECOND DELEGATION TO OTTAWA

In St. John's, the three Newfoundland commissioners, Herbert Pottle, Herman Quinton and Albert Walsh, were now all squarely in the Confederate camp. Governor Gordon Macdonald informed them in conversation soon after the referendum that "the whole effort here should be to overcome the criticism that the terms were unnegotiated." The other challenge, he reminded them, was the composition of the Newfoundland delegation to go to Ottawa: "The Newfoundland Government [the Commission] on its part would do its utmost to ensure that the members of the delegation were the right sort of people with whom the Canadian Government could deal."[1]

The British Commission of Government was primarily concerned with meeting Canadian demands, not with getting the best terms for Newfoundland. In light of the continuing criticism that the terms had not been negotiated, R.A. MacKay advised Louis St. Laurent:

Secret. . . . I feel strongly that any public announcement of the Government's intention to go ahead should indicate that we are prepared to "negotiate" on the basis of the terms with an authorized delegation from Newfoundland, rather than merely to "complete the final arrangements," which would indicate merely dotting i's and crossing t's. One important factor in the vote for Responsible Government was undoubtedly the resentment of Newfoundlanders against being treated as a colony, their self-respect demanding that they should handle their own business. From the standpoint of Newfoundlanders who feel this way, negotiations by a Responsible Government would no doubt be the ideal, but I think they would be prepared to settle for negotiations by a representative group, most of whom presumably would subsequently accept responsibility by standing for election.[2]

If there was going to be a show of negotiation, the word "negotiate" would have to be mentioned. In light of Governor Macdonald's many assurances that "there would be no difficulty at all in finding suitable representatives and finalizing terms" and that, as far as the delegation went, "most of its members would be pro-Confederate" and all would be "the right sort of people with whom the Canadian Government could deal," Prime Minister Mackenzie King felt emboldened to accept MacKay's advice in his final statement. It read: "The Government will also be glad to receive with the least possible delay authorized representatives of Newfoundland to negotiate terms of union on the basis of my letter of October 29, 1947."[3]

Following King's statement, Governor Macdonald announced his selection for the delegation to Ottawa. Albert Walsh was appointed as chairman, J.R. Smallwood as secretary, with Gordon Bradley, J.B. McEvoy, Philip Gruchy, G.A. Winter and Chesley Crosbie as members. To quote Jim Halley:

The Referendum on Confederation was a wrenching experience for Newfoundland. Families and communities were torn apart in the fight to save our nationhood and control our own destiny. We'd fought the war and now we were being denied the very rights we had fought for and won.

My father, Thomas Halley, was also a lawyer and his friends and colleagues were indignant when the Governor appointed the final delegation to Ottawa. It was such a sham. Who gave them the authority to negotiate away our sovereignty? They wanted to know where their authority came from. So the cry went up of "a fix." It made a lot of people angry and desperate. It was a very frustrating feeling to see all this unfolding in front of you, all of it unconstitutional and against the wishes of the National Convention but there was nothing we could do to stop it short of riot.[4]

All the delegates were Confederates, with the exception of Winter and Crosbie, whose appointment was a testament to his popularity and influence. No one was chosen from the Responsible Government League. Winter was perhaps best described as neutral, and, as he confessed later, he was entirely mystified as to why he had been plucked out of private business life and appointed to negotiate Newfoundland's Terms of Union with Ottawa. Philip Gruchy too had not been a member of the National Convention. He was the token out-of-town delegate and, as vice-president and general manager of the Anglo-Newfoundland Development Co., his chief concern was to secure the same tax concessions for his paper mill in Corner Brook as it now enjoyed under British rule. The governor had no worries about these two men, but, as the only non-Confederate in the delegation, Crosbie's actions were watched carefully by Governor Macdonald and Paul Bridle in St. John's. As Bridle wrote to External Affairs on August 26:

> In my despatch No. 386 of August 5th . . . I reported Mr. Crosbie's open letter in which he advised his supporters to remember the urgent necessity of uniting and working together for the good of Newfoundland. . . .
>
> It will be noted that, whereas in his telegrams to his committees Mr. Crosbie said that he felt compelled to agree to serve on the

condition that he reserve the right to withdraw from the delegation if he regarded the terms as unsound or unfair, in his letter . . . to the Governor he limited himself to saying that he reserves the right to object if he regards the terms as unsound or unfair."[5]

The second delegation to Ottawa was better prepared than the first and, before its departure, it held a number of meetings to gather information for the "negotiations" in Ottawa. However, what emerged as the major stumbling block was the budget for the new province. As the minutes from one meeting state: "Provincial Deficits. It was noted that the Budget under consideration envisaged a deficit of over $5,000,000 for each of the first two years of Confederation at least and, in the opinion of some members, this constituted adequate grounds for a request for increased financial assistance from the Canadian Government to enable the Province to bridge this gap."[6] For his part, Smallwood thought there was little chance of the delegation being successful in any request for increased financial assistance. The prime minister had said in his telegram to the governor, and repeated many times after, that the "financial terms were as far as his government could go."

In the intervening months the Canadians had become aware of some glaring omissions and mistakes in the calculations of 1947. As another set of minutes stated:

Errors in Estimates of Revenues.

It is clear that certain of the estimates of probable federal revenues contained in annex IV of The Terms of Union are seriously in error. Estimated revenues from tobacco and liquor taxes are only a fraction of what they should be and customs duties and import taxes are probably much too low also. When these estimates were prepared we did not have access to consumption figures in Newfoundland and greatly underestimated the appetites of this island people.[7]

The Terms of Union as presented to Governor Macdonald and the National Convention in December 1947 envisaged: "the payment to Newfoundland of a Transitional Grant of $3,500,000 annually for the first three years of union, thereafter the amount to diminish annually to $350,000."[8] These grants would be woefully inadequate to cope with an estimated annual deficit of between $5 and $10 million. The problem with all the financial figures in the proposed Terms of Union, apart from the Canadian under-estimates of revenues collected, was that they were based on Smallwood's overly optimistic hypothetical budget from the summer of 1947.

By the time the delegation arrived in Ottawa, the members had been forced to one conclusion:

> Secret. . . . It is apparent that there will be a wide gap between prospective revenue and expenditure, having regard to the amount reasonably required to maintain Provincial public services even at their present level, which is far below that of other Provinces.
>
> It will not be possible for the Province to bridge this gap either by increasing its revenue from Provincial services or by reducing the present level of public services.
>
> The existence of this gap presents a problem which is more than a financial one. It is one the solution of which is a prerequisite to workable union. It should therefore be placed in the forefront of the discussions.[9]

When the Second Delegation to Ottawa arrived in early October 1948, it was received with all the pomp and ceremony of the first delegation. The Canadian negotiating team again consisted of the prime minister, his top ministers from the various government departments, their deputies and aides, along with a raft of bureaucrats from the departments of External Affairs, Finance, and Reconstruction and Supply. The government of Canada was justifiably pleased and proud of the splendid array of officials and experts it had assembled to determine the Terms of Union for Newfoundland.

Sitting opposite this powerful and experienced group at the table were the seven delegates from Newfoundland, chosen by the governor, and their four recently engaged advisers. The lopsided situation of 1947 was reproduced in 1948: "The Canadian team included such stubborn negotiators as the axe-faced economist Mitchell Sharp and the formidable C.D. Howe, whose specialty was driving hard bargains with American multinational corporations in the course of transferring large blocks of the Canadian economy to their management. Such men were unlikely to be generous."[10]

In his memo of October 29 to the deputy minister of finance, Mitchell Sharp, the director of the Economic Policy Division, confirmed that "the figures submitted by the Newfoundland delegation indicate an annual deficit in the area of $10 millions . . . it would be perfectly reasonable . . . if Newfoundland had to draw on her surplus to meet capital expenditures but the surplus would soon be exhausted if it had also to be used to meet a deficit on current account of the magnitude indicated by the Newfoundland estimates." Nevertheless, Sharp concluded: "At this stage I would not say that it would be desirable to offer to increase the scale of transitional grants."[11] And so a stalemate developed: the Canadians refused to consider any changes to the terms of 1947, while the Newfoundlanders insisted that there must be some improvement in the financial package. For weeks the two sides faced each other, but even with the dream delegation from the governor, they remained at an impasse that lasted through October and into November.

Ten months earlier, on December 22, 1947, Ray Atherton at the American Embassy in Ottawa had sent this secret dispatch to the secretary of state in Washington:

Subject: Recent Drilling Results on the Labrador Iron Ore Deposits by Hollinger Mining Interests

I have the honor to refer to the Embassy's report No. 424 dated December 22, 1947 on: The outlook of the Labrador Iron Deposits, and to present additional information revealed in the strictest confidence by Mr. Jules R. Timmins, President, the Labrador Mining and Exploration Company Limited of Montreal, and by Dr. J.A. Retty, chief geologist of this company and the outstanding authority on the ferrous deposits in Labrador and New Quebec where he has been working since 1936.

... Dr Retty substantiated his conclusions that the 1947 drilling results on the Hollinger concessions have been remarkably successful and the iron ore revealed by churn and diamond drilling was "marvellous." The total tonnage of hematite iron ore now proven on the concession of both the Labrador Mining and Exploration Company and the Hollinger North Shore Exploration Company (the latter in Quebec province) could not be divulged but presumably well exceeded 200,000,000 tons of iron ore. John Knox, General Manager of the same company feels that 600,000,000 tons have now been indicated. The target of 300,000,000 tons considered requisite to the final decision of the construction of the 360 mile railway from Seven Islands and the beginning of production is now expected to become proven at the end of next year's drilling program. This reserve would ensure production of 10,000,000 tons annually for 30 years and must be substantial to warrant the initial expenditures.

... Mr. Timmins stated the information given the Embassy's emissary to Montreal had only been divulged to Mr. C.D. Howe, Reconstruction Minister, Mr. Hugh Keenleyside, Deputy Mines Minister, and the directors of the company. Some figures will be released to the shareholders and the public after a meeting next March, but full revelation of the extent of the favorable results might affect the Newfoundland constitutional referendum next year and arouse stock market speculations."[12]

The Newfoundland National Convention. In setting the terms of reference for the National Convention, the British made democracy their pawn in Newfoundland.

J.R. Smallwood dominated the National Convention with his unruly behaviour and a steady stream of propaganda for Confederation.

Major Peter Cashin, a powerful orator and spokesman for the return of responsible government in the National Convention. He spoke the shocking truth but lacked the evidence to support his claims at the time.

On this campaign poster Ches Crosbie as Uncle Sam urges Newfoundlanders to vote Responsible. Fear of Newfoundland joining the United States was the greatest motivating factor behind the Canadian pursuit of Confederation.

James Halley, circa 1948, junior lawyer and co-founder of the Union with America Party. The dynamic events of the period troubled him for the rest of his life.

Crowds outside the CLB Armory in St. John's attending one of the many Responsible Government League demonstrations against the manner in which confederation was being presented to the electorate.

Smallwood with Bradley (on the back of a truck), preaching the Confederate gospel in outport Newfoundland. His campaign took on increasingly Messianic overtones.

Counting the votes in the second referendum on July 22, 1948. Everyone is focused, the strain is evident on all faces.

Smallwood and Bradley getting along with Canadian officials in Ottawa.

Prime Minister Louis St. Laurent addressing the Newfoundland delegation in the House of Commons on the signing of the Terms of Union between Canada and Newfoundland. Seated facing the camera, from left, are: Albert Walsh, Gordon Bradley, John B. McEvoy, and J.R. Smallwood. Gordon Winter and Philip Gruchy are not shown. Missing from the occasion is Ches Crosbie, who refused to sign.

Welcome to Canada! The formal celebration on Parliament Hill to mark Newfoundland's entry into Confederation could well be mistaken for a day of national mourning.

The Daily News

Newfoundland's Only Morning Newspaper

ST. JOHN'S, NEWFOUNDLAND, THURSDAY, MARCH 31, 1949

Five Cents

"God Guard Thee, Newfoundland"

Legend

Discovered by John Cabot
in 1497

Under Star Chamber Government
from 1633 to 1660

Ruled by Fishing Admirals
from 1660 to 1832

Representative Government
from 1832 to 1854

Responsible Government
from 1854 to 1933

Commission Government
from 1933 to 1949

Confederated with Canada
March 31st 1949

NEWFOUNDLAND
The 10th Province

The last edition of the *Daily News* published in the country of Newfoundland. The headline of this souvenir edition, "God Guard Thee Newfoundland," is a refrain from the Ode to Newfoundland. In the end there was only prayer.

This mineral abundance was everything the Canadians had hoped for. Among other things, it was a large enough deposit to trigger the construction of the St. Lawrence Seaway to open up the Canadian heartland. Howe was naturally impressed and careful to keep the valuable information from the Newfoundland delegation, though the good news was not entirely unexpected. In December 1946 the Mackenzie King Record had noted: "St. Laurent was quite strong about bringing the Island in, believing that if we secure Labrador as part of the Dominion territory in connection with terms, Canada might come into possession of valuable mineral deposits."[13]

The Canadians, like the Americans and the Newfoundlanders, suspected there were rich deposits, but the report confirming the "marvellous" size of the expected motherlode had a motivating effect on Howe. Thereafter, bringing the "liability" and "financial burden" of Newfoundland into Confederation became his number 1 priority. One week after Sharp's memo to Finance at the end of October 1948, he asked MacKay what it would take to "carry union through successfully." MacKay replied:

> Personal and Secret. . . . I think these boil down to making provision for Newfoundland's financial gap. That is, this the only issue on which a breakdown of negotiations really threatens, and on which the Newfoundland delegation would be justified in refusing to proceed.
>
> [He advised that:]
>
> As between an increase of some $3½ million to $7 million, and an increase of from $3½ to $5 million, I would strongly recommend the increase to $7 million.
>
> 1. It is justified by the facts of the situation and desirable to speed up the necessary improvement in Newfoundland public service standards.

2. A substantial increase in the proposed subsidy will make it easier to develop an effective provincial tax system—which is the long-run solution.

3. Satisfactory settlement of the financial gap problem (and I think this would be taken as a satisfactory settlement) would make it possible to clear up practically all the other outstanding issues at the departmental official level and put an end to these interminable time-consuming conferences.[14]

The conferences were "interminable" because the Canadians refused to move on the Terms of Union from 1947. In their eyes the Newfoundland people had accepted the terms offered by Mackenzie King when a majority of 52 percent voted in the referendum to join Canada. The Newfoundland delegates were in an impossible position. As journalist Don Jamieson, later to be a federal Cabinet minister, put it: "The already demonstrated weakness in the Convention process became all the more apparent in Ottawa. It was a woefully inadequate instrument from which to launch the complex task of trying to create a new Province."[15]

All the delegates knew the financial provisions were totally inadequate. Although conditions on the Island would improve because of increased federal social benefits, the new province would run large annual deficits, and its own services, such as education and health care, would still be substandard. At this point the delegation, even the die-hard Confederates, felt they could not return to Newfoundland without something more to show the people. Backed into a corner and faced with signing the 1947 terms, they declared that they would "sooner go down as an independent country than an impecunious Canadian province."[16] Even the "right sort of people" have their limits.

Alexander Clutterbuck reported that Smallwood and Walsh told him that, unless Canadians were "more responsive and sympathetic . . . at least three members would refuse to sign the 1947 terms without substantial financial improvement."[17] The three referred to were Crosbie, Winter and Gruchy, but even Walsh and Bradley were resisting. In the end, because its own calculations were obviously wrong and the situation for the province untenable, but finally because the iron-ore deposit in Labrador was "marvellous" and of an excellent grade, Ottawa was obliged to bend its financial provisions. After all, the Canadian government was supposed to be an improvement over English tutelage and much more able than Britain to provide financial stability for Newfoundland. The case then for doing more than the 1947 financial terms was self-evident. But would it be enough?

Jamieson was in Ottawa to report on the negotiations for radio and newspapers back in Newfoundland and also to assist his boss, Ches Crosbie. He described the mood in the capital at the time: "In my interviews with ministers and officials one theme emerged persistently, the need to avoid an expensive settlement. Members of the delegation heard the message constantly from the moment the formal discussions began . . . there were frequent stand-offs on financial provisions with the Newfoundlanders insisting on more and the Canadians claiming there was nothing to give. . . . Such horse trading dragged on for weeks. Instead of being completed in a month as originally expected, the negotiations continued without conclusion through October into November."[18]

Eventually, on December 11, the Canadian government presented its proposed increases in the financial terms—something Mackenzie King had repeatedly emphasized was impossible. The new terms fell short of MacKay's recommendations and would still lead the new province into deficit, but more slowly. At this point all the delegates were under tremendous pressure to sign.

Smallwood regarded the new financial provisions as a bare minimum to be adjusted upwards. Crosbie made his projections on the actual figures offered in the new terms and concluded that they would lead the province into financial catastrophe. Smallwood, Bradley and McEvoy could be counted on to sign. Walsh held out until Canada threw in a redrafted Term 29: "the promise of a Royal Commission within eight years of union to 'review the financial position of Newfoundland and to recommend the form and scale of additional financial assistance, if any, which may be required by the Government of Newfoundland to enable it to continue public services at their prevailing levels without resorting to taxation more burdensome having regard to capacity to pay, than that of the Maritime Provinces.'"[19]

St. Laurent kept insisting the Canadian government would be most sympathetic to Newfoundland when the Royal Commission reviewed Newfoundland's financial situation later on. He kept reassuring Walsh in particular, who, according to the secretary of the delegation, J.W. Channing, was extremely unhappy with the whole process. "Walsh gave every indication of a man who wanted to go home and wash his hands of the entire affair," said Channing. "He would sit stone-faced and listen to the presentations by the Canadian ministers and when they had finished he continued to sit there stone-faced. He didn't react at all, he just sat there, totally shut down. Well, after their presentations these ministers were naturally looking for some reaction from him but there was none. He just sat there unmoved. He made them sweat. They knew he was unhappy. So St. Laurent worked on Walsh continually reassuring him that when the Royal Commission took place Canada would be most sympathetic to Newfoundland. Walsh had gotten an increase from the Canadians but he knew that what was being offered in the end was still not satisfactory."[20] However, as chairman of the delegation and a commissioner of the government, Walsh was hopelessly compromised. He could not allow the negotiations to collapse. He accepted Term 29 and agreed to sign. Gruchy secured the tax concessions he wanted for the Anglo-Newfoundland Development Co., and he too would sign. Crosbie consulted Gordon Winter, who was equally troubled about the shortfall in the financial provisions. But by then Winter felt he had done his best and he had no choice but to sign: that was the task Governor Macdonald had authorized him to do. That left only Crosbie undecided.

Crosbie had contributed significantly to the negotiations, and he

genuinely wanted the best deal for Newfoundland. He was a businessman as well as a nationalist, with no ideological antipathy towards
Confederation itself if the terms were sound, but he had no faith at all in
Term 29. He consulted his large circle of friends and colleagues and
finally summoned his financial adviser Phil Lewis to Ottawa to review all
the relevant documents. Lewis confirmed Crosbie's own doubts about
the inadequacies of the deal.

On the day before the signing ceremony in Ottawa, Crosbie
announced that he could not support the final terms. Smallwood again
offered him any position he wanted in the new administration, but
Crosbie declined and left town. All the other Newfoundland delegates
signed the document, satisfied that a future royal commission would sort
out the intractable fiscal situation that Crosbie believed they were creating. Alexander Clutterbuck's assessment of the final agreement was every
bit as enthusiastic as for the old terms:

> The Newfoundland Delegation were adamant that they would not
> agree to financial terms which in their opinion would confront the
> new province with the prospect of bankruptcy in a few years' time.
> Indeed at one stage in the negotiations it looked as if the negotia-
> tions might reach a deadlock on the question of finance. The
> Canadian Government, however, could not afford to let it be said
> that, when both sides had come so far towards union, they had
> allowed the negotiations to break down on account of a few million
> dollars, and in the end they were persuaded to offer an increase in
> the transitional grant during the first eight years. Under the terms as
> signed the grant is to be increased to $6½ millions in each of the
> first three years, tapering to $2¼ millions in the eighth year. The
> grant for the final four years shows no change from the 1947 offer....
>
> As part of the general settlement, it was acceptable to all
> members of the Newfoundland Delegation, except—as it turned
> out—Mr. Crosbie, who at the twelfth hour refused to sign the

Terms on the ground that the financial arrangements were inadequate. Even his refusal it may be said, "It's an ill wind—" since it has been cynically remarked in Ottawa that, if the entire Delegation had accepted the Terms without any reservation, the existing Provinces would certainly have complained that they were too generous.[21]

In his formal reply to Governor Macdonald, Crosbie laid out his reasons for not signing:

I would like to state here, that the budgets prepared by these gentlemen are in my opinion bare bone. . . .

. . . I must point out also that our surplus account is to be used to cover the deficits . . . over a period of eight years approximately $30,000,000.00 of our surplus will be used for what I call ordinary expenditure. . . . But what of the succeeding years? . . . the province will be left with large deficits in the vicinity of $7,000,000.00 . . . when the disappearing transitional grants are at their lowest. . . .

In my opinion it would be unsound to subscribe to any financial scheme, whether private or public, in which deficits must be met out of accumulated surplus, and this is exactly what we are proposing to do, right from the date of union. . . .

. . . It is true that a Royal Commission will be appointed to study our financial position in the eighth year, after the bulk of our surplus is spent when we are on the verge of bankruptcy. There is no assurance given that this report will be fully implemented, and that the province will be put on a sound financial basis. . . .

. . . The Canadians themselves realized it was doubtful if the financial aid was sufficient, but in spite of this minute nothing further was done. . . .

. . . In view of what I have said I could not possibly sign the terms agreed to by the majority, and only hope that my forecast of the financial position will prove wrong.[22]

Crosbie's forecast did not prove wrong, and the financial record of the first eight years of the new province of Newfoundland would play out exactly as the figures had shown they would. Britain's oldest colony was destined to become Canada's newest have-not province.

The Canadians and the British were thrilled. They did not care about Crosbie's refusal to make the decision unanimous. In fact, it looked good for them: it helped them handle the other provinces and prevented any suggestion of a "fix." Smallwood and the rest of the delegates returned home, where they announced the new final terms and called them "generous." That day marked the successful completion of the Canadian conspiracy with the British to "bounce" Newfoundland into Confederation while she was in constitutional limbo, with no elected government and no legislature of its own to debate the terms and represent Newfoundland's real interests.

CELEBRATION

S hortly after the vote Judge J.G. Higgins wrote to Sir Alan Herbert: "The story of the manner by which Newfoundland has been rail-roaded into confederation is a sordid one, a contemptible piece of political chicanery. . . . If Confederation eventually goes through, there will be a blot on English politics which will never be erased."[1]

Before the Terms of Union could become law, an Act of the British Parliament was required, given the absence of a Newfoundland legisla-ture. On second reading of the bill, Oliver Stanley, the official spokes-man for the Conservative Party of Great Britain, noted: "The sole task of the House was to determine whether, in passing the bill, the House was carrying out the will of the people of Canada and of Newfoundland. There was no dispute about the will of the people of Canada, but I regret that matters were not so clear with regard to the people of Newfoundland." He, concluded, however, that "a rejection from this House might lead to Canada withdrawing altogether from the proposal. It certainly might cause great feeling in Canada as to the extent of interference exercised by this House of Commons with Canadian affairs against the wishes of the people of Canada."[2]

However, the extent of interference exercised in Newfoundland's affairs did not seem to matter to most British parliamentarians any more than did the wishes of the Newfoundland people. Canada's pride trumped Newfoundland's rights. It was left to Sir Alan Herbert to speak for Newfoundland in the only Parliament other than Canada's that voted on the union:

> This house, without prejudice to the merits of the proposed union of the Dominion of Canada and Newfoundland, is not satisfied that the procedure preliminary to the introduction of this Bill has been constitutionally correct and just, is not persuaded that the will of Newfoundland has been established as clearly and unmistakably as is necessary for a surrender of sovereignty and a lasting change of status, and, observing that the terms of union have been debated in the Canadian Parliament for a fortnight but have not been debated in Newfoundland at all, declines to approve the agreement until it has been considered and approved in the Legislature of Newfoundland and an Address presented to His Majesty in accordance with Section one hundred and forty-six of the British North America Act of 1867.[3]

In support of his claim that the Canadian press also disapproved of the process, he quoted from the *Globe and Mail*:

> The procedure by which it is now proposed to unite Newfoundland with Canada it is quite clear violates the British North America Act, it violates the 1934 agreement between Britain and the Island, and ignores or at any rate treats as of no consequence the sovereignty of Newfoundland.[4]

The transfer of sovereignty was not the sort of thing to be put before the electorate in a referendum, said Herbert, and, as for the "poor majority" for Confederation, he stated: "If there is a majority at all it should be two-thirds. Not a comma in the American constitution can be changed unless there is a two-thirds majority, and by the wise rules of the MCC, even the rules of cricket cannot be challenged without a two-thirds majority. . . . Does the right honourable government say that this is a proper majority whereby a dominion is to surrender its sovereignty?"[5] He then challenged the government:

> It is not too late, even now, to change the procedure. There could be a general election as early as this May in Newfoundland to elect a legislature, and a responsible Government of Newfoundland could then go to Ottawa and sign new terms of union—provided of course that the supporters of Confederation obtained a majority in the legislature.
>
> On the other hand, suppose that the Federationists do not win—I believe that the fear that this might happen is at the root of the Bill—and I should not be surprised. Then responsible government will win, and Newfoundland will show that she is capable of running herself forever. So far as I know, her dollar situation is a dammed sight better than ours. She has a secure market for her forest products and her fisheries. Labrador may become another Alaska, because it has the largest iron ore deposits in the world waiting to be exploited, and they will be a terrific thing. Whoever runs them, Labrador will be an Old Age Pension for Newfoundland for a very long time. That is what I suggest. For the life of me, I cannot understand why even now the Government cannot say that this is the best way to do the business and why they cannot do the simple, honourable and constitutional thing.[6]

Sir Alan had fought diligently and passionately for Newfoundland's constitutional rights in the British Parliament for almost the entire period of the Commission of Government between 1935 and 1949. He had come to love the country and its people, whom he praised as "the best tempered, best mannered people walking." His affection for and dedication to Newfoundland is clear in his closing words: "I have done my best for these people, and I can do no more, but I do say this: if the policy of this Bill prevails, I for one shall not be sorry to go out from a Parliament which can so affront a proud, dignified, loyal white people, and the good name and honour of my own beloved country."[7]

In St. John's, three former members of the House of Assembly and three former members of the Legislative Council, including Judge W.J. Browne of St. John's District Court and J.S. Currie, publisher of the *Daily News*, took out a writ in the Supreme Court against the members of the Commission of Government and its chairman, Governor Gordon Macdonald, claiming that the steps taken by the Newfoundland government to pass the National Convention Act of 1946 and the Referendum Act of 1948 were unconstitutional and illegal. The suit was heard by Justice Brian Dunfield, who rejected the claim. Similarly Justices L.E. Emerson and J.A. Winter, both former commissioners, rejected the claim on appeal. The appellants were granted leave to take the case to the Judicial Committee of the Privy Council, but the British Parliament acted to transfer Newfoundland sovereignty to Canada before the case could be heard.

The House passed the Act, but not without much anguish and even resentment. David Gammans, an expert in imperial affairs, charged that the government had "landed the House in an absolutely awkward and unenviable position. . . . As it is, the Bill will leave a very nasty taste behind it."[8]

In January 1949 Major Peter Cashin wrote to Louis St. Laurent, the new prime minister: "I reiterate my statement that your Government has been in collusion with the British Government and the Commission of Government in Newfoundland during the past few years in order to bring about the union. I repeat that both yourself and Prime Minister King have acted dishonestly in this whole matter and I leave it to history to confirm this statement."[9]

But nothing now could stop the machinery of empire. As the great day for transition from one empire to another drew near, Paul Bridle worried that the mood in St. John's was less than celebratory: "Unless Joe Smallwood plans to have some celebration on April 1st, which I hope he will not do, the position will be that April 1st and succeeding days will pass off quietly and the transition of Newfoundland to a Province of Canada will be brought about so quietly it will hardly be noticed here at all."[10] Sir Alexander Clutterbuck, the British high commissioner, who had long experience on the Newfoundland file, though ever optimistic, was not sanguine in the short term: "There is a feeling in Ottawa that the errant and high-spirited son who is now at last joining the family after running wild for so long a period may prove to be both unruly and prodigal but that the sacrifice and inconvenience will be well repaid in the long run."[11]

It is no crime to be a "high-spirited son," but in Clutterbuck's eyes the Newfoundlanders were not only children but "errant" and "prodigal" as well. Canada, as head of the "family," was the grown-up father, taking on the "sacrifice" and "inconvenience" of the troublesome youth in the cause of the British North American family. A sympathetic Clutterback concluded, Canada would in the long term be "well repaid"—C.D. Howe and Mitchell Sharp would make sure of that.

The documents of union were signed in Ottawa on March 31, 1949. Smallwood insisted that the date be moved back a day so that the event was not solemnized on April Fool's Day. But fate cannot be denied, and, as many Newfoundlanders suspected, Newfoundland became at once Canada's newest have-not province and its Confederation an April Fool's joke. The day was marked in Ottawa with a large official celebration, complete with bunting and fine speeches by Prime Minister Louis St. Laurent and Gordon Bradley. The music for the Newfoundland national anthem could not be found, but it didn't seem to matter. The band simply played the national anthem of Canada in its place.

In St. John's there were no celebrations and no disturbances. The populace accepted the results of the referendum with restraint, but the day did not pass without appropriate respect or dramatic gesture. In the silent city the streets gradually filled with supporters of responsible government, all wearing black armbands to mark the passing of the country of Newfoundland.

ALL FOR THE BEST

The final words in the preamble to the Memorandum of Agreement between Canada and Newfoundland of December 11, 1948, state that the Terms of Union have been settled by "authorized representatives of Canada" and "authorized representatives of Newfoundland."[1] But are these words true? This official designation of "authorized representatives" goes to the heart of the Anglo-Canadian plot to deprive Newfoundland of its right to actual self-determination. The statement flaunts an equality between the representatives of both countries which was simply non-existent. The Canadian representatives were certainly authorized by the elected government of Canada with all the power necessary to confederate with Newfoundland. But who had authorized the Newfoundland delegation?

The National Convention elected in Newfoundland in 1946 had authority only to "discuss" and "recommend," and specifically not to "decide" or "negotiate." Beyond that, only four of the seven delegates to Ottawa were elected delegates to that Convention. Albert Walsh, chairman of the delegation, was a commissioner in the Commission of Government that had been rejected in the First Referendum, while Gordon Winter and Philip Gruchy had simply been picked out of private life by the governor. The Newfoundland representatives were "authorized" by the Commission of Government and the British governor who chose them, and would be, as the Governor put it, "the right sort of people with whom the Canadians could deal." None of them had any authority to sign over the sovereignty of their country to Canada. That authority was suddenly granted to them by the British government that had appointed them. The Terms of Union with Canada were accepted by that British government: "that the proposed Terms be reported, with recommendation for adoption by the Newfoundland delegation to the Governor in Commission, which will approve . . . and recommend that they be brought into effect by a United Kingdom statute."[2]

The final Canadian terms were never debated, approved or ratified by any elected Newfoundland body, certainly not by the Newfoundland legislature. It had been suspended by the British in 1933, and it was kept suspended until Confederation with Canada was completed. This setup was confirmed by R.A. MacKay, the chairman of the Steering Sub-Committee of the Interdepartmental Committee on Newfoundland, on September 30, 1948, in his memo on the status of the Newfoundland Delegation: "The delegation last year consisted of the committee of the National Convention, and it was empowered only to enquire whether a fair and equitable basis of union existed. The present delegation will be expressly empowered to negotiate on behalf of Newfoundland. The word 'negotiate' is used in the Prime Minister's statement of July 30, 1948)."[3] MacKay might seem very proud of the inclusion of the word "negotiate," but he continued: "The present delegation should, however, be regarded as representative of the Commission of Government[,] which has reserved to itself the position of principal in the negotiations."[4]

The Dominions Office had ruled early on in this "bizarre experiment in dictatorship" that the secretary of state for dominions affairs was sovereign in all spheres over the Commission of Government in St. John's.[5] The Canadians were therefore negotiating not with any Newfoundland authority but with the British government. The improvised constitutional device of the National Convention and the appointed delegations had been merely a pseudo-democratic screen set up to conceal the real action between London and Ottawa. Although the Commission of Government "reserved to itself the position of principal in the negotiations" between Newfoundland and Canada, at no point in the long and painful process did the Commission of Government or the Commonwealth Relations Office ever question the Canadian terms. Never once did any of their officials say these terms were unfair or inadequate in any respect. The only opinion the British ever expressed about them was that they were "extremely generous," even though it was known that the new province would not be able to exist under them. Clearly there were some British officials who sincerely believed that what they were doing in Newfoundland was the best possible solution. Without doubt, arranging for Newfoundland to enter into Confederation with Canada was a convenient and tidy resolution for the United Kingdom. True democracy, however, is rarely so convenient. When the Newfoundland electorate rejected Confederation in 1889, Governor Hill in Ottawa suggested to the colonial secretary, Lord Granville, that it should be imposed on Newfoundland. Lord Granville replied that the only way Newfoundland could join Canada was by action of the elected Newfoundland legislature, as laid out in the British North America Act of 1867. The Newfoundland Act of 1949 set the BNA Act aside and established a new precedent.

Before the debate on the Newfoundland Act in the British parliament in March 1949, Sir Alan Herbert received a summary of the situation in Newfoundland prepared by the Conservative Party. The conclusion read, "The verdict is likely to be the right thing done in the wrong way."[6] The majority of the written commentaries on Newfoundland's union with Canada in 1949 have concluded that, despite collusion, deception and impropriety, it was "all for the best." As Peter Neary put it: "Arguably, Newfoundland found greater independence within the loose structure of Canadian federalism than it could ever have achieved on its own. . . . All this, of course, means nothing if one believes as an article of faith that Newfoundland was a victim of an Anglo-Canadian plot."[7] But the entire point of the Anglo-Canadian plot was to deprive Newfoundland of regaining self-government and of representing its own interests with Canada on its own authority. Whether the delegates would have negotiated better or worse terms is simply not the point. As a people, Newfoundlanders had the right to self-determination, not British or Canadian determination. To say that manipulation of the democratic process in Newfoundland by Britain and Canada was "all for the best" would have us accept that the end does justify the means and that might makes right, and gives comfort to the same condescending and paternalistic attitudes which informed the Amulree Report and led to the destruction of Newfoundland's democracy and reputation in 1933. Self-determination is, after all, the only protection against the actions of even well-meaning outsiders and autocrats. Commissioner Thomas Lodge, in condemning the entire British scheme in Newfoundland, concluded: "The [Amulree] Royal Commission had been misled in concluding that Newfoundland's ills had stemmed from corrupt and spendthrift administrations rather than from economic causes beyond her control. From this misconception sprang all other errors in judgment on the part of the British Government."[8] History requires that, rather than trusting blindly in the motives of even benevolent dictators, we examine their actions with a jaundiced eye.

We cannot know whether Newfoundland would have been better off as a province of Canada than as an independent country. What we can know is the truth about how it was done—or we can at least come closer to it. That truth was kept from the Newfoundland and Canadian public for almost half a century, and it needs now to be acknowledged—to change minds and to improve attitudes.

In June 1947 Clifford Clark, the deputy minister of finance, remarked to American diplomat Joshua Harrington that he was afraid Newfoundland as a Canadian province would be "a little Ireland," full of "disgruntled people."[9] He was not alone in his concern, and, not surprisingly, there has been discontent ever since on both sides. Given the way the deal was made, it would be incomprehensible if there were not. In all my research on this theme, I have read and heard nothing good about the way Newfoundland's entry into Confederation was handled. The most commonly used words or phrases to describe it are "underhanded," "dishonest," "patronizing," "improper," "shabby," "badly done" and "an unholy deal." Whether the process was legal and binding may still be open to debate, and, if it were to be declared strictly legal, it would be so only because Great Britain wrote the law and could make it so. They could unilaterally void one law, the British North America Act of 1867, by writing another, the British North America Act 1949, and vary the terms of the Newfoundland Act of 1933 without the consent of the original party to that agreement.

It was this particular legal action that troubled Kenneth Wheare and other constitutional experts. After the Imperial Conference of 1926, the parliament of Great Britain could no longer pass laws affecting the dominions without the consent of the parliaments of those dominions. Newfoundland's dominion status was in suspension, and the parliament of Great Britain could not pass the British North America Act 1949 to irrevocably change the status of the Dominion of Newfoundland without the consent of the parliament of Newfoundland. The right of the British parliament to pass such an Act, and the legality of the Act itself, are issues that have never been adequately resolved.

In returning responsible government to Newfoundland, there would have been no winners and no losers, merely the fulfillment of a contract and an occasion of great satisfaction and rejoicing. An elected Newfoundland government would have been a powerful body. By the calculations of the Finance Committee of the National Convention and an analysis by the *Daily News*, among others, an independent government in 1949 would have had a surplus of over $40 million, an expectation of reasonable prosperity for the near future, and no desperate need to join up with anybody. Alexander Clutterbuck and Philip Noel-Baker at the Commonwealth Relations Office presumed that an independent Newfoundland would soon run into financial difficulties. This view was not shared by Lord Beaverbrook, who had already stated publicly that a restored Dominion of Newfoundland had excellent prospects for financial prosperity. In addition, an elected Newfoundland government would have been in a very different position to address many issues not considered in the talks in Ottawa in 1948.

To begin with, an elected Newfoundland government would have become aware of the true significance of the iron-ore deposit in Labrador, elevating it immediately to a much stronger position in its negotiations with Ottawa. But that was precisely what C.D. Howe and Louis St. Laurent were so anxious to avoid. A Newfoundland government, especially one with a strong opposition, would have had to secure either development or a meaningful royalty for that iron ore.

Then, as High Commissioner Scott Macdonald pointed out, there was the issue of "the enormous per capita public debt of Canada which Newfoundlanders would have to share if they entered Confederation."[10] In 1948 the Canadian per capita debt was $1,068, and Newfoundland's was $238. At the conference called to discuss joining Confederation in 1895, the delegation from the Newfoundland government had insisted that Canada take over the whole of Newfoundland's public debt as a condition of union. Five decades later, Macdonald favoured this same arrangement and argued to St. Laurent: "The application now of the same criteria we applied to them in 1895 would result, not only in the assumption of the whole public debt, but in the payment by Canada of a subsidy to compensate them for the amount by which the per capita debt of the Dominion exceeds that of Newfoundland. Interest on this amount even computed at 3% would come to several million dollars per annum."[11] However, the delegation from Governor Gordon Macdonald was in no position to make any such demands, especially given that the vote had already been taken.

Similarly, although the Terms of Union carefully itemize every amount and source of revenue to be assumed by the Canadian government, there is no mention of the considerable revenue that the Canadian government would collect from Newfoundland air space. Newfoundland is on the flight path from North America to Europe, and, even a conservative estimate states it has generated over $8 billion for the federal treasury since 1949.[12] There was no discussion of these potential revenues in the talks or documents leading up Confederation, but an elected government would surely have become aware of them—in the late 1940s or early 1950s.

There are other issues, too, that would have arisen in negotiations between two independent countries, issues that could not arise in the carefully arranged "negotiations" under British authority. Gordon Winter, the reluctant delegate who felt compelled to sign the final terms in 1948, was troubled by the event for the rest of his life. Before he died in 2003, he stated in an interview with CBC St. John's that "there were no negotiations in Ottawa in 48."[13] If responsible government had been restored, it is quite possible that Newfoundland would have become a province of Canada in the fifties, though one of a very different character—not a pauper to be "saved," but a more equal and respected partner in a stronger union. It is probable that a general election in 1948 or 1949 would have produced results similar to those in the referendum, with an evenly divided legislature: a minority pro-Confederate government under Smallwood, perhaps, or a minority pro-independent government under Major Peter Cashin or someone else. Either way, Canada would have had to make an attractive offer to be accepted—certainly better than the one agreed to by Governor Macdonald.

The official correspondence between Canada and Great Britain proves that Newfoundland's right to self-determination was not respected or handled in 1948 in a transparent, fair and democratic fashion by those who held "temporary authority" over the Island. The claim that Great Britain and Canada were involved in a conspiracy to put Newfoundland into Confederation without the knowledge of the people is now a fact grounded in the evidence of their own official documents. This plot was unquestionably harmful to Newfoundland's interests and reputation. As historian Phillip McCann states in his ground-breaking article "British Policy and Confederation," the first work to seriously challenge the official history, "the belief of Peter Cashin and the Responsibles that Britain was engaged in a 'plot' or 'conspiracy' must be given greater credence. There can be little doubt that the situation which brought about Confederation was engineered by the British, almost entirely in secret and largely by the Treasury. Both Newfoundland and Labrador were used as pawns in a deal with the Canadians."[14]

NEITHER WORTHILY NOR WELL

If the extent of Great Britain's connivance with Canada had been known, the mother country would have been exposed to scandal and disgrace. Having gone so far and risked so much, was it plausible that the British would, in the final stage, leave the decision in the hands of Newfoundlanders, when previously they had done everything in their power to decide the matter for them? They established a controversial and troublesome National Convention rather than return the Newfoundland parliament. Is it likely they would risk returning it in a referendum? Conspirators do not conspire to fail.

It was the British who held the referendum in Newfoundland in 1948. They decided what options would appear on the ballot paper, and it was they who counted the votes. Governor Macdonald and the British exercised the tightest control over that process. In 1933 Alexander Clutterbuck wrote in the Royal Commission Report that, for Newfoundland, "considerations of constitutional status were regarded more as a matter for academic discussion than as a practical issue."[1] That thinking was essentially unchanged in 1948. Whether Britain did fix the vote or not, they had put themselves in every position to do so and it would be unrealistic to think they were not prepared to follow through.

There is no official record even in the top secret files of any such plan—but that is not surprising. Nevertheless, over sixty years later, the belief in such a plan is active in Newfoundland and elsewhere. It is supported by personal accounts of those involved, and in personal papers such as those of Charles R. Granger.

Charles R. (Charlie) Granger was the executive assistant to Jack Pickersgill after Confederation, when Pickersgill ran for elected office and became Newfoundland's representative in the federal Cabinet of Lester Pearson. Granger himself later became a minister in the Trudeau government. For a time he was also a member of the Newfoundland provincial government. Throughout his many years in public life, he interviewed people at both the federal and provincial levels about the Newfoundland referendum on Confederation. In all these interviews he found that they commonly did not want to talk about the vote—they found it a painful memory and, overall, described it as a bad business. In the end Granger came to believe that the vote had been tampered with.

Nehemiah Short was the chief electoral officer for the referendum and was stationed at the House of Assembly. He and the British officials with him received the returns there by telephone, and, as they were tallied, a uniformed member of the Newfoundland Constabulary took them across the road to the governor and his officials at Government House. Sir Gordon Macdonald had sole responsibility for compiling and publishing the results. There was no direct communication between the Returning Officer's Office and the governor.[2] According to Granger, it was that secrecy that made the vote tampering possible. As Jim Halley explained: "The British operated on a need-to-know basis. There would be no written record, and only those who absolutely had to know about the plans to change the election results were told. Joey [Smallwood], for instance, was not told. It would have demoralized him. He would have accepted it, but there was more to be gained from his performance by not telling him. The only Newfoundlander who would need to know was Nehemiah Short, the returning officer."[3]

Two days after the vote and long before the results could be confirmed, Governor Macdonald wrote to Sir Eric Machtig at the Commonwealth Relations Office about the successful outcome obtained in the referendum. It would have taken at least a month for a full recount of the close result, but within eight days, in spite of calls for a recount on the west coast, both Great Britain and Canada accepted the results as conclusive.

Within two weeks of the vote, a number of ballots were burned in St. John's. David Butler was a powerful bureaucrat in the Smallwood government after confederation, but during the summer of 1948 he was an assistant to Commissioner Herman Quinton. Shortly after the vote, Butler was ordered by Quinton to take a truckload of ballots to the General Hospital in St. John's and burn them in the furnace there. When Butler arrived at the hospital he decided to open the burlap sacks before he destroyed them. The sacks were filled with ballots, and even the ballot boxes, from the second referendum. Butler was troubled by his orders from Quinton, so he telephoned the chief electoral officer, Nehemiah Short, whom he knew, and told him what Quinton had ordered. Short replied: "The ballots were counted neither worthily nor well. Burn them." Butler burned the ballots but kept one of the boxes for a souvenir.[4] Later on, when Short's secretary was questioned about the ballot count after his death, she became extremely upset, burst into tears and would only say, "You better let sleeping dogs lie."[5]

All these accounts, though unofficial, corroborate each other and are consistent with the official record of deception. The unusual placement of the returning officer at the House of Assembly in isolation from the governor, who received and announced the final results, ensured ample opportunity to tamper with that result. The haste in burning the historic ballots prevented any possibility of a recount. Why were the ballots not preserved for a conclusive recount, and to show off the "fine achievement," as Whitehall called it? In addition, there is no record of any poll-by-poll compilation of results from the second referendum. All these points add credence to the argument that Great Britain conspired to control the result of the second referendum and put Newfoundland into Confederation regardless of the wishes of the people of Newfoundland.

There is also the haunting testimony of Dr. Harold Paddock, a linguist and professor emeritus at Memorial University of Newfoundland from 1972 to 2002. In 1967, when Paddock was a graduate student at the University of London, he became friends with Margot Davies, a journalist who had a popular BBC weekly radio show, *Calling Newfoundland*, which was broadcast in Newfoundland from 1941 until just before her death in 1972. The daughter of D.S. Davies, Newfoundland's trade commissioner in the United Kingdom, Margot Davies loved Newfoundland and devoted her life to helping Newfoundlanders in London.

During the three years he was there, Paddock was a guest on several of Davies' shows and, in February 1967, he was at Bush House, the home of the BBC Overseas Services, waiting to record one of his poems. Seated next to him was an older English gentleman—a friend of Davies. He told Paddock in conversation that he had been in Newfoundland for several years working with the Commission of Government, and that he had married an "unreal" Newfoundlander, meaning a "townie." But the young graduate student knew very little about those years. The Englishman asked about the small outport of Beaumont in Green Bay where Paddock came from and about the poem he was going to record for Davies— "Keep Up the Fince" (see Appendix F). As Paddock recounted:

> The man was quiet for a while after reading the poem and obviously very moved. He then told me he had something he wanted to tell me, that he had a confession to make. He did not have long left to live and he wanted to tell someone from Newfoundland, a "real" Newfoundlander, meaning a "bayman." He said to me, "Your poem is about how badly the Newfoundlanders treated the native Beothuk Indians. But what you don't know is how badly the British treated you. You became the new natives, even though you were white."

In 1948, while working for the Commission Government, he was recalled to Whitehall. "We were told that there would be a Referendum and the result that we would have to announce would be Confederation with Canada, and if there was another result we would have to change it to Confederation. This of course was very unusual and we questioned it and we were told that the reason for this was that it had already been agreed to by Churchill and Roosevelt during the war that Newfoundland must never again be allowed to go unprotected as an ideal advance base for any attack from across the Atlantic. Churchill, wanting to keep Newfoundland in the Commonwealth, brought in Mackenzie King, who staked his claim—to which both Churchill and Roosevelt agreed.

After this directive he returned to St. John's. The two Referenda were held and on the second ballot on July 22 the results were virtually the same as on the first one. Confederation did not win. Responsible Government won by approximately 51% to 49% for Confederation. Those, he said, were the percentages rounded off to the nearest figure. It was a very slight majority for Responsible Government. "We were all very relieved because we didn't know what we would do if we'd had to make a big change. If it had been 55% to 45% or worse, that would have been hard, but the population was virtually split down the middle. We only had to nudge it the other way. I believed at the time that Britain was doing it for the best but I regret it now," he said.

Paddock recalled that at just this moment he was called in to record his poem. He was in such a state of shock that he could barely get through the reading: "I realized that I didn't even know the man's name, but when I got out of the studio both he and Margot had gone." Paddock was so disturbed by what the Englishman had told him that he couldn't work for a week. Confederation was seventeen years old in Newfoundland then, and after much thought he decided not to tell anyone about what he'd heard. "I am sorry now," he said, "that I didn't telephone Margot Davies for the gentleman's name and then get him to put his confession in writing and sign it."[6] Paddock finally shared his story with journalist Ray Guy in 1974 and later with Bren Walsh and Gwynne Dyer. He has since learned a great deal about that period of Newfoundland history.

Paddock's story should surprise no one. It has all the detail of truth and in all aspects conforms to the history of the period as we now understand it. The secret agreement reached early in the war between Roosevelt, Churchill and Mackenzie King is now generally known, but the full implications are rarely drawn. There was no way to predict with certainty which way Newfoundland would vote in the referendum, and both Great Britain and Canada thought it unlikely that Newfoundland would choose Confederation without a push. So, although responsible government might appear on the ballot, it would not be permitted to win. If somehow Britain bungled the referendum process and Newfoundland achieved independence, the Island would be up for grabs by the Americans. But Britain was not about to see Newfoundland and Labrador, that great "bargaining counter," slip out of its hands. Nothing was left to chance.

Shortly after the results of the second referendum were announced, Sir Alan Herbert wrote in the *Times* of London: "I have felt from my first days in this affair that Whitehall (there is no Party question here) was set upon Confederation and stealthily working for it all the time. I am now sure of it."[7]

Thomas Lodge was moved to write in a letter to the *Guardian* newspaper that Confederation had been achieved by "an unholy deal." Lodge, not surprisingly, received neither a silver salver nor a knighthood for his work.

When the British government set up the National Convention in St. John's, it sent out Sir Kenneth Wheare as a constitutional expert to the Convention. Later, when Wheare was rector of Exeter College,

Oxford, he frequently expressed his disapproval of the process employed in Newfoundland.[8]

Harry Winter, the Newfoundland commissioner for justice and defence from 1945 to 1947, wrote that the setting up of the National Convention "was both a breach of contract as regards the Act and Letters Patent and breach of faith with the Alderdice government."[9] Indeed, Prime Minister Frederick Alderdice and all those who accepted the Commission in 1933 would have considered the National Convention and the referenda adopted by the Dominions Office in 1948 an unimaginable violation of both the letter and the spirit of the agreement of 1933.

From London to St. John's there were many who cried foul about Newfoundland's entry into Confederation, but none of them could hold raw power to account. However the "very nasty taste," as one British MP put it, has never gone away.

TO THE VICTORS GO THE SPOILS

It is not uncommon for great powers to abuse the rights of lesser ones, and so it was with Great Britain in Newfoundland in 1948. Newfoundland's becoming part of Confederation falls into the pattern of British decolonization after the war. India was already gone and badly divided along religious lines. Palestine was abandoned to permanent conflict. As for the "problem child" of the Empire, it was traded to another empire, with a legacy of grumbling and discontent ever since. With the successful completion of the plan to "take over Newfoundland," as Mackenzie King had put it, the key players received their rewards.

Charles Burchell was elevated to the Privy Council—the only high commissioner and non-elected official ever so honoured. Sir Gordon Macdonald was sent to the House of Lords. Gordon Bradley became the secretary of state for Canada, and Joey Smallwood the first premier of the new province of Newfoundland. "J.B. McEvoy did not get the senatorship he was seeking. Smallwood never forgave him for his letter to the *Evening Telegram* in February 1948. He was obliged to settle for a one-time payout of $3,000."[1] Herbert Pottle and Herman Quinton, both commissioners from the Commission of Government, and Gordon Winter all received positions in Smallwood's Interim Government. Albert Walsh was knighted and appointed lieutenant governor, and later appointed to the Supreme Court. Leonard Outerbridge was also knighted and became lieutenant governor after Walsh. Nehemiah Short, the chief returning officer, received the Order of the British Empire. Malcolm Hollett went to the Canadian Senate—the pay-off destination for numerous useful party loyalists.

Lesser players received liquor licences or other sinecures. L.E. Emerson died just after the transfer over which he presided as chief justice. Sir Gordon, having wisely decided not to stay on for the "celebrations," returned to England on March 6, 1949. On the occasion of his departure, the *Evening Telegram* printed a poem from a reader thanking the departing Raj. It seemed a flattering verse, but observant readers soon caught on that the first letter of each line spelled out "The Bastard"—a sentiment that pretty well summed up local feelings about Sir Gordon's performance as head of state.

C.D. Howe quietly extracted the billions of dollars' worth of the iron ore out of Labrador West for the Canadian heartland—Ontario and Quebec—with virtually no residual benefit for Newfoundland. Lester Pearson later gave the revenues from the Upper Churchill to Quebec when he refused to require Quebec to allow Newfoundland to transport its power from the Upper Churchill Power Project in Labrador through Quebec to markets in the United States. Instead, Newfoundland was forced to sell its power to Quebec at fixed 1960s' prices. "Smallwood was not allowed to dot an 'i' on the deal, and was forced to support it publicly for the sake of appeasing Quebec and Canadian unity."[2] As a result, Quebec earns from $2 to $4 billion annually from the power it resells from Newfoundland and Labrador to the US market. Newfoundland gets enough to maintain the facility to keep it operating for Quebec's advantage.

If Newfoundland had been allowed the benefit of just one of those two resources, it could have underwritten its independence, including the Swedish social welfare package that Canada adopted. As it was, the full benefit of the Upper Churchill wealth went to the province of Quebec, where René Lévesque boasted it gave economic backbone to its separatist posture. In 1927 the province of Quebec and the federal government, along with the Dominion of Newfoundland, had submitted the Labrador boundary dispute to the Privy Council in London. The Privy Council confirmed Newfoundland's jurisdiction, a decision that was not accepted by the province of Quebec. With Confederation, however, Quebec did finally acquire Labrador's resources. That astonishing transfer of hydro wealth to Quebec both humiliated and impoverished the newest province. Those who were unaware of the fix in 1949 could see it clearly by 1969. As A.P. Herbert remarked: "A Frenchman said that Labrador was the country that God gave to Cain. History may say that it was the country Britain gave to Canada."[3]

For nearly five hundred years since its discovery by the Europeans, Newfoundlanders had prosecuted the fishery. The fishery was the raison d'être for Newfoundland—the reason people came and settled here and went on to develop the culture and lifestyle they enjoyed. Within fifty years of Confederation and federal management, the Newfoundland fishery had collapsed and the great North Atlantic cod stock, the largest biomass on the planet, was on the verge of extinction. But this precipitous decline didn't seem to matter to the Canadians.

The Newfoundland provincial government and the Newfoundland people participated with the rest of the world in the continuous and reckless over-fishing and in the disastrous dragger technology that devastated the ocean floor and the spawning grounds. It was the federal government, however, that bartered away huge fishing quotas to foreign powers for trade concessions. Korea got its fishing quota off Newfoundland when Quebec got a car plant from Hyundai. The Russians got fishing quotas in Newfoundland for buying Canadian wheat. Landlocked Ottawa did not understand the fishery or appreciate its importance, except as a bargaining chip for the heartland. Ultimately, central planning from Ottawa proved to be disastrous for the Grand Banks of Newfoundland. Natural resources should never be controlled by an absentee landlord—in this case Ottawa. The country of Newfoundland may not have been any wiser in its fisheries management, but at least the fishery would have mattered more to Newfoundland.

Canada got what it wanted out of Newfoundland—Labrador and the Grand Banks. These resources far more than paid for the pension and baby bonus cheques from Ottawa. But Ottawa was careful to style itself as the saviour and to portray Newfoundland as a dependant, a second-class province, even a beggar. The myth of Canadian generosity was an easy sell to the Canadian media. The burden, the problem child, had been passed from one empire to another. But Canada had fought long, hard and dirty to acquire it, and, as soon as it had the prize, the extractions could begin.

Ches Crosbie's fears proved only too accurate. Once the resources and the revenues were pouring out of the province to central Canada, Newfoundland was mired in debt after only eight years of Confederation. In 1956 the royal commission to examine Newfoundland's financial position was established, as promised by Term 29 of the Terms of Union. The commission's recommendations fell far short of what Smallwood had hoped for, and what Newfoundland's own royal commission had recommended was necessary to rescue the province from the financial problems created in 1949. But John Diefenbaker's new federal Conservative government was unmoved. It was then that Smallwood, the "Apostle of Confederation," donned the black armband of the Responsible Government League. By that time, there was nowhere left to turn.

Canada failed utterly to develop the new East Coast it had acquired. Geoff Sterling, Newfoundland media magnate and one of Crosbie's lieutenants in the Union with America party, concluded thirty years later that Confederation in Newfoundland had delivered "the worst roads in Canada, no real development money, just handouts."[4] Newfoundland was never adequately connected to the mainland, because no one thought there would ever be any development on the Island. Above all, costs were to be kept to the minimum: the railway was closed, and the poor ferry service kept the province isolated from the mainland. The Liberal culture of dependency there did not begin to change until 1984, when John Crosbie and Premier Brian Peckford negotiated the Atlantic Accord, which attempted to give back to Newfoundland the benefit of some of the resources it had brought with it into Confederation. Interestingly, the federalist John Crosbie was the son of the nationalist Ches Crosbie and a minister in Brian Mulroney's Cabinet. But substantial material change did not come to the Island until Premier Danny Williams was driven on December 23, 2004, to take down the Canadian flag in the Newfoundland legislative building in his fight with Ottawa to give the province more of its offshore oil revenues. His government's support shot up from 41 percent to 86 percent.[5] The Williams government finally forced Confederation to work for Newfoundland and Labrador, and not against it.

As Jim Halley summed it all up:

Newfoundland was a prosperous country in the first part of the twentieth century. We were taken advantage of during the Great Depression in '33, not helped, but taken advantage of, by Great Britain and then again by Great Britain and Canada in '49. When it was suspended in '33, ours was the oldest Parliament in the empire except for the one in Westminster. In the '30s and '40s we were looking at an exciting future for our country. We had TWA, Pan Am, British Airways and Trans-Canada Airways. You could go to Gander, take your pick and fly anywhere in the world. We had two steamship lines, Furness Withy and Furness Red Cross, and twice a month you could put your car on board and cross over to England. We had passenger boats to Boston and New York. We lost all that when we joined Canada, and TCA got a monopoly here. We went from being an international hub to a Canadian backwater overnight.

When we joined Canada, we lost everything. We lost Labrador for all intents and purposes. Canada got the iron ore and the hydro for Ontario and Quebec. We got the cost of running the place. We lost the Grand Banks and all the revenues from that. We brought the Grand Banks into Canada with us when we came. They're the Grand Banks of Newfoundland, not the Grand Banks of Ontario, or even Quebec, and, as Averill Baker wrote, our continental shelf is ten times the size of any other province's, with ten times the potential for jobs, and there should be a separate Newfoundland and Labrador Accord to deal with this vast resource instead of having it all rolled into the Atlantic Accord. If we were independent we'd have 100 percent of our oil and gas, not 40 percent, and we might still have our fishery, as Iceland does.

But we lost everything when we joined Canada, lost the over-fly rights and the revenues from Gander and Goose Bay. Lost our customs revenues. Lost our manufacturing industries to Canadian goods.

We lost our ability to develop our own country or province because we lost control of our resources to Ottawa—which you can see in the official papers is all Ottawa ever wanted out of Newfoundland. So it should not surprise anyone that they had no plans or vision for the newest province. They actually planned for the depopulation of the place so it would cost them less in services.

If we had control of our own resources, we would be one of the most prosperous countries in the West, or the richest province in Canada. According to a UN survey, Newfoundland is the second richest jurisdiction in resources on the planet after Kuwait. Ontario and Quebec have gotten the benefit of that wealth, and they called us a burden, you know. The problem with the fix of '49 is that the crime goes on and on. That's why we need the truth. Justice requires as a bare minimum that we negotiate the Terms of Union with Canada. We cannot say re-negotiate because they were not negotiated in the first place. The people of Newfoundland wanted work, not welfare, but we got welfare. That is changing only recently because Danny Williams fought for 40 percent of our offshore oil. With that 40 percent we've been able to stabilize. If we had what was rightfully ours we wouldn't need Canada. That's the dirty secret Ottawa doesn't want anyone to know. They hit the jackpot when they got Newfoundland and Labrador, and they covered it up with a lot of noise about welfare.

I was at dinner with Jack Pickersgill in 1992 and I asked him why Canada would have wanted to negotiate with a National Convention instead of a duly elected Newfoundland government. Pickersgill smiled and replied: "Because we never would have gotten you so cheap."

So we need control of our Grand Banks back, we need 100 percent of the oil and gas, just as Alberta gets from the tar sands. We need at least joint jurisdiction of our fisheries. There are a lot of things that need to be looked at, such as an elected but equal Senate. And we need to be better connected if we're going to be part of Canada in the twenty-first century. Long ago we should have had a ferry service from Corner Brook into Quebec, but if we can't get any of that, we can separate and put a ferry through to Maine. It might be easier and, as an independent country in the twenty-first century, we might have a better chance than a forgotten region of Canada. Independence would be good for Newfoundlanders, good for our character, good for our self-esteem and good for our children. It's our choice now. Chrétien's Clarity Act gives us that choice. Certainly we are only as valuable as the value we set on ourselves.

If you permit yourself to examine the truth for a moment, you have to consider that responsible government did actually win. Newfoundlanders voted for responsible government and for independence in 1948. If you start with that realization, everything looks very different. Responsible government won in spite of "limitless funds" and the high-pressure tactics and schemes of Great Britain and Canada. From the announcement of the elections for the National Convention in December of '45 to the final vote in July of '48, it took the UK government almost three years to deliver on constitutional obligations, which had already been delayed by another year. It took that long to wear down the Newfoundlanders into accepting Confederation and hopefully achieve the maximum conditions for a win. In spite of all that, responsible government won by a very slim majority, an astonishing achievement for a small but plucky nation. We did well in '48; it was the British and the Canadians who let their end down.[6]

EPILOGUE

In the early 1970s, like so many of my generation, I went to Toronto a Canadian and came back a Newfoundlander. Although we were largely ignorant of, and indifferent to, the events described in this book, we were confronted on arrival with the wall of ignorance and prejudice that followed in its wake. When people discovered I was from Newfoundland, they would laugh openly in my face and ask if I had ever seen a television set and if I really lived in an igloo. At the plant where my brother-in-law worked, every Friday afternoon his co-workers would raise their arms and say to him, "This one's for Newfoundland"— meaning that the afternoon's work would go to support a dependent Newfoundland. They were unaware of the trainloads of iron ore from Labrador that kept the heartland humming and built the skyscrapers of North America.

This unacceptable situation required redress, so my friends and I wrote a theatre show to satirize both Canadians' attitudes and our own. It was called *Cod on a Stick* and it was a hit both in Toronto and at home in Newfoundland. Our company, CODCO, eventually did a TV series on CBC in the late 1980s and early '90s—in Halifax, of course, not St. John's. The weekly show was liberally laced with savage political satire and, eventually, questions were raised about it in the Canadian House of Commons, asking whether it was appropriate for the government, through the CBC, to support such controversial and subversive material. We felt satisfied that in some way we had hit our mark. I am forever grateful to the few brave souls at the CBC who helped us in our "mission" to change attitudes.

Today Newfoundlanders are still on the move, looking for the work that Confederation failed to provide in the newest province. Now they are headed further west, all the way to Alberta. It is with heavy hearts that they leave, and they are confronted on arrival with the same condescension and contempt that confronted us in the early 1970s in Toronto. Too often their children are called "stupid Newfies" in Alberta's schools, exactly as they were in the classrooms of Ontario years earlier. We have paid a heavy personal price for Confederation. However, we cannot be too selfish, for surely no territory needed an influx of fun-loving, hardworking Newfoundlanders more than the humour-challenged heartland. Alberta was for many years a burden on the federal treasury: its newfound respect in Canada comes from a deposit of hydrocarbons north of Edmonton, the controversial tar sands. Newfoundland's rising status can likewise be pegged to deposits of hydrocarbons off our east coast. Alberta gets 100 percent of its resource; we get 40 percent—which is considered generous—and you might say that Newfoundland enjoys about 40 percent of the respect that Alberta does. We all look forward to a future where respect is not pegged to deposits of hydrocarbons or minerals, where people will be respected simply because that is their right as human beings.

As for me, the only firm constitutional conclusion I can come to is that I am from the country of Newfoundland, the Promised Land. I carry a Canadian passport because Newfoundland was occupied by Canada in 1949 by means of a constitutional coup arranged with Great Britain. That said, it is also true that Newfoundland's joining up with Canada made sense, not only geographically, but politically and socially too. It may well have happened later and under different circumstances if it had not been forced on Newfoundland in 1948.

Although Newfoundlanders would make great Americans and would be free in the United States of the negative preconceptions that have hampered them in Confederation, Newfoundland has more in common with Canadian social and political mores than with those in the States. Canadian social policy, leaning to the left on issues such as health care and provincial and human rights (including minority, women's, children's and gay rights), has kept the country compassionate and livable. Our problems with Canada are political, not personal.

It is unfortunate that, in its haste to get Newfoundland on its own terms, Canada did not honour Newfoundlanders' inherent right to self-determination. Newfoundland and Labrador's Confederation is marred by a history of connivance, duplicity, mendacity and abuse. It is hard to see how a union so fraudulently attained can be said to have been attained at all. The Terms of Union are little more than the unilateral conditions of occupation by the stronger power. They were and are unnegotiated and, by any standard of democracy, unbinding on the population of Newfoundland and Labrador. The union, so dreaded by Norman Robertson, is arguably illegal after all, and Newfoundlanders but bastard Canadians. The "various possibilities" of Attlee's violations are unending.

Most Newfoundlanders today are unaware of the connivance and plots of Ottawa and London to grab our province for Canada. Yet we know instinctively that our Confederation with the mainland is in some way crippled. The discovery set out in this book of the real reasons underlying these misconceptions and miseries will, I hope, bring a degree of sanity and understanding to the pain and confusion we have endured since 1949.

In the preface to his volume of Newfoundland documents, 1940–49—a compilation of the top-secret correspondence between Canada and Great Britain on Newfoundland's Confederation with Canada—editor Paul Bridle, the acting high commissioner to Newfoundland at the time of the referendum, was moved to write: "Canadians reveal themselves, at the political level, as remarkably patronizing towards Newfoundlanders."[1]

Then he concluded on a note of hope: "The editor commends the book to his old friends in Newfoundland, confident that the truth that is in it, if it will not make them free, will at least give them food for thought."[2]

It has certainly given us food for thought. The true history of Newfoundland's confederation with Canada has the potential to make us free, in the same way that the articulation of sovereignty and nationhood by the province of Quebec has liberated Quebecers despite their continued federation with Canada. The truth about our history has the power to help us redefine our perspective on our place in the Canadian federation and the world. As Newfoundland slowly gains more control over its resources, it will be empowered to determine its own destiny in a way it was not permitted to do in 1948. Perhaps one day soon the diaspora will return, our sons and daughters will remain at home, and, if they so choose, Newfoundland and Labrador will be an independent country once again, unfettered and free of the attitudes of alien nations off her shores.

The novelist Paul West once described Newfoundland as "a community of Irish mystics cut adrift on the Atlantic."[3] To outsiders standing in seeming security on the mainland, it may appear that we are cut off, but Newfoundlanders see things differently. We are not adrift, we are home, in the place where the Irish mystics dreamed of going.

ACKNOWLEDGEMENTS

I have been fortunate in having the help of a great many people in the process of compiling this book. A special debt of gratitude is owed to all the archivists and librarians in St. John's, London, England, and Ottawa for their unreserved assistance.

Special thanks to historian and friend John FitzGerald for generously sharing his time and considerable knowledge, especially of the referendum process. I am grateful to Bernice Morgan and Lt. Governor John Crosbie, who both read earlier versions of this book and gave me the benefit of their wisdom, and to Gwynne Dyer, who not only read the manuscript and shared his insights but also treated me to lunch at his local in London.

The Halley family, especially Jim's widow, Ethel, and son William have given me their complete co-operation, as has Jim's great friend, John Andrews. Thanks to them and to James A. McGrath, who was very encouraging with his passion for this period of our history.

Thank you to Harold Paddock for his story and his wonderful poem, which he so kindly allowed me to include in the appendix, and to historians Peter Neary, Jim Hiller and Melvin Baker for answering my many questions, and also Larry Felt for his comments.

The staff at the Centre for Newfoundland Studies at Memorial University of Newfoundland could not have been more helpful and I want to thank especially Joan Ritcey, Linda White, Colleen Quigley, Glenda Dawe, Paulette Noseworthy, Bert Riggs and Jenny Higgins and Vince Walsh at the MUN Heritage site. The Provincial Archives of Newfoundland and Labrador at the Rooms is an invaluable resource and the staff, especially Larry Dohey, Joan Mowbray, Sandra Ronayne and Alan Byrne were always most helpful. I appreciate the assistance of Andrea Hyde at the Legislative Library of Newfoundland and Labrador, and of the former legislative librarian, Norma Jean Richards, who told me, "it's what's not in the files that is interesting, Greg."

I would like to acknowledge my dear friend Cathy Jones for her generous support of my research and her general whole-hearted encouragement. Thanks to my friends Don Sharp for his connections; Glen Neary for his contribution to my London research; Howard Granger for helping me access his father's papers; Don Walsh for his swift and hassle-free technical assistance with the maps; and to Marian White and my brother Beni for their steady support.

Special thanks to the staff at Random House of Canada, many of whom I now count as my friends, especially Diane Martin for her continuing support and her introduction to Rosemary Shipton, whose keen interest and expertise I greatly value. And to Jane McWhinney and her eagle eye, my sincerest appreciation and thanks. And to Deirdre Molina and Michelle MacAleese, whom I have relied on throughout the entire process, many, many thanks for all your help.

Finally I wish to thank my redoubtable assistant, Whitey, for her tireless efforts and dedication to this project.

PHOTO CREDITS

Every effort has been made to contact copyright holders; in the event of an inadvertent omission or error, please notify the publisher. Grateful acknowledgement is expressed to the following people and sources for permission to reprint these images.

FIRST INSERT

Page i   The Rooms Provincial Archives Division, St. John's, A47-28

Page ii   The Franklin D. Roosevelt Library, New York

Page iii   National Film Board of Canada, Photothèque, Library and Archives Canada, C-031186

Page iv   Frank Royal, National Film Board of Canada, Phototheque, Library and Archives Canada, C-023266

Page v   United Nations, Library and Archives Canada, C-018532

Page vi   (top, left) Walter Stoneman, © National Portrait Gallery, London; (top, right) Aselstyne/Canada, Department of National Defence, Library and Archives Canada, PA-159575; (bottom, left) Yousuf Karsh, Yousuf Karsh fonds, Library and Archives Canada, Accession number 1987-054, e010679424; (bottom, right) Library and Archives Canada/PA-121703

Page vii   Archives and Special Collections, Queen Elizabeth II Library,
            Memorial University of Newfoundland: File 285 Box 4,5,6

Page viii   The Rooms Provincial Archives Division, St. John's, A67-49

SECOND INSERT

Page i   Archives and Special Collections, Queen Elizabeth II Library,
            Memorial University of Newfoundland, Coll. 307, no.13.03

Page ii   Archives and Special Collections, Queen Elizabeth II Library,
            Memorial University of Newfoundland Coll. 285 Box 31 no. 42

Page iii   Archives and Special Collections, Queen Elizabeth II Library,
            Memorial University of Newfoundland, Coll. 285, Box 4,5,6 no. 28

Page iv   The Rooms Provincial Archives Division, St. John's, NL MG 956.77

Page v   Halley Family Collection, courtesy of Bill Halley

Page vi   Archives and Special Collections, Queen Elizabeth II Library,
            Memorial University of Newfoundland, Coll. 285 Box 7,8,9 no. 45

Page vii   Archives and Special Collections, Queen Elizabeth II Library,
            Memorial University of Newfoundland, Coll. 285, Box 10,11

Page viii   Archives and Special Collections, Queen Elizabeth II Library,
            Memorial University of Newfoundland, Coll. 285, Box 10,11, no.3

Page ix   Archives and Special Collections, Queen Elizabeth II Library,
            Memorial University of Newfoundland, Coll. 285

Page x   Archives and Special Collections, Queen Elizabeth II Library,
            Memorial University of Newfoundland, Coll. 285, Box 13,14,15, no.38

Page xi   Archives and Special Collections, Queen Elizabeth II Library,
            Memorial University of Newfoundland, Coll. 285, Box 28,29,30 no.27

Page xii   Media and Data Centre, Queen Elizabeth II Library,
            Memorial University of Newfoundland

APPENDIX A

Dramatis Personae

Great Britain

Addison, Lord — Secretary of State for Dominions Affairs of Great Britain 1945–47

Ammon, C.G. — Member of Parliament of Great Britain, Chairman Goodwill Mission to Newfoundland 1943

Amulree, Lord — William Warrender Mackenzie, Head of Newfoundland Royal Commission 1933

Attlee, Clement R. — Secretary of State for Dominions Affairs of Great Britain 1942–43
Deputy Prime Minister Great Britain 1942–45
Prime Minister Great Britain 1945–50

Beaverbrook, Lord — William Maxwell Aitken, Lord Privy Seal Great Britain 1943–45
Minister of Aircraft Production Churchill's War Cabinet 1940–41
Minister of Aviation Supply Churchill's War Cabinet 1941–42

Churchill, Sir Winston — Minister Aviation Supply Lloyd George's War Cabinet 1914–15, 1917–19
Prime Minister Great Britain 1940–45

Clutterbuck, P. Alexander — Ass't Secretary Dominions Office of Great Britain 1940–42
Ass't Under-Secretary of State for Dominions Affairs 1942–46
High Commissioner of Great Britain in Canada 1946–52

Cranborne, Lord — Secretary of State for Dominions Affairs of Great Britain 1940–42, 1943–45

Emrys-Evans, P.V. — Parliamentary Under-Secretary of State, Dominions Affairs, Great Britain, 1942–45

Herbert, Sir Allan — Independent Member of Parliament of Great Britain, 1935–50
Member of Goodwill Mission to Newfoundland, 1943

Keynes, John Maynard — Special Advisor to Chancellor of the Exchequer Great Britain
Counsellor to Ministry of Finance Great Britain

Macdonald, Sir Gordon — Governor of Newfoundland for Great Britain 1946–March 1949

MacDonald, Malcolm U.K. High Commissioner to Canada 1941–46

Machtig, Sir Eric Permanent Under-Secretary of State for Dominions Affairs
Great Britain 1940–47
Permanent Under-Secretary of State for Commonwealth
Relations Great Britain 1947–48

Noel-Baker, Philip Secretary of State for Commonwealth Relations of Great Britain
1947–50

Thomas, J.H. Secretary of State Dominions Affairs of Great Britain 1931–35

Walwyn, Vice-Admiral Governor of Newfoundland for Great Britain
   Sir Humphrey 1936–46

Canada

Bridle, Paul A. Third Secretary to High Commissioner in Newfoundland 1945–46
Second Political Division Department External Affairs 1946–48
Secretary Inter-departmental Committee on Canada–
Newfoundland Relations 1946–48
Second Secretary to High Commission in Newfoundland 1948–49
Acting High Commissioner in Newfoundland May–Sept 1948,
March 1949

Burchell, C.J. High Commissioner in Newfoundland Sept 1941–Jan 1944;
High Commissioner in Newfoundland Sept 1948–March 1949

Howe, C.D. Minister of Munitions and Supply 1940–45
Minister Reconstruction and Supply 1944–48
Minister Trade and Commerce 1948–57
Cabinet Committee on Newfoundland 1946–48

Keenleyside, Ass't Under-Secretary of State External Affairs 1941–44
   Hugh L. Acting High Commissioner in Newfoundland Jan–April 1944
Deputy Minister Mines and Resources 1947–50

King, W.L. Prime Minister Canada 1935–48
   Mackenzie Secretary of State for External Affairs 1935–46

Macdonald, J. Scott Counsellor, Department of External Affairs 1940–44
Canadian High Commissioner in Newfoundland 1944–May 1948

MacKay, R.A. Member Second Political Division Dept External Affairs 1945–46
Member Second Political Division Dept External Affairs 1947–48
Inter-departmental Committee on Canada–Newfoundland
Relations 1947–48
Chairman Steering Committee Inter-departmental Committee
on Canada–Newfoundland Relations 1948–49
Head British Commonwealth Division Dept. External Affairs
1948–52

Massey, Vincent Canadian High Commissioner to Great Britain 1935–May 1946

Pearson, Lester B. Under-Secretary of State External Affairs 1946–48
Secretary of State External Affairs 1948–57
Member Cabinet Committee on Newfoundland 1948

Pickersgill, J.W. Private Secretary to Secretary of State External Affairs 1942–45
Special Assistant to the Prime Minister 1945–52

Robertson, N.A. Under-Secretary of State for External Affairs 1941–46
Canadian High Commissioner to Great Britain 1946–Feb 1949
Clerk of the Privy Council and Secretary to the Cabinet
March 1949–52

St. Laurent, Louis S. Minister of Justice 1941–46 Secretary of State for External Affairs
1946–48
Chairman Cabinet Committee on Newfoundland 1946–48
Prime Minister of Canada 1948–57

Sharp, Mitchell W. Director Economic Policy Division Department of Finance
1947–51
Member Interdepartmental Committee on Canada–
Newfoundland Relations 1946–48
Steering Committee on Inter-departmental Committee on
Canada–Newfoundland Relations 1948–49

Wrong, H.H. Assistant Under-Secretary of State External Affairs 1942–44
Associate Under-Secretary of State External Affairs 1944–46
Canadian Ambassador to Washington 1946–53

Newfoundland

Alderdice, Frederick
Prime Minister of Newfoundland 1932–34
Commissioner in Commission of Government 1934–36

Bradley, Gordon F.
Chairman of the National Convention of Newfoundland 1946–47
Member of the National Convention of Newfoundland 1946–48
Chairman of Delegation to London 1947
Chairman of Delegation to Ottawa 1947
President Newfoundland Confederate Association Member
Delegation to Ottawa to the negotiations of Terms of Union in 1948
Secretary of State April 1, 1949–53

Cashin,
Major Peter J.
Member of National Convention of Newfoundland 1946–48
Member Delegation to London 1947
Spokesman for Responsible Government League 1946–49

Crosbie, Chesley A.
Member National Convention of Newfoundland 1946–48
Member Delegation to London 1947
Leader of Party for Economic Union with U.S. 1948
Member Delegation to Ottawa to negotiate final Terms of
Union in 1948

Emerson,
Sir Edward
Commissioner of Justice and Defence Newfoundland 1940–44
Administrator and Chief Justice of Newfoundland 1945–49

Fox, C.F. Chairman
National Convention of Newfoundland Sept–Nov 1946

Gruchy, Philip
Vice-president Anglo-Newfoundland Development Co. Ltd.
Member Newfoundland Delegation to Ottawa to negotiate final
Terms of Union in 1948

Halley, James T., Q.C. Co-founder Party for Economic Union with America

Higgins, Gordon F.
Member National Convention of Newfoundland 1946–48
Member Delegation to Ottawa 1947

Hollett, Malcolm
Member of the National Convention of Newfoundland 1946–48
Member of Delegation to London 1947

Jamieson, Donald
Newfoundland broadcaster Campaign Manager Party for
Economic Union with America 1948

Job, R.B.
Member National Convention of Newfoundland 1946–48
Member Delegation to Ottawa 1947

McEvoy, J.B.	Chairman of the National Convention of Newfoundland 1947–48 Member Newfoundland Delegation to Ottawa to negotiate final Terms of Union in 1948
Perlin, Albert	Columnist with the *Daily News*, St. John's, 1946–59
Pottle, H.L.	Commissioner for Home Affairs and Education Newfoundland 1947–March 1949 Minister of Welfare Provisional Government of Newfoundland April 1–May 1949
Quinton, H.W.	Commission for Home Affairs and Education Newfoundland 1947 Commission for Public Health and Welfare Newfoundland 1947–49 Minister of Public Health, Provisional Government of Newfound- land April–May 1949
Smallwood, J.R.	Member National Convention of Newfoundland 1946–48 Member Delegation to Ottawa 1947 Member of Delegation to London 1947 Campaign Manager Newfoundland Confederate Association 1948 Member Newfoundland Delegation to Ottawa to negotiate the final Terms of Union Aug–Dec 1948 Premier and Minister of Industrial Development, Provisional Government of Newfoundland April–May 1949
Walsh, Albert	Commission for Home Affairs and Education Newfoundland 1944–47 Commissioner of Justice and Defence Newfoundland 1947–49 Chairman Newfoundland Delegation to Ottawa to negotiate the Terms of Union Aug–Dec 1948 Lieutenant-Governor of Newfoundland April 1–Sept 1949
Winter, G.A.	Director T. & M. Winter Ltd, Member Newfoundland Delegation to Ottawa to negotiate final Terms of Union Aug–Dec. 1948 Minister of Finance Provisional Government of Newfoundland April–May 1949

APPENDIX B

CHRONOLOGY OF MAIN EVENTS

1832   Newfoundland wins representative government

1855   Newfoundland granted full responsible government

1907   Newfoundland granted Dominion status

1933   Responsible government suspended in Newfoundland

1934   Commission of Government takes over in Newfoundland

1938   Newfoundland Airport completed at Gander

1939   Defence of Newfoundland Act passed by Commission of Government

1940   Britain transfers control of air bases in Newfoundland to Canada

1941   First American troops arrive in St. John's, January
Leased Bases Agreement signed, March
First Canadian high commissioner appointed to Newfoundland, September

1942   Dominions Secretary Clement Attlee and Alexander Clutterbuck visit Newfoundland

1943   Goodwill Mission from Parliament of Great Britain visits Newfoundland

1945   Labour Government elected in Great Britain, July
Clement Attlee becomes prime minister of Great Britain, July
Clutterbuck arrives in Ottawa for secret talks with Canadians, October
Secretary of state for dominions affairs announces National Convention, December

1946   National Convention elected, June 21
Responsible Government League formed, December 23

1947   Delegation to London, April
Delegation to Ottawa in June–September
Canadian Terms of Union presented to Governor Macdonald

1948   National Convention rejects Confederation as choice on Referendum ballot, January
National Convention dissolves, January
Newfoundland Confederate Association formed, February 21
Economic Union with America Party formed, March 20

First Referendum Vote, June 3
Second Referendum Vote, July 22
Canada accepts results of Second Referendum, July 30
Great Britain and Commission Government accept results, July 30
Newfoundland delegates to negotiate terms with Canada appointed by
Commission of Government, August 5
Writs issued in Supreme Court of Newfoundland against Commission of
Government, November 13
Motion presented in Parliament of Great Britain calls for return of responsible
    government in Newfoundland, November 26
Ches Crosbie announces he will not sign Terms of Union, December 9
Responsible Government League presents resolution against Union to Governor
    of Newfoundland, December 10
Terms of Union signed in Ottawa, December 11

1949   A.P. Herbert tries to present Newfoundland Liberation Bill to House of Commons
    in London, January 28
Bill presented in Canadian Parliament to approve Terms of Union, February 7
Royal Assent is given to Canadian Bill approving Terms of Union, February 18
Commission of Government approves Terms of Union, February 21
Confederation ceremonies held in Ottawa and St. John's, April 1
Albert Walsh sworn in as Lieutenant-Governor of Newfoundland, April 1
Lieutenant-Governor calls on J.R. Smallwood to form provisional government,
    April 1

APPENDIX C

Maps of Dominion of Newfoundland and Labrador and Canada's Atlantic Provinces

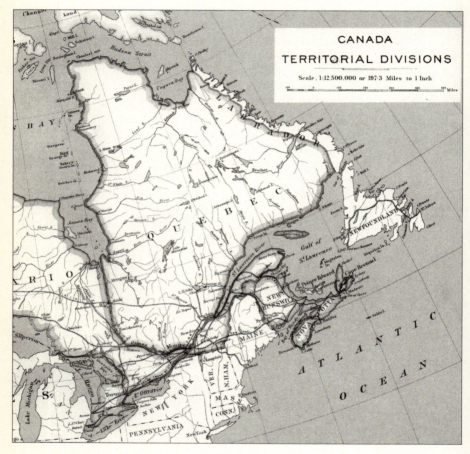

This 1915 map shows Canadian territorial claims to Labrador, which are represented as a part of Quebec with only the narrowest strip of coastline shown as belonging to Newfoundland. In 1927 the Privy Council in London confirmed King George III's grant of 1763 to Governor William Greaves "over the island of Newfoundland and the Coast of Labrador."

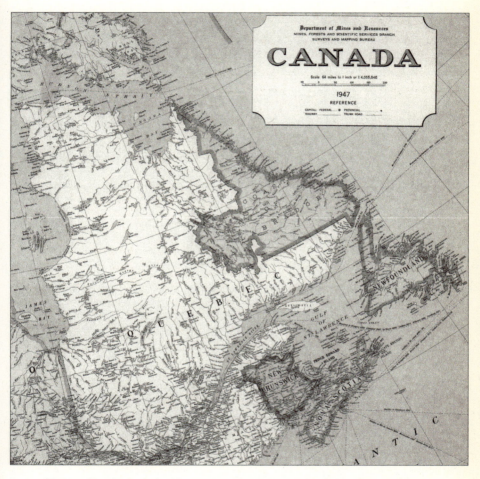

After 1927 Canadian maps for the most part represented Labrador as part of Newfoundland, though this 1947 version still refers to it as the "Coast of Labrador." Labrador is over twice the size of the island of Newfoundland. Together they are over three times the size of the Maritime provinces and a significant addition of territory and resources to Canada.

APPENDIX D

Results of First and Second Referenda

REPORT OF THE CHIEF ELECTORAL OFFICERS RELATING TO THE FIRST POLL OF THE REFERENDUM HELD JUNE 3RD, 1948

ELECTORAL DISTRICTS	NO. OF REGISTERED ELECTORS	NO. OF PERSONS VOTED JUNE 3RD	% VOTE	VOTES FOR COMMISSION OF GOVERNMENT	VOTES FOR CONFEDERATION WITH CANADA	VOTES FOR RESPONSIBLE GOVERNMENT	% FOR COMMISSION OF GOVERNMENT	% FOR CONFEDERATION WITH CANADA	% FOR RESPONSIBLE GOVERNMENT
ST. BARBE	3,755	3,030	80.69	630	1,949	442	21.09	64.32	14.759
WHITE BAY	5,663	5,222	92.21	842	3,327	1,053	16.12	63.71	20.17
GREEN BAY	4,650	3,648	78.45	692	2,208	758	19.70	60.52	20.78
GRAND FALLS	11,458	12,500	109.79	3,025	5,070	4,477	24.05	40.37	35.59
TWILLINGATE	5,513	3,638	65.99	1,544	1,569	525	42.44	43.13	14.43
FOGO	5,652	4,226	74.77	1,004	1,978	1,164	25.65	46.81	27.54
BONAVISTA NORTH	6,743	5,116	75.87	595	3,252	1,269	11.63	63.57	24.80
BONAVISTA SOUTH	7,137	5,734	80.34	1,315	1,944	2,475	22.93	33.90	43.16
TRINITY NORTH	6,983	5,328	76.30	1,048	2,554	1,726	19.67	47.93	32.39
TRINITY SOUTH	5,915	4,386	74.15	471	2,099	1,816	10.74	47.86	41.40
CARBONEAR - BAY DE VERDE	6,843	5,388	78.74	337	2,336	2,715	6.25	43.36	50.39
HARBOUR GRACE	4,172	3,421	81.98	181	1,045	2,195	5.29	30.55	64.16
PORT DE GRAVE	4,603	3,469	75.36	242	1,409	1,319	6.98	40.62	52.40
HARBOUR MAIN - BELL ISLAND	9,168	8,103	88.38	431	982	6,690	5.32	12.12	82.56
ST. JOHN'S WEST	19,586	19,880	101.50	1,874	4,958	13,043	9.43	24.94	65.63
ST. JOHN'S EAST	16,313	16,322	100.05	1,732	3,833	10,752	10.61	23.51	65.87
FERRYLAND	3,791	3,570	94.17	134	206	3,230	3.75	5.77	90.48
PLACENTIA AND ST. MARY'S	5,699	5,127	89.96	313	780	4,034	6.10	15.21	78.68
PLACENTIA WEST	5,488	4,673	94.22	469	1,907	1,617	11.51	48.78	39.70
BURIN	5,683	4,693	82.58	372	3,687	634	7.93	78.56	13.51
FORTUNE BAY AND HERMITAGE	6,267	4,665	74.44	815	2,064	886	17.47	63.54	18.99
BURGEO AND LA POILE	4,814	3,822	79.39	607	2,780	435	15.88	72.74	11.38
ST. GEORGE'S-PORT AU PORT	6,769	6,465	95.51	1,030	3,053	2,382	15.93	47.22	36.84
HUMBER	10,745	11,508	107.84	2,367	6,225	2,996	20.43	53.72	25.85
LABRADOR	2,886	2,283	79.11	162	1,858	263	7.10	81.38	11.52
TOTAL	176,297	155,777	88.36	22,311	64,066	69,400	14.32	41.13	44.55

(Sgd.) N. Short,
Chief Electoral Officer.

I, N. Short, of St. John's, Chief Electoral Officer, hereby make oath and say that the foregoing report made under the provisions of Section 21 of the Referendum Act, 1948, is true and correct.

N. Short,
Chief Electoral Officer.

Sworn before me at St. John's this
day of   , 1948.

Justice of the Peace.

REPORT OF THE CHIEF ELECTORAL OFFICER RELATING TO THE SECOND POLL OF THE REFERENDUM HELD JULY 22ND, 1948.

Electoral Districts	No. of Registered Electors	No. of persons voted July 22nd	% Vote	Votes for Confederation with Canada	Votes for Responsible Government	% Vote for Confederation with Canada	% Vote for Responsible Government
ST. BARBE	3,755	2,986	79.52	2,353	633	78.80	21.20
WHITE BAY	5,663	5,502	97.16	4,171	1,331	75.81	24.19
GREEN BAY	4,650	3,352	72.09	2,392	960	71.36	28.64
GRAND FALLS	11,458	11,030	96.26	6,328	4,802	56.46	43.54
TWILLINGATE	5,453	3,754	68.84	2,524	830	75.25	24.75
FOGO	5,652	3,937	69.66	2,438	1,499	61.93	38.07
BONAVISTA NORTH	6,743	4,653	69.00	3,466	1,187	74.49	25.51
BONAVISTA SOUTH	7,137	5,260	73.70	2,730	2,530	51.90	48.10
TRINITY NORTH	6,983	4,844	69.37	3,153	1,691	65.09	34.91
TRINITY SOUTH	5,915	4,302	72.73	2,593	1,709	60.27	39.73
CARBONEAR-BAY DE VERDE	6,843	5,132	75.00	2,705	2,427	52.71	47.29
HARBOUR GRACE	4,173	3,201	76.71	1,206	1,995	37.68	62.32
PORT DE GRAVE	4,603	3,191	69.32	1,565	1,626	49.04	50.96
HARBOUR MAIN-BELL ISLAND	9,166	8,215	89.61	1,431	6,784	17.42	82.58
ST. JOHN'S WEST	19,586	18,706	95.51	6,193	12,513	33.11	66.89
ST. JOHN'S EAST	16,313	15,679	96.11	4,895	10,784	31.22	68.78
FERRYLAND	3,792	3,965	104.59	612	3,353	15.44	84.76
PLACENTIA AND ST. MARY'S	5,686	5,001	87.95	920	4,081	18.40	81.60
PLACENTIA WEST	5,653	3,771	66.71	2,067	1,704	54.81	45.19
BURIN	5,683	4,801	84.48	4,079	722	84.96	15.04
FORTUNE BAY AND HERMITAGE	6,267	4,515	72.04	3,675	840	81.40	18.60
BURGEO AND LAPOILE	4,814	3,707	77.00	3,296	411	88.91	11.09
ST. GEORGE'S-PORT AU PORT	6,769	6,728	99.39	3,817	2,911	56.73	43.27
HUMBER	10,748	10,378	96.56	7,133	3,245	68.73	31.27
LABRADOR	2,886	3,447	119.44	2,681	766	77.78	22.22
TOTAL	176,297	149,657	84.69	78,323	71,334	52.34	47.66

(Sgd.) N. Short,
Chief Electoral Officer.

I, N. Short, of St. John's, Chief Electoral Officer, hereby make oath and say that the foregoing report made under the provisions of Section 21 of The Referendum Act, 1948, is true and correct.

N. Short,
Chief Electoral Officer.

Sworn before me at St. John's this 26th
day of August, 1948.
    J. P. Mulcahy,
    Justice of the Peace.

APPENDIX E

Terms of Union, 1949

An Act to confirm and give effect to Terms of Union agreed between Canada and Newfoundland.

23rd March, 1949

Whereas by means of a referendum the people of Newfoundland have by a majority signified their wish to enter into confederation with Canada;

And whereas the Agreement containing Terms of Union between Canada and Newfoundland set out in the Schedule to this Act has been duly approved by the Parliament of Canada and by the Government of Newfoundland;

And whereas Canada has requested, and consented to, the enactment of an Act of the Parliament of the United Kingdom to confirm and give effect to the said Agreement, and the Senate and House of Commons of Canada in Parliament assembled have submitted an address to His Majesty praying that His Majesty may graciously be pleased to cause a Bill to be laid before the Parliament of the United Kingdom for that purpose

Be it therefore enacted by the King's Most Excellent Majesty, by and with the advice and consent of the Lords Spiritual and Temporal, and Commons, in this present Parliament assembled, and by the authority of the same, as follows:—

Confirmation of Terms of Union. **1.** The Agreement containing Terms of Union between Canada and Newfoundland set out in the Schedule to this Act is hereby confirmed and shall have the force of law notwithstanding anything in the *Constitution Acts, 1867 to 1940.*

Repeal of Newfoundland Act, 1933. **2.** In accordance with the preceding section the provisions of the *Newfoundland Act, 1933,* other than section three thereof (which relates to guarantee of certain securities of Newfoundland) shall be repealed as from the coming into force of the said Terms of Union.

Short title and citation. **3.** This Act may be cited as the Newfoundland Act.[1]

Schedule: Terms of Union of Newfoundland with Canada

MEMORANDUM OF AGREEMENT ENTERED INTO ON THE ELEVENTH DAY OF DECEMBER, 1948, BETWEEN CANADA AND NEWFOUNDLAND

Whereas a delegation appointed from its members by the National Convention of Newfoundland, a body elected by the people of Newfoundland, consulted in 1947 with the Government of Canada to ascertain what fair and equitable basis might exist for the union of Newfoundland with Canada;

Whereas, following discussions with the delegation, the Government of Canada sent to His Excellency the Governor of Newfoundland for submission to the National Convention a statement of terms which the Government of Canada would be prepared to recommend to the Parliament of Canada as a fair and equitable basis for union, should the people of Newfoundland desire to enter into confederation;

Whereas the proposed terms were debated in the National Convention in Newfoundland and were before the people of Newfoundland when, by a majority at a referendum held on the twenty-second day of July, 1948, they expressed their desire to enter into confederation with Canada;

Whereas the Governments of the United Kingdom, Canada and Newfoundland agreed after the referendum that representatives of Canada and Newfoundland should meet and settle he final terms and arrangements for the union of Newfoundland with Canada;

And whereas authorized representatives of Canada and authorized representatives of Newfoundland have settled the terms hereinafter set forth as the Terms of Union of Newfoundland with Canada:

It is therefore agreed as follows

Terms of Union.

UNION

1. On, from, and after the coming into force of these Terms (hereinafter referred to as the date of Union), Newfoundland shall form part of Canada and shall be a province thereof to be called and known as the Province of Newfoundland and Labrador.

2. The Province of Newfoundland and Labrador shall comprise the same territory as at the date of Union, that is to say, the island of Newfoundland and the islands adjacent thereto, the Coast of Labrador as delimited in the report delivered by the Judicial Committee of His Majesty's Privy Council on the first day of March, 1927, and approved by His Majesty in His Privy Council on the twenty-second day of March, 1927, and the islands adjacent to the said Coast of Labrador.

Application of the Constitution Acts.

3. The *Constitution Acts, 1867 to 1940*, shall apply to the Province of Newfoundland and Labrador in the same way, and to the like extent as they apply to the provinces heretofore comprised in Canada, as if the Province of Newfoundland and Labrador had been one of the provinces originally united except in so far as varied by these Terms and except such provisions as are in terms made or by reasonable intendment may be held to be specially applicable to or only to affect one or more and not all of the provinces originally united.

Representation in Parliament.

4. The Province of Newfoundland and Labrador shall be entitled to be represented in the Senate by six members, and in the House of Commons by seven members out of a total membership of two hundred and sixty-two.

5. Representation in the Senate and in the House of Commons shall from lime to time be altered or readjusted in accordance with the *Constitution Acts, 1867 to 1940*.

6. *(1)* Until the Parliament of Canada otherwise provides, the Province of Newfoundland and Labrador shall for the purposes of the election of members to serve in the House of Commons, be divided into the electoral divisions named and delimited in the Schedule to these Terms, and each such division shall be entitled to return one member.

    (2) For the first election of members to serve in the House of Commons, if held otherwise than as part of a general election, the Governor General in Council may cause writs to be issued and may fix the day upon which the polls shall be held, and, subject to the foregoing, the laws of Canada relating to byelections shall apply to an election held pursuant to any writ issued under this Term.

    (3) The Chief Electoral Officer shall have authority to adapt the provisions of The Dominion Elections Act, 1938, to conditions existing in the Province of Newfoundland and Labrador so as to conduct effectually the first election of members to serve in the House of Commons.

PROVINCIAL CONSTITUTION

7. The Constitution of Newfoundland as it existed immediately prior to the sixteenth day of February, 1934, is revived at the date of Union and shall, subject to these Terms and the *Constitution Acts, 1867 to 1940*, continue as the Constitution of the Province of Newfoundland and Labrador from and after the date of Union, until altered under the authority of the said Acts.

EXECUTIVE

8. *(1)* For the Province of Newfoundland and Labrador there shall be an officer styled the Lieutenant Governor, appointed by the Governor General in Council by instrument under the Great Seal of Canada.

(2) Pending the first appointment of a Lieutenant Governor for the Province of Newfoundland and Labrador and the assumption of his duties as such, the Chief Justice, or if the office of Chief Justice is vacant, the senior judge, of the Supreme Court of Newfoundland, shall execute the office and functions of Lieutenant Governor under his oath of office as such Chief Justice or senior judge.

9. The Constitution of the Executive Authority of Newfoundland as it existed immediately prior to the sixteenth day of February, 1934, shall, subject to these Terms and the *Constitution Acts, 1867 to 1940*, continue as the Constitution of the Executive Authority of the Province of Newfoundland and Labrador from and after the date of Union, until altered under the authority of the said Acts.

10. The Lieutenant Governor in Council shall as soon as may be after the date of Union adopt and provide a Great Seal of the Province of Newfoundland and Labrador and may from time to time change such seal.

11. All powers, authorities, and functions that under any statute were at or immediately prior to the date of Union vested in or exercisable by the Governor of Newfoundland, individually, or in Council, or in Commission,

   (a) as far as they are capable of being exercised after the date of Union in relation to the Government of Canada, shall be vested in and shall or may be exercised by the Governor General, with the advice, or with the advice and consent, or in conjunction with, the King's Privy Council for Canada or any member or members thereof, or by the Governor General individually, as the case requires, subject nevertheless to be abolished or altered by the Parliament of Canada under the authority of the *Constitution Acts, 1867 to 1940*; and

   (b) as far as they are capable of being exercised after the date of Union in relation to the Government of the Province of Newfoundland and Labrador, shall be vested in and shall or may be exercised by the Lieutenant Governor of the Province of Newfoundland and Labrador, with the advice, or with the advice and consent, or in conjunction with, the Executive Council of the Province of Newfoundland and Labrador or any member or members thereof, or by the Lieutenant Governor individually, as the case requires, subject nevertheless to be abolished or altered by the Legislature of the Province of Newfoundland and Labrador under the authority of the *Constitution Acts. 1867 to 1946*.

12. Until the Parliament of Canada otherwise provides, the powers, authorities, and functions vested in or imposed on any member of the Commission of Government of Newfoundland, as such member or as a Commissioner charged with the administration of a Department of the Government of Newfoundland, at or immediately prior to the date of Union in relation to matters other than those coming within the classes of subjects by the *Constitution Acts, 1867 to 1940*, assigned exclusively to the Legislature of a province, shall in the Province of Newfoundland and Labrador be vested in or imposed on such person or persons as the Governor General in Council may appoint or designate.

13. Until the Legislature of the Province of Newfoundland and Labrador otherwise provides, the powers, authorities, and functions vested in or imposed on any member of the Commission of Government of Newfoundland, as such member or as a

Commissioner charged with the administration of a Department of the Government of Newfoundland, at or immediately prior to the date of Union in relation to matters coming within the classes of subjects by the *Constitution Acts, 1867 to 1940*, assigned exclusively to the Legislature of a province, shall in the Province of Newfoundland and Labrador be vested in or imposed on such person or persons as the Lieutenant Governor in Council may appoint or designate.

LEGISLATURE

14. *(1)* Subject to paragraph two of this Term, the Constitution of the Legislature of Newfoundland as it existed immediately prior to the sixteenth day of February, 1934, shall, subject to these Terms and the *Constitution Acts, 1867 to 1940*, continue as the Constitution of the Legislature of the Province of Newfoundland and Labrador from and after the date of Union, until altered under the authority of the said Acts.

   (2) The Constitution of the Legislature of Newfoundland in so far as it relates to the Legislative Council shall not continue, but the Legislature of the Province of Newfoundland and Labrador may at any time reestablish the Legislative Council or establish a new Legislative Council.

15. *(1)* Until the Legislature of the Province of Newfoundland and Labrador otherwise provides, the powers, authorities, and functions vested in or imposed on a Minister or other public officer or functionary under any statute of Newfoundland relating to the Constitution of the Legislature of Newfoundland as it existed immediately prior to the sixteenth day of February, 1934, shall, subject to these Terms and the *Constitution Acts, 1867 to 1940*, be vested in or imposed on such person or persons as the Lieutenant Governor in Council may appoint or designate.

   (2) Until the Legislature of the Province of Newfoundland and Labrador otherwise provides,

   (a) the list of electors prepared pursuant to The List of Electors Act, 1947, shall be deemed to be the list of electors for the purposes of The Election Act, 1913, subject to the provisions of The Election Act, 1913, respecting supplementary lists of electors;

   (b) the franchise shall be extended to female British subjects who have attained the full age of twentyone years and are otherwise qualified as electors;

   (c) the Coast of Labrador together with the islands adjacent thereto shall constitute an additional electoral district to be known as Labrador and to be represented by one member, and residents of the said district who are otherwise qualified as electors shall be entitled to vote; and

   (d) the Lieutenant Governor in Council may by proclamation defer any election in the electoral district of Labrador for such period as may be specified in the proclamation

16. The Legislature of the Province of Newfoundland and Labrador shall be called together not later than four months after the date of Union.

Education.

17. *(1)* In lieu of section ninety-three of the *Constitution Act, 1867*, this Term shall apply in respect of the Province of Newfoundland and Labrador:

    (2) In and for the Province of Newfoundland and Labrador, the Legislature shall have exclusive authority to make laws in relation to education but shall provide for courses in religion that are not specific to a religious denomination.

    (3) Religious observances shall be permitted in a school where requested by parents.[2]

Continuation of Laws.

GENERAL

18. *(1)* Subject to these Terms, all laws in force in Newfoundland at or immediately prior to the date of Union shall continue therein as if the Union had not been made, subject nevertheless to be repealed, abolished, or altered by the Parliament of Canada or by the Legislature of the Province of Newfoundland and Labrador according to the authority of the Parliament or of the Legislature under the *Constitution Acts, 1867 to 1940*, and all orders, rules, and regulations made under any such laws shall likewise continue, subject to be revoked or amended by the body or person that made such orders, rules, or regulations or the body or person that has power to make such orders, rules, or regulations alter the date of Union, according to their respective authority under the *Constitution Acts, 1867 to 1940*.

    (2) Statutes of the Parliament of Canada in force at the date of Union, or any part thereof, shall come into force in the Province of Newfoundland and Labrador on a day or days to be fixed by Act of the Parliament of Canada or by proclamation of the Governor General in Council issued from time to time, and any such proclamation may provide for the repeal of any of the laws of Newfoundland that

        (a) are of general application;

        (b) relate to the same subjectmatter as the statute or pan thereof so proclaimed; and

        (c) could be repealed by the Parliament of Canada under paragraph one of this Term

    (3) Notwithstanding anything in these Terms, the Parliament of Canada may with the consent of the Legislature of the Province of Newfoundland and Labrador repeal any law in force in Newfoundland at the date of Union.

    (4) Except as otherwise provided by these Terms, all courts of civil and criminal jurisdiction and all legal commissions, powers, authorities, and functions, and all officers and functionaries, judicial, administrative, and ministerial, existing in Newfoundland at or immediately prior to the date of Union, shall continue in the Province of Newfoundland and Labrador as if the Union had not been made, until altered, abolished, revoked, terminated, or dismissed by the appropriate authority under the *Constitution Acts, 1867 to 1940*.

SUPPLY

19. Any statute of Newfoundland enacted prior to the date of Union for granting to His Majesty sums of money for defraying expenses of, and for other purposes relating to, the public service of Newfoundland, for the financial year ending the thirty-first day of March, one thousand nine hundred and fifty, shall have effect after the date of Union according to its terms, until otherwise provided by the Legislature of the Province of Newfoundland and Labrador

PATENTS

20. *(1)* Subject to this Term, Canada will provide that letters patent for inventions issued under the laws of Newfoundland prior to the date of Union shall be deemed to have been issued under the laws of Canada, as of the date and for the term thereof.

(2) Canada will provide further that in the event of conflict between letters patent for an invention issued under the laws of Newfoundland prior to the date of Union and letters patent for an invention issued under the laws of Canada prior to the date of Union.

(a) the letters patent issued under the laws of Newfoundland shall have the same force and effect in the Province of Newfoundland and Labrador as if the Union had not been made, and all rights and privileges acquired under or by virtue thereof may continue to be exercised or enjoyed in the Province of Newfoundland and Labrador as if the Union had not been made; and

(b) the letters patent issued under the laws of Canada shall have the same force and effect in any part of Canada other than the Province of Newfoundland and Labrador as if the Union had not been made, and all rights and privileges acquired under or by virtue thereof may continue to be exercised or enjoyed in any part of Canada other than the Province of Newfoundland and Labrador as if the Union had not been made.

(3) The laws of Newfoundland existing at the date of Union shall continue to apply in respect of applications for the grant of letters patent for inventions under the laws of Newfoundland pending at the date of Union, and any letters patent for inventions issued upon such applications shall, for the purposes of this Term, be deemed to have been issued under the laws of Newfoundland prior to the date of Union; and letters patent for inventions issued under the laws of Canada upon applications pending at the date of Union shall, for the purposes of this Term, be deemed to have been issued under the laws of Canada prior to the date of Union.

(4) Nothing in this Term shall be construed to prevent the Parliament of Canada from providing that no claims for infringement of a patent issued in Canada prior to the date of Union shall be entertained by any court against any person for anything done in Newfoundland prior to the date of Union in respect of the invention protected by such patent, and that no claims for infringement of a patent issued in Newfoundland prior to the date of Union shall be entertained by any court against any person for anything done in Canada prior to the date of Union in respect of the invention protected by such patent.

TRADE MARKS

21. *(1)* Canada will provide that the registration of a trade mark under the laws of Newfoundland prior to the date of Union shall have the same force and effect in the Province of Newfoundland and Labrador as if the Union had not been made, and all rights and privileges acquired under or by virtue thereof may continue to be exercised or enjoyed in the Province of Newfoundland and Labrador as if the Union had not been made

(2) The laws of Newfoundland existing at the date of Union shall continue to apply in respect of applications for the registration of trade marks under the laws of Newfoundland pending at the date of Union and any trade marks registered upon such applications shall, for the purposes of this Term, be deemed to have been registered under the laws of Newfoundland prior to the date of Union

FISHERIES

22. *(1)* In this Term, the expression "Fisheries Laws" means the Act No. 11 of 1936, entitled "An Act for the Creation of the Newfoundland Fisheries Board", the Act No. 14 of 1936, entitled "An Act to Prevent the Export of Fish Without Licence", the Act No. 32 of 1936, entitled "An Act to Amend the Newfoundland Fisheries Board Act (No. 11 of 1936)", the Act No. 37 of 1938, entitled "An Act Further to Amend the Newfoundland Fisheries Board Act, 1936", the Act No. 10 of 1942, entitled "An Act Respecting Permits for the Exportation of Salt Fish", the Act No. 39 of 1943, entitled "An Act Further to Amend the Newfoundland Fisheries Board Act, 1936", the Act No. 16 of 1944, entitled "An Act Further to Amend the Newfoundland Fisheries Board Acts, 193638", and the Act No. 42 of 1944, entitled "An Act Further to Amend the Newfoundland Fisheries Board Act, 1936", in so far as they relate to the export marketing of salted fish from Newfoundland to other countries or to any provinces of Canada.

(2) Subject to this Term, all Fisheries Laws and all orders, rules, and regulations made thereunder shall continue in force in the Province of Newfoundland and Labrador as if the Union had not been made, for a period of five years from the date of Union and thereafter until the Parliament of Canada otherwise provides, and shall continue to be administered by the Newfoundland Fisheries Board; and the costs involved in the maintenance of the Board and the administration of the Fisheries Laws shall be borne by the Government of Canada.

(3) The powers, authorities, and functions vested in or imposed on the Governor in Commission or the Commissioner for Natural Resources under any of the Fisheries Laws shall after the date of Union respectively be vested in or imposed on the Governor General in Council and the Minister of Fisheries of Canada or such other Minister as the Governor General in Council may designate.

(4) Any of the Fisheries Laws may be repealed or altered at any time within the period of five years from the date of Union by the Parliament of Canada with the consent of the LieutenantGovernor in Council of the Province of Newfoundland and Labrador and all orders, rules, and regulations made under the authority of

any Fisheries Laws may be revoked or altered by the body or person that made them or, in relation to matters to which paragraph three of this Term applies, by the body or person that under the said paragraph three has power to make such orders, rules, or regulations under the Fisheries Laws after the date of Union.

(5) The Chairman of the Newfoundland Fisheries Board or such other member of the Newfoundland Fisheries Board as the Governor General in Council may designate shall perform in the Province of Newfoundland and Labrador the duties of Chief Supervisor and Chief Inspector of the Department of Fisheries of the Government of Canada, and employees of the Newfoundland Fisheries Board shall become employees in that Department in positions comparable to those of the employees in that Department in other parts of Canada.

(6) Terms eleven, twelve, thirteen and eighteen are subject to this Term.

Financial Terms.

DEBT

23. Canada will assume and provide for the servicing and retirement of the stock issued or to be issued on the security of Newfoundland pursuant to The Loan Act, 1933, of Newfoundland and will take over the Sinking Fund established under that Act.

FINANCIAL SURPLUS

24. *(1)* In this Term the expression "financial surplus" means the balances standing to the credit of the Newfoundland Exchequer at the date of Union (less such sums as may be required to discharge accounts payable at the date of Union in respect of appropriations for the public services) and any public moneys or public revenue (including loans and advances referred to in Term twenty five) in respect of any matter, thing, or period prior to the date of Union recovered by the Government of the Province of Newfoundland and Labrador subsequent to the date of Union.

(2) Newfoundland will retain its financial surplus subject to the following conditions:

(a) one third of the surplus shall be set aside during the first eight years from the date of Union, on deposit with the Government of Canada, to be withdrawn by the Government of the Province of Newfoundland and Labrador only for expenditures on current account to facilitate the maintenance and improvement of Newfoundland public services, and any portion of this onethird of the surplus remaining unspent at the end of the eightyear period shall become available to the Province of Newfoundland and Labrador without the foregoing restriction;

(b) the remaining two-thirds of the surplus shall be available to the Government of the Province of Newfoundland and Labrador for the development of resources and for the establishment or extension of public services within the Province of Newfoundland and Labrador; and

(c) no part of the surplus shall be used to subsidize the production or sale of products of the Province of Newfoundland and Labrador in unfair competition with similar products of other provinces of Canada, but nothing in this paragraph shall

preclude the Province of Newfoundland and Labrador from assisting industry by developmental loans on reasonable conditions or by ordinary provincial administrative services.

(3) The Government of the Province of Newfoundland and Labrador will have the right within one year from the date of Union to deposit with the Government of Canada all or any part of its financial surplus held in dollars and on the thirty-first day of March and the thirtieth day of September in each year to receive with respect thereto interest at the rate of two and five-eights per centum per annum during a maximum period of ten years from the date of Union on the minimum balance outstanding at any time during the six-month period preceding payment of interest

LOANS

25. *(1)* The Province of Newfoundland and Labrador will retain its interest in, and any securities arising from or attaching to, any loans or advances of public funds made by the Government of Newfoundland prior to the date of Union.

(2) Unless otherwise agreed to by the Government of Canada, paragraph one of this Term shall not apply to any loans or advances relating to any works, property, or services taken over by Canada pursuant to Term thirty-one or Term thirty-three.

SUBSIDIES

26. Canada will pay to the Province of Newfoundland and Labrador the following subsidies:

(a) an annual subsidy of $180,000 and an annual subsidy equal to 80 cents per head of the population of the Province of Newfoundland and Labrador (being taken at 325,000 until the first decennial census after the date of Union), subject to be increased to conform to the scale of grants authorized by the Constitution Act, 1907, for the local purposes of the Province and support of its Government and Legislature, but in no year shall sums payable under his paragraph be less than those payable in the first year after the date of Union; and

(b) an additional annual subsidy of $1,100,000 payable for the like purposes as the various fixed annual allowances and subsidies provided by statutes of the Parliament of Canada from time to time for the Provinces of Nova Scotia, New Brunswick, and Prince Edward Island or any of them and in recognition of the special problems of the Province of Newfoundland and Labrador by reason of geography and its sparse and scattered population.

TAX AGREEMENT

27. *(1)* The Government of Canada will forthwith after the date of Union make an offer to the Government of the Province of Newfoundland and Labrador to enter into a tax agreement for the rental to the Government of Canada of the income, corporation income, and corporation tax fields, and the succession duties tax field.

(2) The offer to be made under this Term will be similar to the offers to enter into tax agreements made to other provinces, necessary changes being made to adapt the offer to circumstances arising out of the Union, except that the offer will provide

that the agreement may be entered into either for a number of fiscal years expiring at the end of the fiscal year in 1952, as in the case of other provinces, or for a number of fiscal years expiring at the end of the fiscal year in 1957, at the option of the Government of the Province of Newfoundland and Labrador, but if the Government of the Province of Newfoundland and Labrador accepts the latter option the agreement will provide that the subsequent entry into a lax agreement by the Government of Canada the any other province will not entitle the Government of the Province of Newfoundland and Labrador to any alteration in the terms of its agreement.

(3) The offer of the Government of Canada to be made under this Term may be accepted by the Government of the Province of Newfoundland and Labrador within nine months after the date of the offer but if it is not so accepted will thereupon expire.

(4) The Government of the Province of Newfoundland and Labrador shall not by any agreement entered into pursuant to this Term be required to impose on any person or corporation taxation repugnant to the provisions of any contract entered into with such person or corporation before the date of the agreement and subsisting at the date of the agreement.

(5) If the Province of Newfoundland and Labrador enters into a tax agreement pursuant to this Term the subsidies payable under Term twenty-six will, as in the case of similar subsidies to other provinces, be included in the computation of tax agreement payments.

TRANSITIONAL GRANTS

28. *(1)* In order to facilitate the adjustment of Newfoundland to the status of a province of Canada and the development by the Province of Newfoundland and Labrador of revenue producing services, Canada will pay to the Province of Newfoundland and Labrador each year during the first twelve years after the date of Union a transitional grant as follows, payment in each year to be made in equal quarterly installments commencing on the first day of April, namely,

First year	$ 6,500,000
Second year	6,500,000
Third year	6,500,000
Fourth year	5,650,000
Fifth year	4,800,000
Sixth year	3,950,000
Seventh year	3,100,000
Eighth year	2,250,000
Ninth year	1,400,000
Tenth year	1,050,000
Eleventh year	700,000
Twelfth year	350,000

(2) The Government of the Province of Newfoundland and Labrador will have the right to leave on deposit with the Government of Canada any portion of the transitional grant for the first eight years with the right to withdraw all or any portion thereof in any subsequent year and on the thirty-first day of March and the thirtieth day of September in each year to receive in respect of any amounts so left on deposit interest at the rate of two and five eights per centum per annum up to a maximum period of ten years from the date of Union on the minimum balance outstanding at any time during the six-month period preceding payment of interest.

REVIEW OF FINANCIAL POSITION

29. In view of the difficulty of predicting with sufficient accuracy the financial consequences to Newfoundland of becoming a province of Canada, the Government of Canada will appoint a Royal Commission within eight years from the date of Union to review the financial position of the Province of Newfoundland and Labrador and to recommend the form and scale of additional financial assistance, if any, that may be required by the Government of the Province of Newfoundland and Labrador to enable it to continue public services at the levels and standards reached subsequent to the date of Union, without resorting to taxation more burdensome, having regard to capacity to pay, than that obtaining generally in the region comprising the Maritime Provinces of Nova Scotia, New Brunswick, and Prince Edward Island.

Miscellaneous Provisions.

SALARIES OF LIEUTENANT GOVERNOR AND JUDGES

30. The salary of the Lieutenant Governor and the salaries, allowances, and pensions of the judges of such superior, district, and county courts as are now or may hereafter be constituted in the Province of Newfoundland and Labrador shall be fixed and provided by the Parliament of Canada.

PUBLIC SERVICES, WORKS AND PROPERTY

31. At the date of Union, or as soon thereafter as practicable, Canada will take over the following services and will as from the date of Union relieve the Province of Newfoundland and Labrador of the public costs incurred in respect of each service taken over, namely,

> *(a)* the Newfoundland Railway, including steamship and other marine services;
> *(b)* The Newfoundland Hotel, if requested by the Government of the Province of Newfoundland and Labrador within six months from the date of Union:
> *(c)* postal and publicly-owned telecommunication services;
> *(d)* civil aviation, including Gander Airport;
> *(e)* customs and excise;
> *(f)* defence;
> *(g)* protection and encouragement of fisheries and operation of bait services;
> *(h)* geological, topographical, geodetic, and hydrographic surveys;

(i) lighthouses, fog alarms, buoys, beacons, and other public works and services in aid of navigation and shipping;

(j) marine hospitals, quarantine, and the care of shipwrecked crews;

(k) the public radio broadcasting system; and

(i) other public services similar in kind to those provided at the date of Union for the people of Canada generally.

32. *(1)* Canada will maintain in accordance with the traffic offering a freight and passenger steamship service between North Sydney and Port aux Basques, which, on completion of a motor highway between Corner Brook and Port aux Basques, will include suitable provision for the carriage of motor vehicles:

(2) For the purpose of railway rate regulation the Island of Newfoundland will be included in the Maritime region of Canada, and through-traffic moving between North Sydney and Port aux Basques will be treated as all-rail traffic.

(3) All legislation of the Parliament of Canada providing for special rates on traffic moving within, into, or out of, the Maritime region will as far as appropriate, be made applicable to the Island of Newfoundland.

33. The following public works and property of Newfoundland shall become the property of Canada when the service concerned is taken over by Canada, subject to any trusts existing in respect thereof, and to any interest other than that of Newfoundland in the same, namely,

(a) the Newfoundland Railway, including rights of way, wharves, drydocks, and other real property, rolling stock, equipment, ships, and other personal property;

(b) the Newfoundland Airport at Gander, including buildings and equipment, together with any other property used for the operation of the Airport;

(c) the Newfoundland Hotel and equipment;

(d) public harbours, wharves, breakwaters, and aids to navigation;

(e) bait depots and the motor vessel Malakoff;

(f) military and naval property, stores, and equipment;

(g) public dredges and vessels except those used for services that remain the responsibility of the Province of Newfoundland and Labrador and except the nine motor vessels known as the Clarenville boats;

(h) the public telecommunication system, including rights of way, land lines, cables, telephones, radio stations, and other real and personal property;

(i) real and personal property of the Broadcasting Corporation of Newfoundland; and

(j) subject to the provisions of Term thirty-four, customs houses and post-offices and generally all public works and property, real and personal, used primarily for services taken over by Canada.

34. Where at the date of Union any public buildings of Newfoundland included in paragraph *(i)* of Term thirty-three are used partly for services taken over by Canada and partly for services of the Province of Newfoundland and Labrador the following provisions shall apply:

(a) where more than half the floor space of a building is used for services taken over by Canada the building shall become the property of Canada and where

more than half the floor space of a building is used for services of the Province of Newfoundland and Labrador the building shall remain the property of the Province of Newfoundland and Labrador;

(b) Canada shall be entitled to rent from the Province of Newfoundland and Labrador on terms to be mutually agreed such space in the buildings owned by the Province of Newfoundland and Labrador as is used for the services taken over by Canada and the Province of Newfoundland and Labrador shall be entitled to rent from Canada on terms to be mutually agreed such space in the buildings owned by Canada as is used for the services of the Province of Newfoundland and Labrador;

(c) the division of buildings for the purposes of this Term shall be made by agreement between the Government of Canada and the Government of the Province of Newfoundland and Labrador as soon as practicable after the date of Union; and

(d) if the division in accordance with the foregoing provisions results in either Canada or the Province of Newfoundland and Labrador having a total ownership that is substantially out of proportion to the total floor space used for its services an adjustment of the division will be made by mutual agreement between the two Governments.

35. Newfoundland public works and property not transferred to Canada by or under these Terms will remain the property of the Province of Newfoundland and Labrador.

36. Without prejudice to the legislative authority of the Parliament of Canada under the *Constitution Acts, 1867 to 1940*, any works, property, or services taken over by Canada pursuant to these Terms shall thereupon be subject to the legislative authority of the Parliament of Canada.

Natural Resources

37. All lands, mines, minerals, and royalties belonging to Newfoundland at the date of Union, and all sums then due or payable for such lands, mines, minerals, or royalties, shall belong to the Province of Newfoundland and Labrador, subject to any trusts existing in respect thereof, and to any interest other than that of the Province in the same.

Veterans

38. Canada will make available to Newfoundland and Labrador veterans the following benefits, on the same basis as they are from time to time available to Canadian veterans, as if the Newfoundland and Labrador veterans had served in His Majesty's Canadian forces, namely,

(a) The War Veterans' Allowance Act, 1946, free hospitalization and treatment, and civil service preference will be extended to Newfoundland and Labrador veterans who served in the First World War or the Second World War or both;

(b) Canada will assume as from the date of Union the Newfoundland pension liability in respect of the First World War, and in respect of the Second World War Canada will assume as from the date of Union the cost of supplementing disability and dependants' pensions paid by the Government of the United

Kingdom or an Allied country to Newfoundland and Labrador veterans up to the level of the Canadian rates of pensions, and, in addition, Canada will pay pensions arising from disabilities that are pensionable under Canadian law but not pensionable either under the laws of the United Kingdom or under the laws of an Allied country;

(c) The Veterans' Land Act, 1942, Part IV of the Unemployment Insurance Act, 1940, The Veterans' Business and Professional Loans Act, and The Veterans Insurance Act will be extended to Newfoundland and Labrador veterans who served in the Second World War;

(d) A reestablishment credit will be made available to Newfoundland and Labrador veterans who served in the Second World War equal to the reestablishment credit that might have been made available to them under The War Service Grants Act, 1944, if their service in the Second World War had been service in the Canadian forces, less the amount of any pecuniary benefits of the same nature granted or paid by the Government of any country other than Canada;

(e) Canada will assume, as from the date of Union, the cost of vocational and educational training of Newfoundland and Labrador veterans of the Second World War on the same basis as if they had served in His Majesty's Canadian forces; and

(f) Sections six, seven, and eight of The Veterans Rehabilitation Act will be extended to Newfoundland and Labrador veterans of the Second World War who have not received similar benefits from the Government of any country other than Canada.

PUBLIC SERVANTS

39. *(1)* Employees of the Government of Newfoundland in the services taken over by Canada pursuant to these Terms will be offered employment in these services or in similar Canadian services under the terms and conditions from time to time governing employment in those services, but without reduction in salary or loss of pension rights acquired by reason of service in Newfoundland.

(2) Canada will provide the pensions for such employees so that the employees will not be prejudiced, and the Government of the Province of Newfoundland and Labrador will reimburse Canada for the pensions for, or at its option make to Canada contributions in respect of, the service of these employees with the Government of Newfoundland prior to the date of Union, but these payments or contributions will be such that the burden on the Government of the Province of Newfoundland and Labrador in respect of pension rights acquired by reason of service in Newfoundland will not be increased by reason of the transfer.

(3) Pensions of employees of the Government of Newfoundland who were retired on pension before the service concerned is taken over by Canada will remain the responsibility of the Province of Newfoundland and Labrador.

WELFARE AND OTHER PUBLIC SERVICES

40. Subject to these Terms, Canada will extend to the Province of Newfoundland and Labrador, on the same basis and subject to the same terms and conditions as in the case of other provinces of Canada, the welfare and other public services provided from time to time by Canada for the people of Canada generally, which, in addition to the veterans' benefits, unemployment insurance benefits, and merchant seamen benefits set out in Terms thirty-eight, forty-one, and forty-two respectively, include family allowances under The Family Allowances Act, 1944, unemployment insurance under The Unemployment Insurance Act, 1940, sick mariners' benefits for merchant seamen and fishermen under the Canada Shipping Act, 1934, assistance for housing under The National Housing Act, 1944, and, subject to the Province of Newfoundland and Labrador entering into the necessary agreements or making the necessary contributions, financial assistance under The National Physical Fitness Act for carrying out plans of physical fitness, health grants, and contributions under the Old Age Pensions Act for old age pensions and pensions for the blind.

UNEMPLOYMENT INSURANCE

41. *(1)* Subject to this Term, Canada will provide that residents of the Province of Newfoundland and Labrador in insurable employment who lose their employment within six months prior to the date of Union and are still unemployed at that date, or who lose their employment within a two-year period after that date, will be entitled for a period of six months from the date of Union or six months from the date of unemployment, whichever is the later, to assistance on the same scale and under the same conditions as unemployment insurance benefits.

    (2) The rates of payment will be based on the individual's wage record for the three months preceding his loss of employment, and to qualify for assistance a person must have been employed in insurable employment for at least thirty per centum of the working days within the period of three months preceding his loss of employment or thirty per centum of the working days within the period since the date of Union, whichever period is the longer.

MERCHANT SEAMEN

42. *(1)* Canada will make available to Newfoundland and Labrador merchant seamen who served in the Second World War on British ships or on ships of Allied countries employed in service essential to the prosecution of the war, the following benefits, on the same basis as they are from time to time available to Canadian merchant seamen, as if they had served on Canadian ships, namely,

    (a) disability and dependants' pensions will be paid, if disability occurred as a result of enemy action or counteraction, including extraordinary marine hazards occasioned by the war, and a Newfoundland and Labrador merchant seaman in receipt of a pension from the Government of the United Kingdom or an Allied country will be entitled, during residence in Canada, to have his pension raised to the Canadian level; and

(b) free hospitalization and treatment, vocational training, The Veterans' Land Act, 1942, and The Veterans Insurance Act will be extended to disability pensioners.

(2) Vocational training, Part IV of The Unemployment Insurance Act, 1940, and The Veterans Insurance Act will be extended to Newfoundland and Labrador merchant seamen who were eligible for a Special Bonus or a War Service Bonus, on the same basis as if they were Canadian merchant seamen.

(3) The Unemployment Insurance Act, 1940, and The Merchant Seamen Compensation Act will be applied to Newfoundland and Labrador merchant seamen as they are applied to other Canadian merchant seamen.

CITIZENSHIP

43. Suitable provision will be made for the extension of the Canadian citizenship laws to the Province of Newfoundland and Labrador.

DEFENCE ESTABLISHMENTS

44. Canada will provide for the maintenance in the Province of Newfoundland and Labrador of appropriate reserve units of the Canadian defence forces, which will include the Newfoundland Regiment.

ECONOMIC SURVEY

45. *(1)* Should the Government of the Province of Newfoundland and Labrador institute an economic survey of the Province of Newfoundland and Labrador with a view to determining what resources may profitably be developed and what new industries may be established or existing industries expanded, the Government of Canada will make available the services of its technical employees and agencies to assist in the work.

(2) As soon as may be practicable after the date of Union, the Government of Canada will make a special effort to collect and make available statistical and scientific data about the natural resources and economy of the Province of Newfoundland and Labrador, in order to bring such information up to the standard attained for the other provinces of Canada.

OLEOMARGARINE

46. *(1)* Oleomargarine or margarine may be manufactured or sold in the Province of Newfoundland and Labrador after the date of the Union and the Parliament of Canada shall not prohibit or restrict such manufacture or sale except at the request of the Legislature of the Province of Newfoundland, but nothing in this Term shall affect the power of the Parliament of Canada to require compliance with standards of quality applicable throughout Canada.

(2) Unless the Parliament of Canada otherwise provides or unless the sale and manufacture in, and the interprovincial movement between, all provinces of Canada other than Newfoundland and Labrador, of oleomargarine and margarine, is lawful

under the laws of Canada, oleomargarine or margarine shall not be sent, shipped, brought, or carried from the Province of Newfoundland and Labrador into any other province of Canada.

INCOME TAXES

47. In order to assist in the transition to payment of income tax on a current basis Canada will provide in respect of persons (including corporations) resident in Newfoundland at the date of Union, who were not resident in Canada in 1949 prior to the date of Union, and in respect of income that under the laws of Canada in force immediately prior to the date of Union was not liable to taxation, as follows:

    (a) that prior to the first day of July, 1949, no payment will be required or deduction made from such income on account of income tax;

    (b) that for income tax purposes no person shall be required to report such income for any period prior to the date of Union;

    (c) that no person shall be liable to Canada for income tax in respect to such income for any period prior to the date of Union; and

    (d) that for individuals an amount of income tax for the 1949 taxation year on income for the period after the date of Union shall be forgiven so that the tax on all earned income and on investment income of not more than $2,250 will be reduced to one-half the tax that would have been payable for the whole year if the income for the period prior to the date of Union were at the same rate as that subsequent to such date.

STATUTE OF WESTMINSTER

48. From and after the date of Union the *Statute of Westminster, 1931,* shall apply to the Province of Newfoundland and Labrador as it applies to the other provinces of Canada.

SAVING

49. Nothing in these Terms shall be construed as relieving any person from any obligation with respect to the employment of Newfoundland labour incurred or assumed in return for any concession or privilege granted or conferred by the Government of Newfoundland prior to the date of Union.

COMING INTO FORCE

50. These terms are agreed to subject to their being approved by the Parliament of Canada and the Government of Newfoundland; shall take effect notwithstanding the Newfoundland Act, 1933, or any instrument issued pursuant thereto; and shall come into force immediately before the expiration of the thirty-first day of March, 1949, if His Majesty has theretofore given His Assent to an Act of the Parliament of the United Kingdom of Great Britain and Northern Ireland confirming the same.

Signed in duplicate at Ottawa this eleventh day of December, 1948.

On behalf of Canada:
(signed) LOUIS S. ST. LAURENT
(signed BROOKE CLAXTON

On behalf of Newfoundland:
(signed) ALBERT J . WALSH
(signed) F. GORDON BRADLEY
(signed) PHILIP GRUCHY
(signed) JOHN P. MCEVOY
(signed) JOSEPH R. SMALLWOOD
(signed) G.A. WINTER

SCHEDULE

In this Schedule the expression "District" means District as named and delimited in the Act 22 George V, Chapter 7 entitled "An Act to amend Chapter 2 of the Consolidated Statutes of Newfoundland (Third Series) entitled 'Of the House of Assembly'"

Grand Falls-White Bay: shall consist of the Districts of White Bay, Green Bay, and Grand Falls, and all the territory within a radius of five miles of the Railway Station at Gander, together with the Coast of Labrador and the Islands adjacent thereto.

Bonavista-Twillingate: shall consist of the Districts of Twillingate, Fogo, Bonavista North, and Bonavista South, but shall not include any part of the territory within a radius of five miles from the Railway Station at Gander.

Trinity-Conception: shall consist of the Districts of Trinity North, Trinity South, Carbonear-Bay de Verde, Harbour Grace, and Port de Grave.

St. John's East: shall consist of the District of Harbour MainBell Island and that part of the Province bounded as follows, that is to say: By a line commencing at a point where the centre line of Beck's Cove Hill intersects the North shore of the Harbour of St. John's, thence following the centre line of Beck's Cove Hill to the centre of Duckworth Street, thence westerly along the centre line of Duckworth Street to the centre of Theatre Hill, thence following the centre line of Theatre Hill to the Centre of Carter's Hill, thence following the centre line of Carter's Hill and Carter's Street to the centre of Freshwater Road, thence following the centre line of Freshwater Road to its intersection with the centre of Kenmount Road, and thence along the centre line of Kenmount Road to its intersection with the North Eastern boundary of the District of Harbour MainBell Island, thence along the said North Eastern boundary of the District of Harbour MainBell Island to the shore of Conception Bay and thence following the coastline around Cape St. Francis and on to the Narrows of St. John's Harbour and continuing along by the North Shore of St. John's Harbour to a point on the North shore of the said Harbour intersected by the centre line of Beck's Cove Hill, the point of commencement.

St. John's West: shall consist of the Districts of Placentia St. Mary's and Ferryland, and that part of the Province bounded as follows, that is to say: By a line commencing at the Motion Head of Petty Harbour and running in a straight line to the Northern Goulds Bridge (locally known as Doyle's Bridge) thence following the centre line of Doyle's Road to Short's Road, thence in a straight line to a point one mile west of Quigley's, thence in a straight line to the point where the North Eastern boundary of the District of Harbour MainBell Island intersects Kenmount Road, thence along the centre line of Kenmount Road and Freshwater Road to Carter's Street, thence down the centre line of Carter's Street and Carter's Hill to Theatre Hill and thence along the centre line of said Theatre Hill to the centre line of Duckworth Street and thence easterly along the centre line of Duckworth Street to the top of Beck's Cove Hill, thence from the centre line of said Beck's Cove Hill to the shore of St. John's Harbour and thence following the shore of St. John's Harbour and, passing through the Narrows by the North of Forth Amherst and thence following the coastline Southerly to the Motion Head of Petty Harbour, the point of commencement.

Burin-Burgeo: shall consist of the Districts of Placentia West, Burin, Fortune Bay-Hermitage, and Burgeo and La Poile and all the unorganized territory bounded on the North and West by the District of Grand Falls, on the South by the Districts of Burgeo and La Poile and Fortune Bay-Hermitage, on the East by the Districts of Trinity North, Bonavista South and Bonavista North.

Humber-St. George's: consist of the Districts of St. George's Port au Port, Humber, and St. Barbe, and all the unorganized territory bounded on the North by the District of Humber, on the East by the District of Grand Falls, on the South by the District of Burgeo and La Poile, and on the West by the District of St. George's-Port au Port.

APPENDIX F

"Keep Up the Fince,"
Harold Paddock

1.   h'Uncle Jake Rowser was proud o' de part
    'e'd played in de birt' of our village called Beau
    An' late winter nights wi' fire all flickerin'
    De bol' tale 'e tol' een de days long ago:

2.   "Well, me zun, 't was on Zunday I virs' zeed de harbour,
    Een de vall o' de year wi' de water like oil—
    I wus zhovin' long zhore wi' me eyes on de bottom
    Lookin' vor someplace where a kettle 'ould boil,

3.   "Whin zudden I hared up een Rid Cliff a clatter—
    Like vounderin' rocks an' a pourin' o' gravel,
    An' whin I looked up where de stalligans grow
    A h'Injun wus perked on a little small level.

4.   "I dropped bot' the paddles as quick as a wizzle,
    I cocked de ol' inch-bore tucked tight 'gin me zhou'der,
    An' whin I pulled trigger zix vingers o' powder
    Kicked back wi' zich vorce dat I barely could 'old 'er.

5.   "Dat ridskin jus' zeemed to stan' stiell vor a h'instant
    Wit a bloody big miss where 'is vorehead 'ad been,
    An' din 'e jus' crumpled like cut grass een zummer
    An' vell off dat lidge like a deer I once zeen.

6.   "I loaded agin an' I looked all aroun' me
    But I zeed no more Injuns alive on dat day,
    Zo I rowed up to Long-Beach where I under a birch tree
    I boiled me kittle where de brook meets de zea.

7.   "An as I wus eatin' I noticed how nice 'twus:
    Up 'ere in een de bottom 't wus all level lan',
    "Gains win' from de zuth-eas' an' noth-eas' 'twus sheltered—
    De bes' place to zittle in all Newfoundland.

8. "Zince I'd left de Old Country dat spring wi' me new bride
    I'd been zearchin' vor timber real close to de vish;
    An', now, 'ere it wus wid lan' vor a garden
    An' close to de cod-grouns as any might wish.

9. "Well, de very nix wik, zon, I broughd up de missus
    An' we t'owed up a tilt 'gains' dat virst winter's col';
    An' dough we worked 'ard vor a vew years 'twus wort' it
    An' zince dere's come oders – til we'm ninety all tol'.

10. "Dat church on de hiell wus mos'ly my doins:
    I loves de ol' gospel an' all dat it stans vor:
    It keeps us vrom zinkin' as low as de headen,
    Dis great good be broughd whin we come 'cross de water."

11. An' Uncle Jake's body was laid to res'
    Near de new graveyard fince whose rails he had peeled,
    An' as up the Pigs-Droke dey spelled his frish pine box
    Beneat' 'is two quintals de four bearers reeled.

12. De years dey rolled pas' like de swells on the sunker
    As day after day rises and dies,
    An' children was barn and faders forgot
    As ol' nature call an' man a'ways replies.

13. Din h'up in St. John's dey decided dat Beau
    'ad need of a road along de h'eas' side,
    So whin all de fish 'ad been made for de summer
    De min below Rid-Cliff would work at low tide.

14. I was on'y a boy an' could jus' swing a pickaxe,
    I was workin' above where the gravel chute starts;
    Whin cuttin' een under to make a bank founder
    I uncovered someting dat rose up me heart.

15. 'e was lyin' all sprawl wid 'is feet stickin' upwards
    Two dark impty holes starin' back at de sky
    An' his ochre stained teet' grinned 'orrible at me,
    An' was fangs bared at dose who h'answered me cry.

16. Ol' Hard 'Arry Parsons (young Bob is 'is gran'son)
    Lit out his coarse laugh an' swung 'ard with 'is pick—
    De soun' o' de h'iron as it crushed t'rough de dry bone
    Was awful revoltin' – it nigh made me sick.

17. 'e holed up de skull de len't' of de handle
An' 'e shouteed out "h'Injun" wid all of his might;
Sich a h'icho come back from de Rid-Cliff above us
Dat all of us shivered an' looked up een fright.

18. An' outside de graveyard we dug a small 'oller—
'Twas barely knee deep (Gearge Sparkes said 'twould do)—
An' we buried de bones widout any service—
Ol' Gearge, our lay reader, said 'twas what we should do.

19. On'y Davy John said dat we shouldn' 'ave done it:
Dat de h'Injun 'ad right to be h'inside the fince,
But out good man of God turned an' looked at 'in nasty
An' as'ed 'is intintions of larnin' some since.

20. As for me, I be glad dat 'e's not een de graveyard:
I don't want no h'Injuns up dere een de sky;
So keep up de fince, boys, whin I'm gone an' rotted
So dere'll be no mistakes whin de judgemint comes by.

NOTES

Prologue

1. St. John's *Daily News*, Dec. 12, 1945.
2. Jim Halley, Personal Interviews, 2008.
3. P.V. Emrys-Evans to J.H. Thomas, June 10, 1942, in Paul A. Bridle, ed., *Documents on Relations Between Canada and Newfoundland*, vol. 2, part 1, p. 24.
4. St. John Chadwick, *Newfoundland: Island to Province*, p. xi.

Chapter One

1. St. John Chadwick, *Newfoundland: Island to Province*, pp. 5–6.
2. A.H. McLintock, "The Establishment of Constitutional Government in Newfoundland 1783–1832," in Chadwick, *Newfoundland*, p. 5.
3. D.W. Prowse, *A History of Newfoundland*, p. 466.
4. Bren Walsh, *More Than a Poor Majority*, p. 268.
5. Peter J. Cashin, "My Fight for Responsible Government," in J.R. Smallwood, ed., *The Book of Newfoundland*, vol. 3, p. 105.
6. O.D. Skelton to W.D. Herridge, Nov. 24, 1933, in Walsh, *Poor Majority*, p. 92.
7. Frederick Alderdice, "Manifesto to the Electors of Newfoundland," June 1932, in John Edward FitzGerald, ed., *Newfoundland at the Crossroads*, pp. 2–9.
8. Paul A. Bridle, ed., *Documents on Relations between Canada and Newfoundland, 1940–1949*, vol. 2, pt. 1, p. xxvii.
9. *Who Was Who*, 1971–80, Clutterbuck, p. 156, in Peter Neary, *Newfoundland in the North Atlantic World, 1929–1949*, p. 16.
10. The Report of the Newfoundland Royal Commission, chaired by Baron Amulree (Amulree Report*)* 1933, page 42.
11. Ibid., p. 43.
12. Ibid., p. 71.
13. Ibid., p. 86.
14. Ibid., pp. 223–24.
15. John Edward FitzGerald, "Dying 'Beyond Its Means,'" p. 8.
16. Neary, *Newfoundland in the North Atlantic World*, pp. 24–28.
17. C.A. Magrath to Lord Amulree, Sept. 30, 1933, LAC, Charles A. Magrath Papers, in Walsh, *Poor Majority*, p. 88.
18. F.C. Alderdice to Baron Amulree, Amulree Papers, Bodleian Library, Oxford, Dec. 2, 1933, in Peter Neary, *Newfoundland in the North Atlantic World*, p. 36.
19. Ibid., p. 36.
20. Karl E. Mayer and Shareen Blair Brysac, *Tournament of Shadows*, p. 7.
21. W.D. Herridge to O.D. Skelton, Nov. 1933, Skelton papers, LAC, in Walsh, *Poor Majority*, p. 92.
22. Bridle, ed., *Documents*, vol. 2, pt.1, p. xxix, n. 8.

23. J. Holland Rose, A.P. Newton and E.A. Benians, *The Cambridge History of the British Empire*, vol. 6, p. 683.

24. In fact, Newfoundland and Finland were the only two countries to pay off their war debt—and at what cost to Newfoundland? John FitzGerald, "'Dying Beyond Its Means': Newfoundland's War Debts, Its Loss of Self-Government, and Confederation," p. 11.

25. *Newfoundland Royal Commission Report, 1933*, paragraph 555.

26. Clement Attlee, Dec. 12, 1933, *Parliamentary Debates*, PRO, Kew, cols. 223-31, quoted in Neary, *Newfoundland in the North Atlantic World*, p. 38.

27. Morgan Jones, Dec. 12, 1933, quoted in Walsh, *Poor Majority*, p. 93.

28. J.H. Thomas, Dec. 12, 1933, ibid.

29. Neary, *Newfoundland in the North Atlantic World*, p. 26.

30. David Hale, "The Newfoundland Lesson," *International Economy Magazine*, April 28, 2003. Available at www.international-economy.com

31. Bridle, *Documents*, vol. 2, pt. 1, p. xxix.

32. Alderdice to Amulree, Amulree Papers, Bodleian Library Oxford, Dep. C. 391, p. 135, quoted in Peter Neary, *Newfoundland in the North Atlantic World, 1929–1949*, p. 42.

Chapter Two

1. Jim Halley, Personal Interviews, 2008.

2. "Agreement between the governments of the United Kingdom and the United States . . ." March 27, 1941, PRO, Cmd. 6259.

3. Lord Cranborne note, PRO, CAB 98/17, Feb. 12, 1941, in Peter Neary, *Newfoundland in the North Atlantic World*, p. 45.

4. W. Churchill to L.E. Emerson, March 1941, DO 114/111 22, p.16, in Neary, *Newfoundland in the North Atlantic World*, p. 146.

5. Neary, *Newfoundland in the North Atlantic World*, p. 144.

6. Joe Garner, *The Commonwealth Office 1925–1968*, pp. 250–51.

7. P.A. Clutterbuck memo, DO 35/740/157/53, in Neary, *Newfoundland in the North Atlantic World*, p. 108.

8. Thomas Lodge, *Dictatorship in Newfoundland*, p. 1.

9. Ibid., p. 265.

10. Paul A. Bridle, ed., *Documents on Relations between Canada and Newfoundland, 1940–1949*, vol. 2, pt. 1, pp. 5–6.

11. Governor Walwyn to E. Machtig, March 4, 1944, DO 35/1376, in Neary, *Newfoundland in the North Atlantic World*, p. 213.

12. A.B. Butt interview, April 27, 1979, Charles R. Granger Collection, LAC, MG32–C48.

13. J.W. Herbertson to Sir Charles Dickson, Sept. 23, 1939, Avia 2/2285, PRO, National Archives, Kew.

14. Ibid., Oct. 13, 1939.

15. Mackenzie King to O.D. Skelton, Aug. 28, 1940, LAC, in Walsh, *Poor Majority*, p. 305.

16. Extract from MacKenzie King Record of a meeting between Roosevelt and King in Washington, Dec. 5, 1942, quoted in Bridle, *Documents*, vol. 2, pt. 1, p. 45.

17. David Murray, ed., *Documents on Canadian External Relations, 1939–1941*, vol. 7, pt.1, pp. 10–12, in John FitzGerald, *Newfoundland at the Crossroads*, p. 22.
18. Ibid., pp. 13–16, in FitzGerald, *Newfoundland*, p. 26.
19. Walsh, *Poor Majority*, p. 19.
20. St. John's *Daily News*, Sept. 19, 1941.
21. *Fishermen-Workers Tribune*, Sept. 19, 1941, C.J. Burchell to N.A. Robertson, memorandum, LAC, MG26-31.
22. C.J. Burchell to N.A. Robertson, Dec. 11, 1941, in Bridle, *Documents*, vol. 2, pt. 1, p. 7.
23. Robertson to Burchell, Jan. 3, 1942, ibid., p. 9.
24. P.V. Emrys-Evans to Dominions Office, June 10, 1942, ibid., pp. 23–26.
25. E. Machtig to C. Attlee, June 13, 1942, ibid., pp. 26–29.
26. C.J. Burchell to N.A. Robertson, June 9, 1942, ibid., pp. 17–23.

Chapter Three

1. N.A Robertson to C.J. Burchell, Aug. 22, 1942, in Paul A. Bridle, ed., *Documents on Relations between Canada and Newfoundland*, vol. 2, pt. 1, p. 33.
2. Robertson to Burchell, Aug. 24, 1942, ibid.
3. Burchell to Robertson, Sept. 3, 1942, ibid., p. 34.
4. Burchell to Robertson, Sept. 18, 1942, ibid, p. 38
5. Burchell to Robertson, Sept. 18, 1942, ibid., pp. 38–40.
6. C. Attlee to Gov. Walwyn, Nov. 25, 1942, ibid., pp. 42–43.
7. Gov. Walwyn to C. Attlee, Jan. 7, 1943, ibid., pp. 53–54.
8. C.A. Burchell to H.L. Keenleyside, Feb. 16, 1943, ibid., pp. 56–57.
9. J.W. Pickersgill to C.A. Burchell, May 1943, ibid., pp. 69–70.
10. Mackenzie King, Extracts from Debates of House of Commons, June 1943, ibid., p. 74.
11. P.A. Clutterbuck to E. Machtig, July 23, 1943, ibid., p. 77.
12. Jim Halley, Personal Interviews, 2008.
13. J.K. Hiller, *Confederation: Deciding Newfoundland's Future*, p . 47.
14. Burchell to Robertson, Sept. 13, 1943, in Bridle, *Documents*, vol. 2, pt. 1, p. 79.
15. House of Commons Debates, Dec. 1943, quoted in A.P. Herbert, *Independent Member*, p. 295.
16. Ibid.
17. C. Attlee to War Cabinet of Great Britain, March 9, 1943, Bridle, *Documents*, vol. 2, pt. 1, pp. 81–84.
18. DO 35/1142/1/12, note, Dec. 8, 1943, quoted in Neary, *Newfoundland in the North Atlantic World*, p. 217.
19. Draft Minutes of Second Meeting between Dominions Secretary [Lord Cranborne] and Commissioners of Newfoundland, Aug. 8, 1944, Bridle, *Documents*, vol. 2, pt. 1, p. 118.
20. Memorandum by Lord Privy Seal to War Cabinet of Great Britain, Nov. 18, 1943, ibid., pp. 88–89.
21. Gov. Walwyn to C. Attlee, Feb. 12, 1944, ibid., pp. 104–08.
22. Ibid.
23. Richard Gwyn, *Smallwood: The Unlikely Revolutionary*, p. 59.

24. "Agreement between the Governments of the U.K. and the U.S.A. relating to bases leased to the U.S.A. concerning the defence of Newfoundland," March 27, 1941, Cmd 6259, in St. John Chadwick, *Newfoundland: Island into Province*, p. 179.

25. Walwyn to Attlee, Feb. 12, 1944, in Bridle, *Documents*, vol. 2, pt. 1, pp. 104–07.

26. Ibid., p. 106.

27. N.A. Robertson to Dominions Office, DD35/1376/N665/35, June 27, 1944, in Neary, *Newfoundland in the North Atlantic World*, p. 201.

28. R.A. MacKay to Norman Robertson, Jan. 8, 1944, in Bridle, *Documents*, vol. 2, pt. 1, pp. 98–101.

29. Ibid.

30. Malcolm MacDonald to Lord Cranborne, Nov. 7, 1944, ibid., p. 129.

31. Cranborne to MacDonald, Nov. 8, 1944, ibid.

32. Alexander Clutterbuck to Malcolm MacDonald, Nov. 17, 1944, ibid., pp. 129–30.

33. P.A. Clutterbuck, "The Approach to Canada," Nov. 8, 1944, ibid., vol. 2, pt. 1, pp. 130–33.

34. Malcom MacDonald to Cranborne, Dec. 9, 1944, ibid., p. 137.

35. Extract from Memorandum by Foreign Exchange Control Board, Canada, ibid., pp. 135–36.

36. Lord Cranborne to John Anderson, Feb. 20, 1945, ibid., p. 141.

37. Anderson to Cranborne, Feb. 27, 1945, ibid., p. 142.

Chapter Four

1. Charles Burchell to Norman Robertson, March 19, 1943, in Paul A. Bridle, ed., *Documents on Relations between Canada and Newfoundland*, vol. 2, pt. 1, p. 62.

2. Ibid., March 5, 1945, pp. 143–45.

3. H.H. Wrong to J.E. Read, June 6, 1945, ibid., pp. 151–52.

4. Alexander Clutterbuck to Sir Eric Machtig, Aug. 9, 1945, ibid., pp. 161–63.

5. Lord Addison to Prime Minister Clement Attlee, Sept. 5, 1945, ibid., pp. 166–67.

6. C. Attlee to Lord Addison, Sept. 7, 1945, ibid., p. 167.

7. N.A. Robertson to Macdonald, Sept. 25, 1945, Ibid, p. 170.

8. N.A. Robertson to J.S. Macdonald, July 9, 1945, ibid., p. 157.

9. J.S. Macdonald to N.A. Robertson, July 14, 1945, ibid., p. 160.

10. Ibid.

11. Bren Walsh, *More Than a Poor Majority*, p. 72.

12. Mackenzie King to J.S. Macdonald, Sept. 10, 1945 in Bridle, *Documents*, vol. 2, pt. 1, p. 167–68.

13. E. Machtig to Malcolm MacDonald, Sept. 11, 1945, ibid., p. 168.

14. P.A. Clutterbuck to Lord Addison, Sept. 20, 1945, ibid., p. 168.

15. Peter Neary, *Newfoundland in the North Atlantic World*, p. 182.

16. Clutterbuck Report, Oct. 19, 1945, in Bridle, *Documents*, vol. 2, pt. 1, pp. 173–78.

17. Ibid.

18. Ibid.

19. *Globe and Mail*, Dec. 30, 2006.

20. T220/60, Keynes note, Dec. 18, 1944, in Peter Neary, *Newfoundland in the North Atlantic World*, p. 228.

21. Lord Addison to Cabinet of Great Britain, Oct. 18, 1945, in Bridle, *Documents*, vol. 2, pt. 1, pp. 180–82.

22. Extract from the Mackenzie King Record, ibid., p. 182.

23. Lord Addison to Cabinet of Great Britain, Nov. 21, 1945, ibid., p. 190.

24. Extract from Draft Statement to be made in House of Lords, Dec. 1, 1945, ibid., p. 193.

25. Norman Robertson to Prime Minister Mackenzie King, Dec. 1, 1945, ibid., p. 192.

26. Memorandum by Prime Minister Mackenzie King, Dec. 2, 1945, ibid., p. 194,.

27. Vincent Massey to Lord Addison, Dec. 10, 1945, ibid. p. 194–95.

28. Addison to Massey, Dec. 11, 1945, ibid., p. 195.

Chapter Five

1. Scott Macdonald to Mackenzie King, Dec. 12, 1945, in Paul A. Bridle, ed., *Documents on Relations between Canada and Newfoundland 1940–1949*, vol. 2, pt. 1, pp. 195–96.

2. Dominions Secretary to War Cabinet of Great Britain, Nov. 8, 1943, ibid., pp. 80–85.

3. Albert Perlin, "The Wayfarer," May 8, 1946, in Francis Hollohan and Melvin Baker, eds., *A Clear Head in Tempestuous Times*, pp. 21–22.

4. Paul Emrys-Evans, Dec. 2, 1943, House of Commons Parliamentary Debates, vol. 395.

5. Robert Holland and J.K. Hiller, "Newfoundland and the Pattern of British Decolonization," ed., p. 142.

6. Halifax *Herald*, Dec. 12, 1945, James Maxton, House of Commons Parliamentary Debates.

7. Perlin, "Wayfarer," in Hollohan and Baker, eds., *Clear Head*, p. 22.

8. Lord Addison to Cabinet of Great Britain, Nov. 21, 1945, in Bridle, *Documents*, vol. 2, pt. 1, p. 189.

9. W.J. Bourne interview, Aug. 8, 1980, Charles R. Granger Collection, LAC, MG32-C48.

10. Scott Macdonald to Secretary of State External Affairs, July 4, 1945, ibid., p. 155.

11. Memorandum by Secretary of State for Dominion Affairs to Prime Minister, Nov. 21, 1945, DO 35/1345/N402/43 in Peter Neary, *Newfoundland in the North Atlantic World*, p. 234.

12. [Scott Macdonald,] High Commissioner in Newfoundland to Under-Secretary of State for External Affairs, January 17, 1944, in Bridle, *Documents*, vol. 2, pt. 1, pp. 102–03.

13. Extracts from Memorandum from Special Assistant to Under-Secretary of State for External Affairs to Acting Under-Secretary for External Affairs, June 29, 1945, ibid., pp. 152–54.

14. *Newfoundland Act* of 1933, p. 7.

15. R.A. MacKay to J.B. McEvoy, Feb. 19, 1946, in Bridle, *Documents*, vol. 2, pt. 1, pp. 211–12.

16. Ibid., p. 212.

17. Jim Halley, Personal Interviews, 2008.

18. Harold Horwood, *Joey*, pp. 9–16.

19. Richard Gwyn, *Smallwood: The Unlikely Revolutionary*, pp. 5–7.

20. Ibid., p. 34.

21. Horwood, *Joey*, p. 67.

22. Jim Halley, Personal Interviews, 2008.

23. G. Bradley to B. Dunfield, GN 13/1 Box 233 File 95, Nov. 8, 1935, in Neary, *Newfoundland in the North Atlantic World*, p. 282.

24. Perlin, "Wayfarer," in Hollohan and Baker, *Clear Head*, pp. 37–39.

25. J.K. Hiller and Michael F. Harrington, eds., *Newfoundland National Convention, 1946–1948*, vol. 5, pp. 93–96.

26. Scott Macdonald to N.A. Robertson, Nov. 4, 1946, in Bridle, *Documents*, vol. 2, pt. 1, pp. 316–17.

27. Perlin, "Wayfarer," in Hollohan and Baker, *Clear Head,* pp. 41–42.

28. Hiller and Harrington, *National Convention Debates*, 13 Sept.–Dec. 1946, p. 117.

29. Macdonald to Robertson, Nov. 7, 1946, in Bridle, *Documents*, vol. 2, pt. 1, pp. 322–23.

30. Lester Pearson to Cabinet Committee on Canada Newfoundland Relations, Nov. 16, 1946, ibid., pp. 330–31.

31. Memorandum of a Discussion on Newfoundland between the Under-Secretary of State for External Affairs and the High Commissioner for the United Kingdom in Ottawa, Nov. 19, 1946, ibid., pp. 334–36.

32. Scott Macdonald to Louis St. Laurent, Jan. 8, 1947, ibid., pp. 377–79.

33. Lester B. Pearson to N.A. Robertson, Feb. 28, 1947, ibid., p. 400.

34. Robertson to Pearson, March 4, 1947, ibid., pp. 402–03.

35. Scott Macdonald to Pearson, March 13, 1947, ibid., pp. 408–09.

36. Macdonald to Pearson, April 1, 1947, ibid., p. 437 (initials and first names of delegates added).

37. Memorandum by Second Political Division, April 1947, ibid., pp. 443.

38. Ibid., p. 443.

39. Memorandum by Second Political Division, May 22, 1947, ibid., p. 478.

40. Ibid.

41. Jim Halley, Personal Interviews, 2008.

Chapter Six

1. Extract from Despatch from High Commissioner in Newfoundland to Secretary of State for External Affairs, March 22, 1947, in Paul A. Bridle, ed., *Documents on the Relations between Canada and Newfoundland 1940–1949*, vol. 2, pt. 1, pp. 415–16.

2. J.R. Smallwood to Secretary of State for External Affairs, March 21, 1947, ibid., pp. 414–15.

3. Ibid., p. 449.

4. Albert Perlin, "The Wayfarer," in Francis Hollohan and Melvin Baker, eds., *A Clear Head in Tempestuous Times*, p. 56.

5. Scott Macdonald to Governor Macdonald, April 19, 1947, in Bridle, *Documents*, vol. 2, pt. 1, pp. 450–51.

6. A.A. Butt, "Interview with Charlie Granger," Charles R. Granger Papers, 1979.

7. London *Daily Express*, May 9, 1947, quoted in Peter Cashin address, J.K. Hiller and M.F. Harrington, eds., *The Newfoundland National Convention, 1946–1948*, vol. 1, pp. 534–35.

8. Harold Horwood, *Joey*, p. 85.

9. London *Daily Express*, June 26, 1947, in Phillip McCann, "British Policy and Confederation" in J.K. Hiller, ed., *Newfoundland Studies*, vol. 14, no. 2, p. 164.

10. Charles R. Granger interview with W.J. Browne, Aug. 8, 1980, Charles R. Granger Collection, LAC, MG32-C48.

11. Hiller and Harrington, eds., *Newfoundland National Convention*, May 19, 1947, vol. 1, pp. 533–34.

12. Ibid.

13. Paul A. Bridle to Secretary of State for External Affairs, Minute on Despatch No. 259 of May 21, 1947, in Bridle, *Documents*, vol. 2, pt. 1, p. 477.

14. Perlin, "Wayfarer," May 19, 1947, in Hollohan and Baker, *Clear Head*, pp. 64–65.

15. Peter Neary and Melvin Baker, eds., "Allan M. Fraser's 'History of Participation by Newfoundland in World War II,'" pp. 29–30.

16. Ibid., p. 30.

17. Scott Macdonald to Louis St. Laurent, May 26, 1947, in Bridle, *Documents*, vol. 2, pt. 1, pp. 479–80.

18. Extracts from Memorandum from Head, Second Political Division, to Under-Secretary of State for External Affairs, June 2, 1947, ibid., p. 485–86.

19. Scott Macdonald to Secretary of State for External Affairs, May 30, 1947, ibid., pp. 483–84.

20. "Report on the Legal Procedure Which Might Be Adopted for the Admission of Newfoundland as a Province," ibid., pp. 490–91.

21. Secret Memorandum by Secretary of Cabinet Committee on Newfoundland Relations to Cabinet, June 16, 1947, ibid., pp. 496–99.

22. Ibid., pp. 499–500.

23. Hunt, C.E., "What of the Future," Dec. 31, 1946, St. John's *Daily News*, quoted in Bridle, *Documents*, pp. 511–12.

Chapter Seven

1. Bren Walsh, *More Than a Poor Majority*, p. 137.

2. Extracts from a Memorandum by Second Political Division on Speech by the Prime Minister at the Dinner in Honour of the Delegation from the National Convention of Newfoundland on June 24th, in Paul Bridle, ed., *Documents on Relations Between Canada and Newfoundland*, vol. 2, pt. 1, p. 520.

3. Memorandum by Second Political Division, March 8, 1947, ibid., p. 404.

4. Extracts from Memorandum from Head, Second Political Division, to Under-Secretary of State for External Affairs. Ottawa, July 4, 1947, ibid., p. 553.

5. Richard Gwyn, *Smallwood: The Unlikely Revolutionary*, p. 87.

6. Ibid., p. 88.

7. Memorandum by Second Political Division, August 19, 1947, Minute on Despatch no. 399 from the Office of the High Commissioner for Canada, St. John's, dated Aug. 19, 1947 in Bridle, *Documents*, vol. 2 pt. 1, pp. 622–23.

8. Memorandum by Department of External Affiars, Aug. 25, 1947, ibid., p. 623.

14. Jim Halley, Personal Interviews, 2008.
15. Horwood, *Joey*, pp. 113–15.
16. Extract from the Mackenzie King Record, June 3, 1948, in Bridle, *Documents*, vol. 2, pt. 1, p. 885.
17. Bridle to St. Laurent, June 8, 1948, ibid., pp. 886–87.
18. Ibid., p. 890.
19. Jim Halley, Personal Interviews, 2008.
20. J.B. McEvoy, K.C., LL.B., Letters of June 5 and June 7 to R.A. MacKay, June 9, 1948, in Bridle, *Documents*, vol. 2, pt. 1, p. 892.
21. Jim Halley, Personal Interviews, 2008.
22. Don Jamieson, *No Place for Fools*, p. 101.
23. Mr. J.B. McEvoy, K.C., LL.B., letters of June 9, 1948, in Bridle, *Documents*, pp. 891–93.

Chapter Ten
1. John FitzGerald, "The Confederation of Newfoundland with Canada, 1946–1949," p. 225.
2. N.A. Robertson to Louis St. Laurent, July 2, 1948, in Paul A. Bridle, ed., *Documents on Relations between Canada and Newfoundland, 1940–1949*, vol. 2, pt. 1, p. 916.
3. Ibid. Emphasis added.
4. Ibid.
5. N.A. Robertson to Louis St. Laurent, July 2, 1948 (#2), ibid., p. 918.
6. Sir Eric Machtig to Sir Alexander Clutterbuck, July 1, 1948, PRO DO 35 34/58, quoted in John FitzGerald, "Confederation of Newfoundland with Canada," p. 225.
7. N.A. Robertson to Louis St. Laurent, July 2, 1948, in Bridle, *Documents*, vol. 2, pt. 1, p. 919.
8. Bren Walsh, *More Than a Poor Majority*, p. 33.
9. Memorandum by Department of External Affairs, June 22, 1948, in Bridle, *Documents*, vol. 2, pt. 1, p. 911.
10. N.A. Robertson to Louis St. Laurent, July 2, 1948 , in Bridle, *Documents*, vol. 2, pt. 1, pp. 918–19.
11. Lester B. Pearson to N.A. Robertson, July 16, 1948, ibid., p. 928.
12. Philip Noel-Baker to Governor Macdonald, July 12, 1948, MA PRO DO 35/3460, quoted in FitzGerald, "Confederation of Newfoundland with Canada," p. 228.
13. Governor Macdonald to Sir Eric Machtig, 13 July, 1948, MA.PRP PREM 8/1043, ibid., p. 227.
14. Paul A. Bridle to R.A. MacKay, June 21, 1948, in Bridle, *Documents*, vol. 2, pt. 1, pp. 906–09.
15. N.A. Robertson to Louis St. Laurent, July 2, 1948, ibid., p. 915.
16. Extract from St. John's *Evening Telegram*, Feb. 9, 1948, ibid., p. 815.
17. Paul A. Bridle to Louis St. Laurent, July 17, 1948, ibid., p. 931.
18. J.B. McEvoy to C.D. Howe, June 21, 1948, ibid., p. 911. Emphasis added.
19. H. Porter to F.M. O'Leary, July 29, 1948, in FitzGerald," Confederation," pp. 253–54.
20. Ibid., p. 255.
21. Ibid., p. 220.

22. Ibid., p. 277.
23. Harold Horwood, "How We Got Confederation," St. John's *Evening Telegram*, March 28, 1969, p. 37.
24. Gordon Higgins to Leo Jackman, Aug. 26, 1948, J.G. Higgins Papers, in FitzGerald, "Confederation of Newfoundland with Canada," p. 208.
25. Peter Neary, *Newfoundland in the North Atlantic World*, p. 323.
26. A.B. Butt, Interview, Jan. 11, 1980, Charles R. Granger Collection, LAC, MG32-C48.
27. FitzGerald, "Confederation of Newfoundland with Canada," p. 174.
28. Bridle to Secretary of State External Affairs, July 19, 1948, in Bridle, *Documents*, vol. 2, pt. 1, p. 936.
29. St. John's *Evening Telegram*, June 28, 1948, ibid., p. 930.
30. Bridle to St. Laurent, July 20, 1948, ibid., p. 937.
31. Extract from Mackenzie King Record, July 20, 1948, in Bridle, *Documents*, vol. 2, pt. 1, p. 940.
32. Bridle to Governor Macdonald, July 30, 1948, ibid., p. 977.
33. Wainwright Abbot to Secretary of State for War, 2 Aug. 1948, LAC, RG 59, 843.00/8-248, quoted in Neary, *Newfoundland in the North Atlantic World*, p. 324.
34. Bridle to St. Laurent, July 24, 1948, in Bridle, *Documents*, vol. 2, pt. 1, p. 953.
35. FitzGerald, "Confederation of Newfoundland with Canada," p. 227.
36. Noel-Baker to Lord Hall, 3 July, 1948, ibid., p. 227.
37. Secretary, Responsible Government League to Prime Minister, July 25, 1948, ibid., p. 955.
38. Prime Minister to Secretary, Responsible Government League of Newfoundland, July 30, 1948, ibid., p. 978.
39. Sir Eric Machtig to Sir Alexander Clutterbuck, July 26, 1948, ibid., pp. 961–62
40. Draft Statement by Prime Minister, July 30, 1948, ibid., p. 975.
41. Ibid.

Chapter Eleven

1. Second Conversation with Governor and Commissioners Pottle, Quinton and Walsh, July 27, 1948, in Paul A. Bridle, ed., *Documents on Relations between Canada and Newfoundland, 1940–1949*, vol. 2, pt. 1, p. 991.
2. Memorandum from Head, British Commonwealth Division to Under-Secretary of State for External Affairs, July 29, 1948, ibid., p. 981.
3. Extract from St. John's *Daily News*, July 31, 1948, ibid., p. 994.
4. Jim Halley, Personal Interviews, 2008.
5. Acting High Commissioner in Newfoundland to Secretary of State for External Affairs, August 26, 1948, Bridle, *Documents*, vol. 2, pt. 2, p. 1010.
6. Extracts from Minutes of a Meeting of the Delegation of Newfoundland to the Negotiations of the Terms of Union, Sept. 13, 1948, ibid., p. 1064.
7. Memorandum by Director Economic Policy Division, Department of Finance, Sept. 13, 1948, ibid., p. 1070.
8. Report by Sub-Committee on Finance and Economic Policy, Interdepartmental Committee on Newfoundland. A Background On Financial Terms Contained In

Proposed Arrangements for the Entry of Newfoundland into Confederation, Sept. 30, 1948, ibid., p. 1107.

9. Extracts from Memorandum by Delegation of Newfoundland to Meeting with Cabinet Committee, Oct. 13, 1948, ibid., p. 1130.

10. Harold Horwood, *Joey*, p. 135.

11. Extracts from memorandum by Director, Economic Policy Division, Department of Finance, to Deputy Minister of Finance, Oct. 29, 1948, ibid., p. 1163.

12. Ray Atherton to Secretary of State in Washington, Dec. 22, 1947, in FitzGerald, *Newfoundland at the Crossroads*, pp. 101–04.

13. Extract from Mackenzie King Record, in Bridle, *Documents*, vol. 2, pt. 1, p. 371.

14. Memorandum from Director General, Economic Research Branch, Department of Reconstruction and Supply, to Minister of Reconstruction and Supply, Nov. 2, 1948, ibid., vol. 2, pt. 2, pp. 1174–78.

15. Don Jamieson, *No Place for Fools*, p. 369.

16. Peter Neary, *Newfoundland in the North Atlantic World*, p. 327.

17. Sir Alexander Clutterbuck telegram, 15 Oct. 1948, DO 114/103 1, pp. 200-1, in Neary, *Newfoundland in the North Atlantic World*, p. 327.

18. Jamieson, *No Place for Fools*, pp. 131–32.

19. Privy Council Office to Cabinet Comitteee on Newfoundland, Report by Sub-Committee on Finance and Economic Policy, Interdepartmental Committee on Newfoundland. A. Background On Financial Terms Contained In Proposed Arrangements For The Entry Of Newfoundland Into Confederation, Oct. 1, 1948, in Bridle, *Documents*, vol. 2, pt. 2, p. 1107.

20. J.W. Channing interview, June 19–26, 1981, Charles R. Granger Collection, LAC, MG32-C48.

21. High Commissioner of Great Britain to Secretary of State for Commonwealth Relations of Great Britain, Dec. 23, 1948, ibid., pp. 1300–01.

22. C.A. Crosbie, Esq. to Governor Macdonald, Feb. 7, 1949, ibid., p.1515–17.

Chapter Twelve

1. Higgins to A.P. Herbert, March–Dec., 1948, RG LP3.01.027, Correspondence, J.G. Higgins, in John FitzGerald, "The Confederation of Newfoundland with Canada 1946–1949," p. 277.

2. Debate on Second Reading in the House of Commons, March 2, 1949, quoted in Paul A. Bridle, ed., *Documents on Relations between Canada and Newfoundland 1940–1949*, vol. 2, pt. 2, pp. 1546–47.

3. Debate on Second Reading in the House of Commons, March 2, 1949, in Bridle, *Documents*, vol. 2, pt. 2, pp. 1546–47.

4. *Globe and Mail*, March 1949, in A.P. Herbert, *Independent Member*, p. 438.

5. Herbert, *Independent Member*, pp. 437–39.

6. Debate on Second Reading in the House of Commons, March 2, 1949, in Bridle, *Documents*, vol. 2, pt. 2, pp. 1546–47.

7. Ibid., pp. 1548–49.

8. House of Commons Parliamentary Debates, March 2, 1949, in St. John Chadwick, *Newfoundland: Island into Province*, p. 220.
9. Peter J. Cashin to Prime Minister, Jan. 26, 1949, in Bridle, *Documents*, vol. 2 , pt. 2, p. 1363.
10. C.J. Burchell to R.A. MacKay, Feb. 25, 1949, ibid., p. 1531.
11. Sir Alexander Clutterbuck to Philip Noel-Baker, Dec. 23, 1948, ibid., p. 1302.

Chapter 13
1. Memorandum of Agreement Entered into on the Eleventh Day of December 1948 Between Canada and Newfoundland, quoted in Paul A. Bridle, ed., *Documents on Relations between Canada and Newfoundland* 1940-1949, vol. 2, pt. 2, p. 1244.
2. Extracts from Report of Sub-Committee on Law and Procedure, October, 1948, ibid., p. 1153.
3. Memorandum from Chairman, Steering Sub-Committee, Interdepartmental Committee on Newfoundland, to Cabinet Committee on Newfoundland, September 30, 1948, Bridle, *Documents*, vol. 2, pt. 2, p. 1101.
4. Ibid., p. 1101.
5. Thomas Lodge, *Dictatorship in Newfoundland*, p. 249.
6. A.P. Herbert, *Independent Member*, p. 435.
7. Peter Neary, *Newfoundland in the North Atlantic World*, p. 345.
8. Lodge, *Dictatorship*, p. 70.
9. Harrington to Foster, 23 June, 1947, LAC RG 84, file 800, in Peter Neary, *Newfoundland in the North Atlantic World*, p. 358.
10. J.S. Macdonald to N.A. Robertson, March 30, 1946, in Bridle, *Documents*, vol. 2, pt. 1, p. 234.
11. Ibid., Dec. 11, 1946, p. 357.
12. D.J. Fox, "Summary of Potential Air Space, Gross Revenue Newfoundland 1949–2006."
13. The Royal Commission on Renewing and Strengthening our Place in Canada, Jan. 16, 2003, Transcript of Proceedings, The Expectations Roundtable Meeting.
14. Phillip McCann, "British Policy and Confederation," in J.K. Hiller, ed., *Newfoundland Studies*, vol. 14, no. 2, p. 166.

Chapter Fourteen
1. The Newfoundland Royal Commission Report, 1933, p. 196.
2. Charles R. Granger Papers.
3. Jim Halley, Personal Interviews, 2008.
4. David Butler, Personal Interview with John FitzGerald, 1995.
5. Jim Halley, Personal Interviews, 2008.
6. Harold Paddock, Personal Interview, March 23, 2010.
7. Sir Alan Herbert, "Letter" to London *Times*, Sept. 1948, in Herbert, *Independent Member*, p. 409.
8. Kenneth C. Wheare, *The Constitutional Structure of the Commonwealth*. .
9. Harry Anderson Winter, *The Political Memoirs of Harry Anderson Winter*, quoted in Bren Walsh, *More Than a Poor Majority*, p. 228.

Chapter Fifteen

1. Jim Halley, Personal Interviews, 2008.
2. Jim Halley, Personal Interviews, 2008.
3. A.P. Herbert, *Independent Member*, p. 272.
4. Walsh, *Poor Majority*, p. 316.
5. http://en.wikipedia.org/wiki/Danny_Williams
6. Jim Halley, Personal Interviews, 2008.

Epilogue

1. Paul A. Bridle, ed., *Documents on Relations between Canada and Newfoundland 1940–1949*, vol. 2, pt. 1, p. xiii.
2. Ibid., p. xv.
3. Paul West, in Richard Gwyn, *Smallwood: The Unlikely Revolutionary*, p. viii.

BIBLIOGRAPHY

Manuscript Sources

Bridle, Paul A., ed. *Documents on Relations between Canada and Newfoundland 1940–1949.* Vol. 2, parts 1 and 2. Ottawa: Supply and Services Canada, 1984.

Centre for Newfoundland Studies: Queen Elizabeth II Library, Memorial University, St. John's
    The Newfoundland Act of 1933
    The Newfoundland Royal Commission 1933 Report
    Hiller, J.K. and M.F. Harrington, eds. *The Newfoundland National Convention, 1946–1948: Debates, Papers and Reports.* Two vols. Montreal: McGill-Queen's University Press, 1995.

The Rooms Provincial Archives
    Charles R. Granger Papers

A.C. Hunter Library, Newfoundland Collection, St. John's
    Daily News. St. John's
    Evening Telegram. St. John's
    Fishermen-Workers Tribune. St. John's

Public Records Office, Kew, London, England
    Air Ministry Files, AVIA 2/2285.

Library and Archives Canada
    Charles R. Granger Audio Collection
    Charles A. Magrath Papers
    Mackenzie-King Record.

Newspapers and Periodicals
Daily Express. London
Globe and Mail. Toronto

Personal Interviews
Jim Halley, 2008.
John Edward FitzGerald, 2009–2012.
Harold Paddock, 2009, 2012.

Secondary Sources

Aitken, H.G.J. "Defensive Expansionism: The State of Economic Growth in Canada." In H.G.J. Aitken, ed., *The State and Economic Growth*. New York: Social Science Research Council, 1959.

Chadwick, St. John. *Newfoundland: Island into Province*. London: Cambridge University Press, 1967.

FitzGerald, John Edward., ed. *Newfoundland at the Crossroads: Documents on Confederation with Canada*. St. John's: Terra Nova Publishing, 2002.

————. "Dying 'Beyond Its Means': Newfoundland's War Debts, Its Loss of Self-Government, and Confederation." Unpublished Paper. St. John's: Memorial University of Newfoundland, Department of History, 1998.

————. "The Confederation of Newfoundland with Canada 1946–1949." Master of Arts Thesis. St. John's: Memorial University of Newfoundland, Department of History, 1992.

Garner, Joe. *The Commonwealth Office 1925–1968*. London: Heinemann, 1978.

Gywn, Richard. *Smallwood: The Unlikely Revolutionary*. Toronto: McClelland & Stewart, 1968.

Hale, David, "The Newfoundland Lesson," *International Economy Magazine*, April 28, 2003. www.international-economy.com.

Herbert, A.P. *Independent Member*. London: Methuen & Co. Ltd., 1952.

Hiller, J.K. *Confederation: Deciding Newfoundland's Future, 1934–1949*. St. John's: Newfoundland Historical Society, 1998.

Holland, Robert, and J.K. Hiller, eds. "Newfoundland and the Pattern of British Decolonization," *Newfoundland Studies*, vol. 14, no. 2. 1998.

Hollohan, Francis, and Melvin Baker, eds. A *Clear Head in Tempestuous Times*. St. John's: Harry Cuff Publications, 1986.

Horwood, Harold. *Joey*. Toronto: Stoddart Publishing, 1989.

Jamieson, Don. *No Place for Fools: The Political Memoirs of Don Jamieson*. Vol. 1. Carmelita McGrath, ed. St. John's: Breakwater Books, 1989.

Lodge, Thomas. *Dictatorship in Newfoundland*. London: Cassell and Company Ltd., 1939.

MacKenzie, David. "The Terms of Union in Historical Perspective." *Newfoundland Studies*, vol. 14, no. 2, 1998.

Mayer, Karl E. and Shareen Blair Brysac, *Tournament of Shadows: The Great Game and the Race for Empire in Central Asia*. Berkeley, California: Counterpoint, 1999.

McCann, Phillip. "British Policy and Confederation," *Newfoundland Studies*, vol. 14, no. 2, 1998.

Neary, Peter. *Newfoundland in the North Atlantic World, 1929–1949*. Montreal: McGill-Queen's University Press, 1988.

————, ed. *White Tie and Decorations*. Toronto: University of Toronto Press, 1996.

————, and Melvin Baker, eds. "Allan M. Fraser's 'History of Participation by Newfoundland in World War II,'" *Newfoundland Quarterly*, vol. 102, no. 4, 2010.

Prowse, D.W. *A History of Newfoundland*. London: Eyre and Spottiswoode, 1896.

Rose, J. Holland, A.P. Newton and E.A. Benians, *The Cambridge History of the British Empire*. Vol. 6. Cambridge: Cambridge University Press, 1929.

Smallwood, J.R., ed. *The Book of Newfoundland.* Vols. 1, 2 and 3. St. John's: Newfoundland Book Publishers, 1967.

—————. *I Chose Canada: The Memoirs of the Honourable Joseph R. "Joey" Smallwood.* Scarborough, Ontario: New American Library of Canada, 1975.

Walsh, Bren. *More Than a Poor Majority.* St. John's: Breakwater Books, 1985.

Webb, Jeff. "Confederation, Conspiracy and Choice: A Discussion." *Newfoundland Studies,* vol. 14, no. 2, 1998.

Kenneth C. Wheare, *The Constitutional Structure of the Commonwealth.* Oxford: Clarendon Press, 1960.

Will, Gavin. *The Big Hop: The North Atlantic Air Race.* Flatrock, Newfoundland: Boulder Publications, 2009.

INDEX

on union with US, 167
Wayfarer column, 31–2, 38, 81–2, 97
Dalton, Hugh, 73
Davies, D.S., 225
Davies, Margot, 225, 226, 227
defence, 23, 25–6, 53–4
delegation to Ottawa (1947; first), 128–49
  Committee on Newfoundland and,
    123–5
  conclusion of, 136
  Inter-Departmental Committee on
    Canada-Newfoundland Relations
    and, 123
  lack of negotiating power, 131, 138, 185
  J.S. Macdonald and, 59, 95
  Pearson on, 98–9
  postponement of, 97, 102–3
  press reaction to, 106–7
  Smallwood and, 95–7, 101
delegation to Ottawa (1948; second),
    198–207
  authorization of members, 214–15
  and budget for new province, 197–8
  Canadian negotiating team and,
    198–9
  choice of members, 162, 183–4, 194,
    195–6, 215
  Commission of Government and,
    183, 215
  Labrador ore and, 201
  as negotiation between Canadian and
    British governments, 215–16
  preparedness of, 197
  results of second referendum and, 193
  Terms of Union, 199, 202–4
delegation to UK, 102–5, 108, 112–20
delegation to US, 101, 107–8
delegations
  ignorance of Anglo-Canadian
    understandings, 102
  MacKay's summary of, 215
  resolutions passed by National
    Convention, 105

sequencing of, 104–5, 108
strategic deployment of, 102–3
democracy
  Amulree Report and, 9–10, 13
  Commission of Government and, 21
  debt rescheduling/restructuring and,
    14–15
  Great Depression and, 12–13
  Machtig on, 30
  postwar restoration to Newfoundland,
    30
Depression. *See* Great Depression
Dictatorship in Newfoundland (Lodge), 21
Dixon, Sir Charles, 20, 23, 47
dominion status, 4, 22, 32, 44–6, 105, 147–8
Dominions Office
  British Parliament and, 82–3
  Clutterbuck's report re visit to Ottawa,
    69–73
  and Commission of Government, 21
  and Confederation, 100, 114
  and delegation to Ottawa, 130
  and delegation to UK, 104, 112–13,
    117–18
  and future of Newfoundland govern-
    ment, 37, 62
  and National Convention terms of
    reference, 43
  and Newfoundland public opinion, 82
  and not returning responsible govern-
    ment to Newfoundland, 40
  plans for Confederation, 114
  and reconstruction in Newfoundland,
    43–4, 56–7
  and responsible government, 40
  and reversal of Newfoundland to crown
    colony, xiv
  as running Newfoundland, 10–11
  and self-determination, 99–100
  and US-Newfoundland link, 57
  and wording of Amulree Report, 9
Dunfield, Brian, 85, 211
Dyer, Gwynne, 227

Greg Malone is probably best known for his satire on the WGB and CODCO TV shows and his wicked impersonations of political icons, like the Queen and Barbara Frum, for which he has received many awards. As a political activist, Malone has championed many causes such as the campaign that stopped the privatization of Newfoundland and Labrador Hydro. He is the author of the acclaimed memoir *You Better Watch Out*, and is currently a director and actor who lives in St. John's.